CRITICAL STUDIES IN PRIVATE LAW

Law and Philosophy Library

VOLUME 16

The titles published in this series are listed at the end of this volume.

THOMAS WILHELMSSON
Department of Private Law, University of Helsinki

CRITICAL STUDIES IN PRIVATE LAW

A Treatise on Need-Rational Principles in Modern Law

KLUWER ACADEMIC PUBLISHERS
DORDRECHT / BOSTON / LONDON

Library of Congress Cataloging-in-Publication Data

Wilhelmsson, Thomas, 1949-
[Social civilrätt. English]
Critical studies in private law : a treatise on need-rational principles in modern law / Thomas Wilhelmsson.
p. cm. -- (Law and philosophy library ; v. 16)
Rev. translation of: Social civilrätt. 1987.
Includes bibliographical references and index.
ISBN 0-7923-1659-2 (HB : acid free paper)
1. Contracts--Social aspects--Finland. 2. Civil law--Social aspects--Finland. 3. Critical legal studies. 4. Sociological jurisprudence. I. Title. II. Series.
KJT858.W5513 1992
340'.115'094897--dc20 92-3911

ISBN 0-7923-1659-2

Published by Kluwer Academic Publishers,
P.O. Box 17, 3300 AA Dordrecht, The Netherlands.

Kluwer Academic Publishers incorporates
the publishing programmes of
D. Reidel, Martinus Nijhoff, Dr W. Junk and MTP Press.

Sold and distributed in the U.S.A. and Canada
by Kluwer Academic Publishers,
101 Philip Drive, Norwell, MA 02061, U.S.A.

In all other countries, sold and distributed
by Kluwer Academic Publishers Group,
P.O. Box 322, 3300 AH Dordrecht, The Netherlands.

Printed on acid-free paper

Printed in the Netherlands

TABLE OF CONTENTS

PREFACE

In discussions of legal theory in the Nordic countries in the early 1980s, one of the foreground questions concerned the possibilities of, and the limits to, a reorganizing, "critical", "alternative" legal dogmatics. The discussion tended to remain at a theoretical level, however, and concrete examples of this kind of dogmatics were few. The position was just such a one as described by the East German legal philosopher *Hermann Klenner* in criticizing the attempts in his own country to make methodological legal research independent of legal scholarship: he objects to "such a division of labour that some people know *how* to research (but cannot) and others can indeed do research (but do not know *how*)..." (Staat und Recht 1/1986 p. 57).

I myself had in various contributions to the discussion stated the view that private-law research ought to be developed, among other ways, by placing greater weight upon the general principles. Such statements incur obligations: sooner or later one is in a position where one has to do something oneself, not merely tell others how. The Swedish-language original of this work (*Social civilrätt*, 1987) represented an attempt to fulfil this moral obligation.

The English version is not a direct translation of the Swedish original. Large parts have been rewritten: the theoretical parts have been expanded while parts of the concrete dogmatics have been cut out.

The two works contain an attempt to adopt a new perspective upon certain topics of general importance within contract law. What is essential in them is their pervading theme: the possibility of developing the need-oriented elements in the general principles of contract law. Much of the detail could naturally be deepened and altered: it has nonetheless been my hope that the works are sufficiently well developed to permit scrutiny of the central ideas by the learned community and the legal audience. Ultimately, it is not worth improving the strain too much before one can see whether the seeds will grow at all. The law develops in small steps: too large a single step, and the legal scholar easily falls outside the field of what is legally possible.

I wrote parts of the original *Social civilrätt* during a fairly long stay, in 1986, funded by the Deutsche Forschungsgemeinschaft and the Academy of Finland, at the Zentrum für Europäische Rechtspolitik, University of Bremen. I wish to repeat here my thanks to the collaborators and staff of the department, and particularly to its Director, Professor *Norbert Reich*, for their support. In Finland I am indebted for the ideas developed in the book chiefly to the now defunct discussion circle for critical private law, with, among others, *Niklas Bruun* and *Juha Pöyhönen* as members.

The English-language version of the work has come about through the initiative of Professor *Aulis Aarnio* and with the help of his unfailing international contacts. This is but a small example of his tireless work for the benefit of Finnish legal theory.

The translation has been carried out expertly and rapidly by *Tim Crosfield*, Stockholm. It has been funded by the Academy of Finland, the University of Helsinki and Oskar Öflunds stiftelse. The finishing work is performed within the large research project "*Social Contract Law in Europe*", also funded by the Academy of Finland.

Helsinki, August 1990

Thomas Wilhelmsson

CHAPTER I

INTRODUCTION

1. BACKGROUND: THE NORDIC DISCUSSION OF ALTERNATIVE LEGAL DOGMATICS

Critical legal research, that is, research that questioned the dominant legal-dogmatic paradigm, experienced a heyday in many places in the world during the 1960s and 1970s. The Nordic countries were no exception: here too, the barb of critical discussion pointed at the way legal research was being carried on. The normativity of legal science and its isolation from social reality were criticized in terms that were partly, but only partly, reminiscent of the attack of the American realists some decades earlier on traditional "law in books".[1] At the same time, critical discussion in the Nordic countries was also receiving strong impulses from Marxist legal theory.

Even at this stage there were some critics who contented themselves with demands for qualitative changes within legal dogmatics, such as more open argumentation, an extension of the legal sources in the direction of the social sciences, etc. The more radical wished, however, to abandon legal dogmatics as unscien-

---

[1] The demand of the American realists for reform of legal studies, for integration of material from other social sciences with legal science, for a study of the law in its social context, for a re-systematization of legal problems in line with the problem complexes occurring in real life, and so on, are very familiar to a participant in the Finnish legal debate of the 1970s. On this comparison, see Wilhelmsson 1976.

tific. They stated openly that they were not prepared to concede the basic problem of traditional legal dogmatics, the endeavour to elucidate the content of valid law, a status as a scientific issue.[2] Legal science was to become "real science" through the loan of issues and methods from the other social sciences.

Since the end of the 1970s there has been a reorientation within parts of the tradition of critical thought in Nordic legal science. Legal dogmatics has been "rediscovered" and critical researchers have asked whether this could be developed in an emancipatory direction.[3] Was it possible to create an "alternative" or "critical" legal dogmatics whose political ambition would be to contribute to an emancipatory upheaval of the legal system and whose scientific aim would be a natural integration, into itself, of the types of legal science that were inspired by the social sciences?

The debate in the Nordic countries on an alternative legal dogmatics has received inspiration from many quarters. One of the sparks that ignited the discussion was experience from Italy where, since the beginning of the 1970s, discussions both theoretical and practical have been going on regarding the possibilities of "l'uso alternativo del diritto".[4] Further fuel later came from German alternative jurisprudence[5] and from the American Critical Legal Studies movement.[6] Women's law research, in which the dividing line between dogmatics and other legal science is very rapidly being erased, has, again, tended to draw its impulses from other

---

[2] Perhaps the chief example in Finnish doctrine of a total denunciation of the traditional presentation of the problem - what is the standpoint of valid law? - is Kivivuori's noted doctoral thesis on the development of the law of torts (1969), specially page 26.

[3] An important starting point for this discussion, which has been carried on chiefly in the columns of the journal Retfaerd, was Eriksson's draft for a Marxist jurisprudence (1979), later deepened in his doctoral thesis on Marxist theory and legal science (1980).

[4] This line of thought was introduced into the Finnish discussions through Eriksson's article on the Magistratura democratica and the Italian lawyer opposition (1977).

[5] Particularly Reifner 1979.

[6] Particularly Unger 1983.

women's research.

The debate on alternative legal dogmatics was long to centre on issues of principle. Thus doubt was expressed regarding what was "*alternative*"[7] in the new models, and objections were raised regarding the *desirability* of an alternative legal dogmatics.

Some critics of the theories of the alternative use of law have claimed that the model does not differ theoretically from traditional legal dogmatics. At the very beginning of the discussion it was pointed out that the structure of decision-making is the same whether the judge or the author takes his stand on a question of interpretation in the traditional way or whether he claims to do so in an alternative fashion. Alternative legal dogmatics chooses between different possibilities of interpretation as well as traditional dogmatics does. The difference lies only in the ground for making the choice, that is, in the content of the interpretative sentences, not in their structure.[8] Against this it may be asserted that the critique, rather, appears to express a truism, since all legal dogmatics *per definitionem* endeavours to produce, among other things, interpretative propositions: the differences between traditional legal dogmatics and alternative legal dogmatics should be sought elsewhere.

Other critics wondered whether even the grounds for making the interpretative choice could be entirely different in kind within alternative legal dogmatics. Was it not rather a question of a difference in degree in relation to traditional legal dogmatics? Is the new legal dogmatics something different from the normal, sensible juridical work already being done by normal, sensible, liberal and radical jurists?[9]

---

[7] Initially the term "Marxist" legal dogmatics was also used, thus for example in Eriksson's work mentioned in note 3 above and in Pöyhönen 1980. This terminology could not but give rise to a verbal battle over the correctness of using the term in the present context. Now this terminological issue has lost relevance in discussions in the Nordic countries and need not be touched on here either.

[8] Aarnio 1978 p. 231 ff.

[9] Mathiesen 1980 p. 71.

Whether an alternative legal dogmatics was desirable was also questioned on several grounds. It was asserted that alternative legal dogmatics would contribute to strengthening the social position of legal ideology, and such a juridification of political issues was viewed as dangerous.[10] In addition there was criticism of alternative legal dogmatics as a new theoretical model. Particularly for researchers, who tended to doubt the status of legal dogmatics as legal science, it was easy to represent the new models as an over-intellectualization of legal dogmatics.[11]

In its original form[12] the present work represented a contribution to this discussion. The aim has been to develop further in certain respects the Nordic theories relating to alternative legal dogmatics, in connection with more recent international discussion; and, as well, to test the theory on a concrete issue. Now a general feature of the earlier Nordic discussion was that it was carried on at a high level of abstraction. Models for alternative legal dogmatics were created in theory and counter-arguments formulated in general terms, while concrete legal-dogmatic studies were absent.[13] The question of how alternative legal dogmatics can and should differ from traditional, and how alternative-dogmatics work can and should be intellectualized, cannot, however, be answered without such concrete paradigmatic examples.

2. WHAT IS "ALTERNATIVE" LEGAL DOGMATICS?

Legal dogmatics has traditionally been viewed as having two chief tasks: to interpret and to systematize legal norms. The activity focuses on the *normative content* of valid law. The result

---

[10] Mathiesen 1980 p. 73 f.

[11] Dalberg-Larsen 1979 p. 88.

[12] Wilhelmsson 1987.

[13] Now worthy of mention as another such concrete study in Finnish law is Pöyhönen 1988. Outside the Nordic countries there naturally exist such applications of alternative legal-dogmatic theories: an eminent example is Reifner 1979.

is given in the form of norms or norm systems. The primary interest of knowledge in such activity may be assumed to be technical or hermeneutic.[14] The questions now are, whether it is possible to produce and apply to this work a new paradigm which would also have an emancipatory potential, and what this emancipatory legal-dogmatic paradigm would look like.

In international and Nordic discussion, a number of proposals have been made for a new legal dogmatics of this kind. They have been characterized in various ways, so that one speaks of "Marxist", "critical" and "alternative" dogmatics etc. The differences in terminology are not quite arbitrary: certain of the terms, such as "Marxist" and, at least by some scholars, "critical", accentuate a connection with special background theories of law and society. In the Nordic countries the term "alternative" later became the most usual, appearing as an umbrella term for the various proposals for legal dogmatics of an emancipatory cast. Since in many cases the connection between the new models and the theories possibly underlying them has not emerged particularly clearly in the concrete proposals presented - the associated background theory has not formed a necessary basis for the emancipatory-legal-dogmatic model in question - this use of language also seems justified. In the present work, however, in consideration of accepted international usage, "critical legal dogmatics" is used in parallel with "alternative legal dogmatics". The terms are used as synonyms: "critical" does not refer to any special background theory.

Within the framework of what may be characterized as alternative or critical legal dogmatics there lies, if the matter is considered from an international perspective, a relatively broad spectrum of different currents of thought. Common to the adherents of all the forms of legal dogmatics that can be termed alterna-

---

[14] Reference is made here to Habermas' (1968) description of the three basic interests of knowledge: a technical interest, whose purpose is to give man the tools to control his environment, a hermeneutic interest through which one strives to understand texts and cultures, and an emancipatory or liberating interest.

tive in the present meaning, however, are the following characteristics, at least:

(i) The realization that the idea of a value-free (objective) legal dogmatics is an illusion.[15]

(ii) Based on this realisation, a relatively strong emphasis on the wide discretion which the legal system gives judges and other legal decision-makers.[16]

(iii) The view that traditional legal dogmatics (mainstream legal dogmatics) is based implicitly on conservative social values.

(iv) The desire to build one's own activity on values and ideals that are perceived as being more emancipatory.

(v) The belief that, through legal-dogmatic activity, one can achieve social change towards the ideals one has embraced.

(vi) A greater reliance than in traditional forms of dogmatics on the fruitfulness of the interdisciplinary project of infiltrating theories and results of social science into legal dogmatics.

These criteria are patently diffuse. No clear demarcation can be made between alternative forms of legal dogmatics and progressive variants of traditional dogmatics; nor is it meaningful to attempt to do so. As will emerge from what follows it is by no means evident that all, even in "alternative" quarters, wish to stress the differences between an "alternative" paradigm and a "traditional" one.

Even among legal researchers who possess the characteristics listed above there exist opinions according to which the problem is primarily a *practical/political* one. It becomes a question of how well a progressive judge and legal scientist can use his wide discretion concerning interpretation and application of the legal

---

[15] This realization is of course not the sole property of the "alternative" or "critical" jurists: in many legal cultures, as for example in Finland, it is fairly generally accepted - at least among legal theoreticians. For this reason, among others, e.g. Tuori 1988 p. 201 ff. has queried the difference between alternative legal dogmatics and at least some parts of the dominant *legal-theoretical* discussion.

[16] A central postulate of American Critical Legal Studies supporters is "the Indeterminacy of the Law". See on this, e.g. Yablon 1985.

norms to promote his ideals. The actual significance of the individual decision with regard to the environment, oppressed social groups, the working class, etc. determines the outcome of the case. The link between politics and the law is direct and contextually bound.[17] The difference between "context of discovery" and "context of justification" is stressed. Even if the radical judge or dogmatist can achieve his result through a heuristic process that differs from that of his traditional colleague's, because of the open-ended nature of the legal system he has no need of new theoretical structures of argumentation. Alternative law is thus something that appears primarily in the legal work of radical jurists: it means *critical legal practice*. This model does not presuppose any dogmatic substructure, even though progressive standpoints regarding individual issues in the doctrine can, it is granted, support such a practice.

When determining the sought-for objective in the context of discovery one can employ social-science models for how society is built up and developed. For practice to lead to the best possible result in terms of the objective selected, one should have access to empirical research regarding the significance of the legal rules and their influence on the area of life affected by the decision. Firm anchorage in the social sciences can thus easily be reconciled with critical practice.

Naturally, such a pragmatically oriented model for critical practice is not, and does not set out to be, "alternative" in any more profound sense. A legal dogmatics that implies mere critical practice presents its results in a structure that resembles that of traditional dogmatics. Assertions concerning the theoretical concordance of alternative legal dogmatics with other dogmatics have also, presumably, had precisely a critical practice model of this kind as their object. If one wishes seriously to explore the possibilities of creating an alternative paradigm for legal dogmatics, then, it is not enough to argue for critical practice in the interpretation of the law in single cases. Attention must also be drawn to the

---

[17] See e.g. Mathiesen 1980 p. 71.

second task of legal dogmatics: *systematization* of the legal system.

Moreover, in the alternative legal dogmatics debate many have been unwilling to settle for a non-theoretical model for critical practice. There has been a wish to create a more total frame of reference for alternative dogmatics. The real issue is the way of funnelling the political (and sociological) element into law. The desire has been to go beyond the individual decisions and the individual questions of interpretation and, rather, to *incorporate the political element into law via the system*, or via some systematic whole. Consequently there is great interest in the *general principles and concepts* ("the general doctrines", die allgemeine Lehren) of the legal system or of the relevant branch of the law. From the rest of social science are taken, primarily and openly, within the framework of the context of justification, qualitative analyses of society's and its sub-systems' developmental tendencies and stages; though this does not rule out the use of empirical knowledge at micro-level.

The pure variant of this model for alternative legal dogmatics is a doctrine in which the connection between the legal decision and the subjective political viewpoint is made as indirect as possible. Politics is introduced into law via the *developmental structures* of the law and of society. The starting point is a *fundamental critique* (Prinzipielle Kritik; a critique in principle) of the legal system. There is an attempt to show how central elements in the system or in single areas conflict with structures developed or in course of development in society. *Udo Reifner's* alternative civil law affords a good example of such a way of approaching the problems.[18] Reifner maintains that traditional civil law as an ideal type expresses a power exercised through the private ownership of the means of production, and shows how this form of civil law,

---

[18] Reifner 1979 p. 68 ff. Also Eriksson 1980 p. 108 f. starts *partly* from a fundamental criticism of the kind meant here, when he links different models for legal argument to the development of the societal base: the subsumptional-logical model of argument corresponds to the exchange-value rationality of early capitalism while the goal-rational and need-rational models have their roots in the competing use-value rationality of late capitalism (see below III.3.1).

based on exchange between equal and free individuals, has come into conflict with the need for planning and control that follows from the increasingly social nature of production; how this also includes a conflict between minority interests represented by traditional civil law and the political pressure from general social interests. This double conflict creates the basis for re-structuring civil law. This critique, however, does not go the whole way: it should be supplemented with a concrete legal analysis of new elements in which the law reflects the processes of social development just mentioned. Reifner terms this analysis *symptomatic criticism.*[19]

The form of alternative legal dogmatics just described presupposes reliance on a *general theory* (a "Grand Narrative") of the development of society.[20] Society changes tendentially in a certain direction and this pressure of change is reflected in elements of the law. Using his knowledge of the logic of development the researcher can create an adequate, future-oriented legal dogmatics. One could speak of a *systematic-fundamental* alternative dogmatics.

Systematic-fundamental alternative legal dogmatics is an extreme form - extreme is used without negative connotation - in relation to its opposite, critical practice. These two extremes are, however, not the only possibilities available. One can imagine intermediate forms where one tries to reconcile the view that the law is a *pragmatic instrument* for influencing society with the realization that the law is a whole that must also be scrutinised at the level of a *system*. One can see the law as a box of tools the critical judge must work with in his practice, at the same time

---

[19] Reifner 1979 p. 80 ff.

[20] Dogmatics of this type is therefore also vulnerable to a post-modern deconstructivist critique which stresses the unavoidability of a conceptual duality in our discourses. Every view put forward has a suppressed "dangerous supplement" which undermines it. An interesting analysis of American contract law based on a critique of this type has been presented by Dalton 1985, who stresses *inter alia* the impossibility of separating public from private in contract doctrine.

noting that legal ideology (the system) both influences the use of the tools and is itself a tool.

Pragmatic alternative legal dogmatics of this kind cannot construct its system *on the basis of* a general theory of the development of society and law. Here, instead, it is natural for symptomatic criticism to assume a relatively prominent position. In the concrete legal material - legislation, judgments, *travaux préparatoires*, doctrine, etc - elements are traced which break with traditional legal thinking. From these elements, new general concepts and principles are developed which can support other decisions in the same direction. The new principles are seen as instruments for use as needed by the critical judge. The interplay between juridical "theory" and practice is experienced as strong: the new theory offers arguments supporting a critical practice, which in turn supports further development of the theory. The question of what elements of the concrete legal material should be taken as a starting point in the construction of the general principles depends on the actual social situation, and the answer will therefore be changeable. The general theories of society and law are considered merely to supply *one* group of arguments for the choice of strategy, a choice which in the last analysis is perceived as *political-moral*. A model like this for alternative dogmatics could perhaps be termed *systematic-practical*.

An alternative legal-dogmatic paradigm cannot be shaped independently of the social and legal environment in which it is intended to operate. The dominant view of the role and functions of law cannot but influence alternative-dogmatic points of attack. If for example one is traditionally more inclined to attach weight to formal views in one legal system while substantive patterns of argument are given more weight in another,[21] this cannot avoid influencing, in each system, the creation of (the line of criticism in) the alternative models, which by definition must be substantive-

---

[21] See Atiyah - Summers 1987, who have attempted to show that this very difference obtains between the more formal British law and the more substantive American law.

ly characterized. It is hardly an accident that systematic-theoretical alternative legal dogmatics germinated in the German environment, where civil law (= Bürgerliches Gesetzbuch) to a far greater degree than in the Nordic countries is seen as a closed system with a "correct" theoretical basis, and where general thinking on society and law is greatly marked by model-building. The modern Nordic view of law, for its part, stresses fairly heavily the instrumental side of law at the expense of its systemic qualities (see section 4 below for more detail). In this environment it has appeared natural to attempt to explore the concrete possibilities of alternative legal dogmatics along *systematic-practical* lines.

3. THE PROBLEM

3.1 The model

This work has two purposes. First, as will already be clear, it represents a contribution to the legal-theoretical discussion on the creation of *alternative models for legal dogmatics*. The analysis does not remain at the theoretical level, however, since the usefulness of the systematic-practical model chosen is elucidated through a concrete legal-dogmatic study. Secondly, through the concrete study, the book seeks to achieve a *material result*: to develop certain new concepts and principles, of need-oriented content, which are used in building an alternative doctrinal structure of private law, "social private law".

The importance of scrutinizing law at the system level, as legal ideology, has already been stressed. For future-oriented legal dogmatics seeking alternative legal solutions in a deeper sense, this level must be the focus of research. The field of vision of legal science is delimited by its approved concepts, the general principles of law and the system: only by developing these can legal science adequately take account of the possibilities social development offers. This point of departure is analysed more closely in Chapter II.

The material object of the present work is the *general*

principles of private law and particularly of *the law of contract*. The analysis is future-oriented. The aim is to clarify certain new possibilities for the development of the systematic contents of contract law that can be discerned in the concrete legal material both from this area and from other areas of private law. A central point of attack here is the *conceptual apparatus* of contract law. The concrete legal material in the areas of private and contract law contains the embryo of new systematic concepts, admitting consideration of new issues. This is indicated in Chapter V. The discussion then turns to whether and how far this concrete material can serve as a basis for a "switching of principles" (on this concept see below II.3.3). Under what conditions and in what way can and should one endeavour to create more general principles out of the attempts at a new thinking that may be traced in the concrete legal material (Chapters VI-VII)?

An alternative legal dogmatics, even when theoretically slanted, should also have a practical goal. Its practitioner must work on the assumption that he through his work can somehow influence legal practice (in a broad sense), for otherwise his work would be meaningless. The concluding chapter, Chapter VIII, contains a discussion, based on the model constructed, of what developmental features of modern society and the law permit the assumption that an alternative dogmatics of this kind can lead to changes in practice.

3.2 The concepts of contract law

A common criticism of the general principles and concepts of private law is that they are insensitive to the concrete needs that the legal system ought to fulfil (see below II.2.2). Private law is criticised on good grounds for its excessively high level of abstraction. The abstract concepts used in private law hamper discussion of the actual parties' economic and social needs and the importance of these for the legal decisions. It can also be maintained that the use of more general concepts of law increases the relative autonomy of the legal system in relation to society. One goal of an emancipatory dogmatics of private law, attempting to bring juridical discourse closer to societal (to give the substantive elements greater weight in relation to the formal elements of the legal system), should therefore be to create *new* concepts of law and new arguments which break through the abstract façade of private-law principles. It is not enough merely to use the accepted concepts in a new way.

The high abstraction level of private law is maintained by, among other things, the *concepts of juridical roles* (more on this in Chapter IV). One speaks of seller A and buyer B, creditor C and debtor D, owner E and non-owner F, and so on, without regard to who in the actual case is hidden behind these concepts; thus in a traditional analysis of private law we less frequently run across Professor of Law A, docker B, the big industrial company C, Fatty D, small-town resident E, etc. The criticism just mentioned of the general principles of private law obviously focuses on precisely the way the parties have been described within the system of private law.[22] This becomes an important point of attack for a legal dogmatics that is attempting to enhance the potential of private law to deploy substantive arguments in connection with the circumstances of the actual parties. The objective is to lessen "the gap between legal subjectivity ... and life-factual subjectivity".[23]

When discussing the possibilities for an alternative legal dogmatics it has often been stressed that many issues would be fairly immune to a socially conditioned juridical analysis simply because the juridical features (roles) of the parties as such rule out

---

[22] Cf. also Zinke 1982, p.163 ff., who considers just this concretization of the parties a precondition for a "political" way of arguing in private law.

[23] Broekman 1986 (the quotation from p. 85) maintains the existence of this "gap". He himself appears to assume that it cannot be bridged. This is one reason why "alternative dogmatic figures" only "bring about changes in the sense of a contextually sufficient justification", not "in the sense of deep-justification" (p.94).

any regard to the social position of a party.[24] It seems, however, that such a view fails to observe that the very selection of the juridical roles that are to be used as the basis of systematization implies the adoption of a position. The legal description of the parties' relevant characteristics can be developed, and is de facto being developed all the time. The possibilities of creating, at the level of system, certain more concrete descriptions of the parties are one subject of discussion in this book. Differently expressed, the work concerns the possibilities of increasing the weight of certain new types of person-related argument in the discourse of private law.

The abstract role concepts in traditional private law, as indicated, screen off private law from other social sciences. Both a critique of private law based on empirical knowledge and a constructive use of such knowledge in legal argumentation are rendered more difficult by this abstract conceptual apparatus of private law. New person-related concepts in private law can function as intermediaries between legal dogmatics and the social sciences.

3.3 Towards a "social private law"

The creation of a new systematics for private law posits a choice of objectives that in the final instance is political-moral. The reasons for the choice underlying the present work are discussed more closely in Chapter III. The goal is to work towards a private law in which the ideology of the "*welfare state*" is taken at its word; the production of *certain elements* of a *social private law*.[25]

Much used in the literature of private law, this term "social private law" generally expresses mainly the materialization

---

[24] See e.g. Aarnio 1979 p.196 f.

[25] Cf. the concept of "Social law" in Ewald 1986, used in a broader sense as an umbrella term "for the legal practices that typify the Welfare State" (p. 40).

of private law in the form of norms for protecting the weaker party in a legal relationship. The goals of the welfare state are perceived as appearing in private law through precisely this principle of protection. As shown below (section III.1), however, such regulations of contract law, in which the principle of protection appears, can only partly be viewed as realizing this social idea: redistributive welfare goals are not realized through such rules. The question is, however, how far such goals, typical for social security law, could be promoted directly *within the framework* of private law and contract law.[26] How far can one speak of *social private law in this sense* (or perhaps even further on of "private social law")? Or, to use a more pretentious formulation: how far can the *autonomy* of traditional contract law be replaced with the *solidarity* of social law when creating general principles of contract law?

In more concrete terms the issue is here formulated as follows: *to what extent can and should a party's economic and social position be taken account of as a legal fact in contract law*? Can norms of contract law be developed which strengthen the position of economically and socially weak social groups or - using a different formulation - which (to some extent) fulfil the economic and social needs of such groups? The key concept in what follows is thus *need-orientation*: the work represents an attempt to develop the general principles of the law of contract in a more need-oriented direction.

3.4 Perspective

The concrete legal material used in this work (see Chapter V) has been taken chiefly from *Finnish law*. This material is used as *examples* of how an alternative law of contract could be established on the basis of the points advanced above.

As the *similarity of the law in the Nordic countries* (of

---

[26] The social-security function of private law - and primary of the law of succession - are analysed in Kangas 1982.

which more details in Section 4 below) is considerable, particularly regarding the general principles of private law, authoritative material from Sweden and, to some extent from the other Nordic countries, has been used where needed. In the development of social and legal values the Nordic countries are so similar that the development of the general principles can be examined and alternative models developed from a common perspective.

The book is *not* intended to be, and should not be read as, an all-round introduction to certain features of Finnish and Nordic law. Alternative dogmatics merely indicates, on the basis of certain given value premises, a legal opportunity for the critical judge.

The concrete material is intended not only to exemplify how an alternative dogmatics could be created in concrete terms. The material is also used as a starting point for a *general discussion, divorced from Finnish law*, of the substantive problem of how far and with what limitations need-orientation can be brought out as a central element of an alternative private law in the welfare state (see Chapter VI). To show that similar considerations are not inconceivable outside the Nordic countries, concrete legal material from other countries is advanced at various points.

4. ON NORDIC LAW

As stated above, a discussion of legal theory that is not operating at a very high level of abstraction cannot but be coloured by certain basic features of a national legal order. A theory is always partly bound to the practice in its country of origin, and can seldom be transferred to another legal environment entirely without modification.[27]

---

[27] As Atiyah-Summers 1987 state on page 416 as a conclusion to their comparative analysis of form and substance in English and American law: "It now seems to us that legal theorists would do well to approach many of the standard questions of jurisprudence at a lower level of abstraction, a level that at least takes account of basic variations in the phenomena of law from system to system - such as variations of valid law, in the role of judges, and in the methods of statutory interpretation

The alternative model constructed in this work has its background in *Nordic law*. Although the major part of the concrete legal material is Finnish, the basic approach to law, and the structure and legal sources of private law, are so similar in the Nordic countries that using such generalization of background for this model is justifiable.

This does not imply that the normative content of the alternative principles developed coincides in every detail in the various Nordic countries. However, *Nordic legal community* in private law renders an exchange of dogmatic ideas between legal science in the different countries a natural occurrence. In practice one often sees a more or less direct transfer of statements on legal principles and concepts from one Nordic country to another. It is typical, particularly in works on general principles, to rely heavily upon literature from the rest of the Nordic area.[28]

In what follows are mentioned - extremely briefly - some of the central features of the Nordic legal system with which the reader should be familiar if he is to understand correctly the content of the model outlined here, and to relate it to conditions in his own legal system.

First concerning *sources of law*, Nordic law belongs to the Continental tradition of strongly emphasizing *legislation* as the primary source. The paradigmatic model for legal decision-making is perceived as being the application and interpretation of written law. As opposed to what prevails in typical Continental legal systems, however, Nordic law is not based on a comprehensive civil code such as the Bürgerliches Gesetzbuch.[29] Important parts

---

(to cite just a few examples). We believe that the answers to most such questions will depend in major part upon the degree to which a given legal system is (appropriately) more formal or (appropriately) more substantive, matters that cannot be ascertained in the abstract."

[28] To give but one example: When the Danish scholar Lyngsø in his thesis of 1971 on the right to cancel a contract (p. 2 ff.) speaks of "Danish and Nordic law" as opposed to "foreign law", this is entirely consonant with the prevailing juridical paradigm.

[29] The old Swedish-Finnish code of 1734 is casuistic and today of very little importance.

of private law are codified in several more or less independent acts, such as the Contract Act, the Promissory Notes Act, the Sale of Goods Act, etc.[30] Other parts, and especially the general principles of private law, are uncodified and will probably remain so. A comprehensive codification of "the general part" of private law is not in line with Nordic traditions.

This circumstance, the central significance of legislation and the lack of a general code, make the method of constructing the general principles on the basis of analogies ("induction") from individual pieces of legislation a relatively natural one. The question of whether any piece of legislation with formally limited scope expresses a "general principle" is not uncommon in Nordic doctrine.

In the absence of a general code other accepted sources of law assume, of course, central significance,[31] not merely in the application of individual acts but also in the construction of the general principles. In Nordic law considerable weight is placed upon the *travaux préparatoires* to the legislation, and also of course to *legal practice*, particularly that of the supreme courts. In material of this kind there also occur from time to time explicit statements on the general principles considered to apply to an issue.

To supplement these authoritative sources there is reason to note particularly the weight of what are termed "real arguments", substantive arguments concerning the consequences of a decision.[32] Stressing 'real arguments' has been considered typical of Scandinavian realism with its strong emphasis on legal science as a form of *social engineering*.[33] This opening of argumentation

---

[30] The examples mentioned in the text are at the same time examples of acts which are more or less identical or at least very similar in the Nordic countries.

[31] Aarnio 1987 p. 78 ff. gives an overview in English.

[32] What are called "goal reasons" in Summers' well-known distinction between rightness reasons and goal reasons. See Summers 1979.

[33] See e.g. Helin 1988 p. 253 f.

in the direction of substantive argument occurred later in Finnish law than in that of the other Nordic countries. *Markku Helin* in his great thesis on the influence of Scandinavian realism on Finnish private-law research dates the breakthrough of social-engineering law and the strengthened position of real arguments in Finland to the 1940s.[34]

The substantive sources of law mentioned are not necessarily always secondary to the authoritative (formal) sources. There may well be situations where substance precedes form.

The relatively *low degree of formality* in Nordic law is further underlined by the fact that the hierarchy of legal sources is very little formal.[35] There exists no binding rule that would establish the internal balance between different authoritative and substantive arguments in Nordic law apart from legislation, which normally is considered to be the primary source. Consequently the pattern of assessment varies to some extent from court to court and among writers on legal science.

Despite the lack of a general civil code, a Nordic jurist tends *from a structural point of view* to perceive the law in Continental manner as a systematic whole, a *doctrinal structure*. Since, however, the parts of this structure - its general principles and concepts - are not laid down by legislation, they are not perceived as a "given" theoretical framework using which legislative measures that do not fit could be rejected as "juridically incorrect".[36] The doctrinal structure is subordinate to the primacy of legislation; this is connected with the instrumental view of the law that prevails within Scandinavian realism.

The absence of a general civil code also allows legal science relatively great latitude in building a theoretical structure

---

[34] Helin 1988 p. 368 ff.

[35] The concept of formality is here used in the same sense as in Atiyah - Summers 1987.

[36] Such a way of arguing as used in West German doctrine on Sonderprivatrecht and its congruence with private law (= BGB), see e.g. Chapter II, at Footnote 20, below for more detail, would hardly be possible in the Nordic countries.

of law. Particularly in these systematical questions the authoritative weight of legal dogmatics is significant in Nordic law.

It will be clear from the above brief overview that Nordic law - despite its Continental points of departure in the emphasis on legislation, system and legal dogmatics - exhibits features that lead one's thoughts in the direction of an Anglo-American way of looking at law. As examples of this one could perhaps mention the absence of a statutory general part of private law and the readiness to accept pragmatic-instrumental argumentation. A model for alternative dogmatics based on such an "intermediate form" of legal system can to some extent use models from both Continental and Anglo-American law. For the same reason the model can hopefully, in its turn, find some understanding among critical jurists within both these types of legal system.

CHAPTER II

"GENERAL PRINCIPLES" AS THE PRIMARY OBJECT OF ALTERNATIVE STUDIES

1. REMARKS ON THE TERMINOLOGY

As was stressed in the Introduction, any model of legal dogmatics that is alternative in a deeper sense must direct attention to the way legal dogmatics systematizes its research object. This does not mean systematization in a merely pedagogical sense, but something more: the general principles and concepts of the legal order or the relevant branch of law stand at the centre of interest. These are the instruments with whose help the systematization is carried out.

In continental legal discourse the concept "*general doctrines*" (in German "allgemeine Lehren") is widely used. The content of the concept, however, can be understood in different ways. Often the attribute "*general*" is stressed. The "general doctrines" of private law then affect norms and concepts that emerge within all or at least many of the particular fields of private law.[1] Such general doctrines may be formed not only by legal science but by the legislator as well. But the emphasis can also be placed upon the noun "*doctrines*". The "general doctrines" are perceived as something developed by those learned in the law,

---

[1] Thus e.g. Tolonen 1973 p. 12.

in other words chiefly by *legal science*. They constitute the system created by legal science within which individual statutes, legal cases and other legal source material can be arranged.[2] When speaking of the systematizing contribution of legal dogmatics, it is precisely this aspect of the "general doctrines" that one thinks about. In the present work, the general doctrines of private law are conceived in the latter sense. Consequently, it is not "*general* doctrines", but rather "general *doctrines*" that are treated here. Even principles that belong within only some particular branch of private law can therefore be included in this concept.

The subject of an alternative legal dogmatics of the kind developed here is therefore those concepts and legal principles developed by legal science that hold together both private law in general and its particular sub-areas. In other words, we are dealing with the *integrative* element within each branch of law. Using the concepts and principles, the individual fragments of law are connected together: through them is created a system of law.[3]

This could be rendered concrete with a metaphor, halting in places yet illuminating: if one compares the legal system with a building, the individual norms or rather the legal source material of statutes, cases, statements in *travaux préparatoires* etc. represent the bricks and other parts (more important statutes such as the Contract Act can be understood as entire building elements) of which the building can be constructed. The plan one uses to erect a building of the parts must all the same be created by legal science. It is this plan, or parts thereof, that represents what are here termed "general doctrines". Of present interest is not only the

---

[2] When in such a definition interest is directed towards legal science, this does not of course imply depriving e.g. the legislation of importance as an influence on the general principles. It is obvious that the legislator, particularly through general regulation such as in the Nordic countries the Contract Act or, in German law, the general part of Bürgerliches Gesetzbuch, can guide the legal-scientific development of general doctrines.

[3] They constitute the aids with which in Juha Pöyhönen's terminology *the legal order* is transformed into a *legal system*. This distinction between legal order and legal system which has been stressed by Pöyhönen in various contexts will not be consistently employed in this book.

structure of the entire building (the markedly "*general*" doctrines), but also individual details - for example the siting of the bathrooms.

"General doctrines" as the English form of the Continental "allgemeine Lehren" is not a very adequate term. In what follows therefore, "*general principles*" is used to refer to the content of the system-building elements - both *legal concepts* and "*legal principles*" - which were stated above to form parts of "the general doctrines" of civil law. Thus for "general principles" in what follows, unless otherwise clear from the context, read "legal principles and concepts".

There is, however, reason to stress that the term "legal principle" is by no means unambiguous. It is often used undefined in legal writing and can refer to different features. A "legal principle" can conceivably be distinguished from a "legal rule" on at least the following different grounds:[4]

(i) One can refer to the degree of *generality* in the norm in question. Norms with a broader sphere of application would be principles while more closely delimited norms would be rules.

(ii) Sometimes reference is made to the *way in which the norm has originated*. Legislation contains rules, while the principles arise through legal practice, legal writing and so on.

(iii) It may also be a matter of the degree of explicit *binding to values*. Principles are more openly value-bound than rules are.

(iv) Further, one can also describe as principles norms that in some respect are more *typical* of the relevant legal system, while rules represent only exceptions from, or are neutral with regard to, the systematic entirety.

(v) One view is that only rules are perceived as true legal norms, while principles are seen only as *bases for norms*, justifications of norms or as indicators of the values to be observed when applying norms.

---

[4] This list is developed on the basis of the analysis in Pöyhönen 1988 p. 20 f.

(vi) Lastly one can distinguish on the basis of the position of the norm within legal decision-making, of the way in which the norm is theoretically[5] considered *to determine* the result of a legal inference. One can with *Robert Alexy*[6] view the principles as *optimization commands* (Optimierungsgebote), which should be followed as closely as possible but which in individual decisions must be weighed against other principles. Thus they can be applied to a greater or a lesser extent, while rules must be applied "in an all-or-nothing fashion".[7] In Nordic legal theory a corresponding distinction has already been made using the terms rules and *guidelines*.[8]

The "general principles" with which the present work is concerned are as mentioned the structure that legal science has created by joining the elements of the law into a system. The defining of the object of investigation is thus based primarily upon the distinction mentioned in point (ii): alternative legal dogmatics is interested in the normative structure that has arisen and is continuously being renewed through legal science. "General principles" are in this context "*legal principles and concepts created by legal doctrine*". At the same time they naturally also incorporate traits of the distinction mentioned in points (i) and (iv): the systematic elements are always to some degree general and typical ones. The question is precisely when and how new individual elements in the legal order can be generalized to form new, more or less typical, general principles.

It should be particularly stressed that the distinction between principles and rules which is made in point (vi) and which today appears to be dominating legal-theoretical discussion of legal principles does not form a basis for defining the term "general

---

[5] Granted that interpretation of the norm is presumed to be unproblematic.

[6] Alexy 1985 p. 19ff. Alexy has further developed Dworkin's distinction between rules and principles, see Dworkin 1981 p. 24 ff.

[7] Dworkin 1981 p. 24.

[8] Eckhoff - Sundby 1976.

principles" as used in this work. The "general principles" intended here may be both "principles" and "rules" in Dworkin's and Alexy's terminology. As will emerge from Chapter VI, the new systematic proposals developed here must in the majority of cases be given in the form of guidelines; in Chapter VII, however, a problem complex is also presented where new formulations with the character of rules can be arrived at.

2. THE SIGNIFICANCE OF THE GENERAL PRINCIPLES

2.1 General principles as juridical arguments

The general principles (the systematization) have not been created merely for theoretical or pedagogical ends: they are also of significance for practical legal decision-making. Even if we do not today consider a purely conceptual-juridical method (Begriffsjurisprudenz) - drawing concrete juridical conclusions from the general concepts constructed by legal science - to be presentable, it is not considered unsuitable to use the general principles and concepts in juridical argument in a more uncommitted way.[9] General legal principles and other systematic arguments represent one - but only one - group of arguments that can be used for justifying a legal decision.

In his analysis of the Finnish (Nordic) doctrine of legal sources, *Aulis Aarnio* places general legal principles in the group of arguments (legal sources) described as permitted arguments. The legal decision-maker would not be obliged to observe these arguments - as opposed to the arguments statute, custom, *travaux préparatoires* and court decisions - but it would be permitted to adduce them when necessary.[10] This actually acceptable analysis of prevailing normative legal ideology should not, however, conceal the fact that general legal principles in certain situations -

[9] See e.g Helin 1985 p. 91 f.

[10] See Aarnio 1987 p. 89 ff.

primarily of course where the concrete legal material is incomplete - can acquire a very significant position in legal reasoning.

It is partly a political question as to how strong an argument value one wishes to concede to general legal principles. It has been claimed that these often assume a static character.[11] The more one then stresses the value of general legal principles as a source of law, the stronger become the arguments that can be adduced against a legal practice and a legal science which seek to introduce new elements in the law.[12]

This view of the political role of general legal principles is based on the conviction that they are lagging behind changes in the legislation and other concrete legal material. Theoretically, this need by no means be the case, and has not always been the case historically, either (see for more detail below 5.iii). In principle, legal science can also function as a forerunner and develop general principles that are more in line with the times than is an obsolete legislation. From criticism of the retarding effect of the general principles, therefore, one does not necessarily need to conclude that their position should be (further) played down; one can just as well maintain that the *content* of the principles should be *modified* instead.

The analysis of the express use of general principles as source of law, which quite correctly classifies them as permittled arguments only, is also misleading. In fact, general principles are always present in the application of law, as the application does not take place in a value-free vacuum. Many traditional general principles are just considered as so self-evident, that no express reference to them is needed. They are only impliedly present in

---

[11] See e.g. Kivivuori 1983 p. 58 f.

[12] An illuminating example can be taken from the West-German discussion regarding the development of rules of consumer law, where certain advocates of improved protection for consumers have stressed the danger that such rules, if included in the Bürgerliches Gesetzbuch, would be interpreted on the basis of obsolete general principles. See e.g. Damm 1978 p. 176; cf. however, regarding possibilities of influence in the other direction, e.g. Gilles 1980 p. 6.

the legal decision.

Total elimination of the general principles as a source of juridical argument can therefore not be achieved, as long as there is a desire to maintain the notion of a systematic legal science. The very systematization of juridical material influences legal argumentation. Behind every analogy there lies a certain perception of the design of the juridical system - an implicit "general principle".[13]

2.2 *The significance of the conceptual apparatus*

Systematization of the law affects not only the conclusion reached through legal reasoning but also its starting point. The legal conceptual apparatus controls the *formulation of the problems* that are perceived as juridically relevant.

The analytical criticism of the substantive concept of ownership in conceptual jurisprudence is here the traditional example. Analytically dividing the concept of ownership into its various elements allows us to ask new and more precise questions when examining problems connected with the transfer of this right.[14] It is easy to illustrate from contract law, too, the significance of the conceptual apparatus for the way problems are formulated. While within a traditional law on the sale of goods - with certain exceptions - juridical problems were examined in the relationship between seller and buyer in general, one can now, following the development of the conceptual pair merchant/consumer assess the questions in different ways depending on whether the matter is one of a purchase between merchants or a contract

---

[13] It may be mentioned that the Finnish Supreme Court often formulates analogical inferences in such ways that the court claims support from a "legal directive" which emerges from a legal rule not directly applicable to the case (see e.g., as an example, HD 1969 II 18). The analogy, then, is explicitly given the following structure: inapplicable legal rule -> general principle with broader application -> analogous conclusion.

[14] In Finland this analytical critique was carried out by Zitting in 1951.

between a merchant and a consumer.[15] This naturally makes possible a larger spectrum of conceivable answers.

Nor, either, can the juridical conceptual apparatus be dispensed with as long as one remains true to a systematic legal science. This is not to say that the conceptual apparatus must of necessity be the most general one possible. A general system of regulation has been said to be more insensitive to citizens' particular needs and circumstances.[16] The same may be said of the general concepts of the general principles. The answer to this criticism cannot, however, be an attempt to achieve the impossible (as long as law is not abolished), that is, to eliminate the juridical conceptual apparatus. The criticsm should, rather, be taken into account in such a way as to attempt to develop *new* less general juridical *concepts* that more adequately reflect the needs they are dealing with.

Such a lowering of the level of generality of the juridical conceptual apparatus involves at the same time a reduction of the relative autonomy of the law in relation to society.[17] The more juridical concepts approach those concepts with whose help concrete social reality can be described, the more sensitive the law also becomes to more occasional demands made by different groups in society. This is a development for good and evil: the more concrete concepts make possible both a critical reshaping of the law and its more effective use in the interest of the predominant social groups. The reduction in the relative autonomy of the law can therefore also be evaluated in various ways (see also below III.4).

---

[15] The third category, contracts between private persons, has attracted less interest.

[16] Thus e.g. Kivivuori 1983 p. 58.

[17] "The same events that subvert the generality also tend to destroy the relative autonomy of the legal order", writes Roberto Mangabeira Unger, 1976 p. 199. See also Friedman 1986 p. 16, who stresses the connection between the formal rationality of traditional law and its autonomy, and also Wilhelmsson 1986.

2.3 *The de lege ferenda significance of systematization*

What has just been said already contains a hint that the general principles have a more far-reaching significance than merely to function as aids to the application of the law in force. They control not only the activity of those who apply the law *de lege lata*, they also draw limits for the law drafter's activity *de lege ferenda*.[18]

This holds good in both political[19] and technical respects. It goes without saying that it is far harder to put through legislation that conflicts with established legal principles than legislation that is easy to fit into the generally-embraced system. That the legal conceptual apparatus also influences problem formulations at de-lege-ferenda-level is, in addition, more or less self-evident.

As a typical example one might mention the West German discussion of whether a general system of regulation for consumer protection ought to be introduced. One of the main arguments of the opponents here has been that regulation of this nature would "burst the system", would be irreconcilable with the prevailing order of private law.[20]

---

[18] Esser 1964 p. 57 prefers the formulation that the general principles protect "gegenüber juristischem Pointillismus und legislativer Selbstherrlichkeit".

[19] A similar train of thought from quite different starting-points clearly underlies the theories of law as an autopoietic system: "The autopoietic closure sets effective limits to the political instrumentalization of law", Teubner 1988 p. 4. See also e.g. Broekman 1986 p. 80: "law cannot accept legal measures which endanger the unity of law".

[20] See on this point e.g. Reich 1977 p. 196, Westermann 1983 p. 11.

3. THE COHERENCE AND CHANGEABILITY OF THE GENERAL PRINCIPLES

3.1 Contradictions within the law

In traditional juridical doctrine one often understands the legal system as an, at least in theory, conflict-free whole built upon a relatively uniform foundation of values.[21] The consistency of the law is stressed as the central legal value. The differences in substantive values, which, because of the varying ages of the concrete legal material if for no other reason, must underlie the positions taken in legislation and legal practice, are pushed into the background by general principles extracted from the material and claimed to provide a generally accepted system of juridical values. The concrete building blocks that are the working material of legal science, can, consequently, according to this view be joined only in *one* acceptable way. At any one time there exists only one set of building plans - fairly small variations can naturally occur - that represents the system of general principles "in force".

In many parts of the world legal science has begun to question this view of the legal system as something basically harmonious - which view is naturally grounded in a feeling that society is an organic whole without (deep) inner contradictions - and, instead, asserted the conflict-filled character of the law. This aspect has in fact been strongly stressed by the representatives of an alternative legal dogmatics. It may also be claimed that *this very emphasis on the internal contradictions of the law is the feature that most clearly differentiates various forms of alternative dogmatics from traditional dogmatics.*

Some examples of such alternative dogmatic formulations that have their starting point in the notion of the internal contradictions of the law will be mentioned in what follows.

---

[21] Goodrich 1986 p. 4 ff. connects this perceived unity of the legal system with the need for an "ideational source of law" such as God, reason, nature etc.

In the Federal Republic of Germany, *Udo Reifner* has, as mentioned before, published a theoretical model for alternative legal dogmatics in a large study on consumer credit. The starting point of his analysis is the conflicts arising from the private law system. The author emphasises the existence of contradictions on both the economic and the political levels: first, there is a conflict between the individualism of private law and the need for a social regulation of production which has become increasingly social and, secondly, between general private law, as a formulation of the interests of a minority, and the political pressure from other interests.

Because of these conflicts, to an increasing extent private law itself corresponds to a legal form which mirrors the process of sociality (Vergesellschaftung).[22] Existing legal dogmatics, however, has not noticed this development and, therefore, strives to explain the new features of private law as exceptions. Reifner offers another solution: one should reject the prevailing views concerning the formulation of main rules and exceptions from the conflicting material. The aim should be a social interpretation with the starting point being a material rather than a formal conception of the ideals of freedom, equality and certainty.[23] The ideals underlying bourgeois law should be taken seriously as a basis for substantive legal demands.

In the USA similar perceptions, from an entirely different philosophical starting point, have been presented by *Roberto Mangabeira Unger*. In his model, too, Unger emphasizes the contradictions within the legal order.

There are conflicts between the different levels of abstraction (principles and rules, etc) as well as conflicts within the same level. The critical (or deviationist) doctrine should start "by conceiving a broad field of law as the expression of a system of principles and counter-principles whose actual or proper relation to

---

[22] Reifner 1979 p. 79.

[23] Reifner 1979 p. 99.

each other can be represented in clashing ways".[24]

Deviationist doctrine wants to bring these instabilities in the legal system to the surface and not suppress them. It thereby becomes possible for the doctrine to rearrange the relation between the traditional leading principles and their counter-principles. Instead of the principle of freedom to contract, Unger emphasizes the counter-principle of community, and instead of the principle of freedom of contract, the counter-principle of fairness.[25] On this basis he creates a counter-vision which "implies that obligations do arise primarily from relationships of mutual dependence that have been only incompletely shaped by state-imposed duties or explicit and perfected bargains".[26]

In Nordic doctrine *Lars D. Eriksson* builds his theory of alternative use of the law on an analysis of the different models of legal reasoning which he claims prevail in late capitalism. He distinguishes between the model of subsumptional logic and the goal-rational model and alleges that the importance of the latter is growing; in many fields of the law it has already gained a dominating position.[27] The social content of the legal decisions comes to the fore in the legal argumentation. In some fields progressive goals have been formulated within the law; social and collective values have central positions as principles, e.g. in environmental law, social law, planning law, etc. There are, however, contradictions between these progressive values and other elements of the legal order.

The new jurisprudence should make use of these contradictions within the law. Its task is to take seriously the social needs and interests which are formulated in the capitalist legal order as real and primary goals for this order, instead of treating them just

---

[24] Unger 1983 p. 646.

[25] Unger 1983 p. 618 ff.

[26] Unger 1983 p. 639.

[27] Eriksson 1979 p. 42 ff., 1980 p. 108 ff.

as instruments for preserving the system.[28] Or expressed somewhat differently, legal dogmatics ought to strive towards a deformalization and de-objectivization of the law "through a *disarticulation*, a breaking-down into their smallest components, of valid principles, theories, constructions, systematizations, etc, on the one hand, and on the other a *re-articulation*, i.e. these smallest components being reassembled but now on the basis of a new integrative principle".[29]

All the authors mentioned above stress the idea of the law being full of internal contradictions. When adopting a perspective that thus stresses conflict, it is not for the purpose of increasing interest in possible juridical-technical conflicts between concrete norms. What is more interesting here is the realization that various elements of the law can express ethical, social-philosophical and social-political starting points that contradict each other.

The contradictions within the law that are of interest for alternative legal dogmatics can be vertical or horizontal. The contradiction can exist between different levels of legal regulation or may be read from different legal elements on the same level. The following types, at least, of contradictions *within* the law can be distinguished:

(i) One can, as e.g. Eriksson does, take a starting point in the vertical conflict between intralegal *goal formulations* and *concrete legal norms*. If such goal formulations which are incorporated into the law are taken literally, they often prove to go much further than the legal measures through which the goals are intended to be realized.

(ii) *Different branches of law* can be characterized by partially differing social values. Such contradictions exist not only between traditionally counterposed fields such as private law and public law: within private law, too, corresponding conflicts have arisen. Today's private law "embodies a multiplicity of special

[28] Eriksson 1979 p. 46.

[29] Eriksson 1985 p. 91 (translated here).

private laws, long without conceptual, dogmatic unity".[30]

(iii) The conflict can also be located to the relationship *between legal elements* within the same branch of law. Within the law of contract, for example, there may occur separate statutes, legal cases and other concrete legal material that express mutually conflicting values.

3.2 Causes of contradictions: an example

Contradictions within the law are a consequence of the social nature of law. Law cannot be developed as an isolated whole, detached from the rest of society: it is always to some degree a result of (conflicting) social interests and interest combinations prevailing at any one time.[31] For this reason it is obvious that the balancing-off of interests petrified in concrete legal material at a certain point in time is not necessarily the same as what is expressed in material from a different point in time. The

---

[30] Teubner 1989 p. 414. In Teubner's analysis of the conflicts within modern law (p. 416 ff.) the conflicts between separate legal fields are mentioned as the central form of system conflicts internal to law (at partly extra-legal levels conflicts occur between "autopoietic social systems" such as between politics, economy, family, religion, science and culture and between State law and "the quasi-law of various social fields" such as standardized terms of trade). The internal conflicts between separate legal fields are a consequence of the legislator's and the courts' *ad hoc* striving for compromises between outer and inner goals and requirements, which "results in very separate legal fields, administered by specialized legal experts, who identify with the corresponding social spheres at least as strongly as with the law" (p. 419). - Teubner's way of exploiting the conflicts departs, however, from those of the alternative dogmaticians mentioned in the text. The described dissolution of the law into a number of special laws without conceptual and dogmatic unity is something that, in Teubner's model, one should not attempt to overcome through an integration of the elements with the help of (new) uniform values and concepts. Rather, one should recognize "the relative autonomy of legal fields": "the mutual recognition of each field's basic principles buffers the further development of principles, yielding an overall coherence" (p. 420).

[31] Cf. also e.g. Ewald 1986 p. 58: "the law is no longer so much the expression of the general will as the form taken on by the endlessly renewed settlements of society with itself".

social strengths of the respective interests when a piece of regulation was introduced must affect its formulation.

Explanations of the internal contradictoriness of the law should not of course be sought only in the varying ages of the concrete legal material. Different combinations of contemporary interests can also result in different concrete legal elements; different parts of the legislative apparatus (e.g. different ministries) and the judicature can be affected in different ways by different background interests. One and the same legal instrument (an act, for example) can also represent such a genuine compromise between differing interests that it contains within itself conflicting parts.

The *temporal aspect* of the internal conflicts of the law is well illustrated in the West German discussion about a possible reform of the Bürgerliches Gesetzbuch. It is often maintained that the BGB is based on an obsolete "social model" from the 1800's which is incompatible with the new model underlying the development of modern private law.[32] If, as often happens, one equates BGB and "Privatrecht" the same conflict also emerges in the banner "Wirtschaftsrecht als Kritik des Privatrechts".[33] It is, to mention still one more formulation, basically the same contradiction as when one asserts as today's central conflict within the law the dual character of the law: on one hand as organizer of economic processes that run according to market principles, and on the other as a state instrument for influencing these processes and introducing social-state goals into them.[34] This conflict between "the models" is perceived precisely as a consequence of the different interests behind the legislation. While different social groups can nowadays at least partially influence legislative change, the

---

[32] This view, presented by the grand old man of German private-law history Franz Wieacker already in the 1950's (see Wieacker 1974 p. 9 ff.), is discussed in detail in e.g. Westermann 1978 and Schmidt 1985 p. 17 ff.

[33] See Assmann - Brüggemeier - Hart - Joerges 1980.

[34] Reich 1977 p. 65.

BGB is said to be dominated by the interests of one social class.[35]

As already indicated, the temporal aspect is not the only source of conflict within the law. As a consequence of social compromise contradictory values often infuse concrete legal material from the same period. This is the case today: the "dual character" of German private law is of course continuously being reproduced and confirmed in modern material. But the same goes for older norms: the relatively uniform value background to the BGB could, for example, be achieved only be referring many labour-law issues, and also the problems of hire-purchase, for regulation in special legislation.[36] But not even with these measures was it possible to produce an entirely coherent BGB. It has in fact been said that this codification in individual details both maintains authoritarian or patriarchal features and leaves scope for the social demands of the future.[37]

3.3 Consequences for the systematization of the law

The emphasis on the contradictory nature of the law is of essential importance when the design of the general principles is discussed. Only as far as the concrete legal material of a branch of law is based on a uniform value system is it possible to elaborate general principles that objectively reflect the whole of this material. If however - as claimed above - contradictory values are represented in the statutes, legal cases and other legal source material the legal dogmatician is to use, the development of a system, of general principles, always presupposes a choice: what values are to be elevated into main principles and what are to be viewed merely as exceptions from the main principle? If one wishes to draw any general conclusion from the international discussion of the self-contradictory nature of the law and the significance of this for legal dogmatics, it boils down to the

---

[35] "Das besitzende Bürgertum", see Wieacker 1974 p. 16.

[36] See e.g. Kindermann 1981.

[37] Wieacker 1974 p. 22.

demand that the prevailing view of main principles and exceptions need not necessarily be respected. From what has previously been perceived as an exception one can, if this seems justified, create new main principles. Concepts and distinctions earlier viewed as applying to special cases may be generalized to form leading systematic points of departure.

Therefore, the emphasis on the contradictions in the law need hardly have as a consequence a denial of the possibility of a systematic legal science as such. One goal of legal dogmatics can (and should) continue to be to create a consistent set of general principles starting from the available concrete legal material. The fact that one recognizes the existence of contradictions in this material entails, however, certain consequences for the status one grants these principles. These consequences are as follows:

(i) One must recognize the possibility of building up *many different systems* of general principles on the basis of the concrete legal material. The systematization offered by traditional doctrine (*communis opinio*) is only *one* possible systematization. Referring back to the building metaphor it may be said that not one, but many, building plans can be drawn up using the same amount of material. - Yet this does not mean that the general principles could be formulated in an entirely arbitrary fashion starting from the concrete legal material. To some extent they must contain *a-priori* elements which of necessity follow from the link with the form of society the principles are to serve. Or, to use the building metaphor again: the surrounding landscape and the environment always limit to some extent the architect's options.

(ii) The choice between different systematizations cannot be made using criteria from within the law: the key to the system must be found *outside the law*.[38] The building's social purposes, etc, are decisive for how the given material is arranged in the drawing.

---

[38] See also the plea of Goodrich 1986 p. 216 "for systematizations of the law that will take into account more than the singular internal logic of legal texts themselves".

The attempt of traditional legal dogmatics to seek the key to its systematization within the law is illusory, and in practice means only an emphasis, grounded outside the law, on legal tradition: a formerly accepted principle is upheld almost regardless of the, perhaps growing, number of exceptions to that principle.

(iii) The system elaborated by legal science necessarily takes on a more *momentary* character. The traditional legal-dogmatic view of the legal system as a slowly changing whole in which more important systematic rearrangements are effected only on the basis of gradually accumulated massive changes in the concrete legal material cannot be upheld. Both new building blocks and changes in circumstances outside the law can at any time make a re-examination of the systematization justifiable.

Analysis by the representatives of alternative legal dogmatics cited above consequently leads to a demand for a kind of "*switching of principles*". To the extent socially justifiable, there is a wish to have the system's main rules and the exceptions change places. The recognition of such a possibility for a "switching of principles" is a central point of departure for a systematically directed alternative legal dogmatics. This realization makes it possible within the framework of legal dogmatics to call parts of the prevailing professional legal ideology in question - to draw legal ideology into the struggle for social-ideological hegemony.

Naturally, this switching of principles cannot be an end in itself. For a legal dogmatician striving for renewal of the general principles but *not* believing in any completely linear theory of evolution where *each* new development necessarily represents something more modern and therefore better than what went before, a fundamental problem is therefore to decide on those cases for which such renewal is socially justified. The decision requires an answer to two problems: first a statement on what new elements in the concrete legal material one wishes to consider as valuable steps forward - not everything new is good; secondly determination of whether the good new values are of such importance that one should strive for generalization of the legal elements containing such values.

These choices, which, as stated above, cannot be made using only criteria from within the law, are ultimately *politico-moral* ones. The criteria for the development of the general principles are always to some extent linked with the researcher's view of society, which naturally can and should be based on a scientific analysis of society, and with his view of what social group's interests the legal order can and should protect. One systematization can favour certain social groups while others may be favoured by another approach. There is no meta-criterion, detached from the researcher's politico-moral choice, to determine which of the two alternatives is the "more correct".[39]

This "decisionist" view has been criticized for "raising its hands" in defeat when faced with the demand for rational justification of the choice.[40] Even if those elements of the choice that relate to scientific analyses of the effects of legal rules and the structure of society, etc., are rational, the final position on the question of what interests the researcher wishes to promote will indubitably be "decisionist". This criticism, however, if it is to hit the mark, presupposes that one imagines that the alternative principles, too, would be produced with the same demand for recognition as the only correct systematization as traditional dogmatics makes. But if the above consequences of the contradictory nature of the law are taken seriously, this is impossible. An alternative dogmatics cannot in my view, without betraying itself, seek any "one and only" way of building a new system of general principles. An alternative doctrine presents only a *possible* new model, to be used or rejected by different parts of the juridical auditorium.[41]

---

[39] This is also stressed in West German critical theory: see e.g. Joerges 1989 p. 619: "The normative problematic of the materialization process appears rather to consist in the fact than no meta-criteria are available for decisions between the internally contradictory statutes and legal principles".

[40] Tuori 1988 p. 203 in a direct comment on the Swedish edition of the present work.

This possible alternative systematization, having been determined by a key from outside the law, must also itself, as mentioned above, openly have a *momentary* character. When changes occur in the socially or legally possible (see below 5.iii), the alternative legal doctrine may and should create a new system which better reflects the new conditions. The less the doctrine feels itself bound by the systematical solutions of traditional legal dogmatics, the less it can be tightly bound by its own earlier redefinitions. The building of a stable new system of law - in the same sense as traditional legal dogmatics creates the legal system - is impossible for the alternative use of law, if it wants to remain true to its own point of departure.

If the facultative and instable nature of the new systematizations is conceded in this way, it is clear that the criticism sometimes made of critical legal science, that it attempts to do the impossible in building up a system where such a system, given the fundamental contradictions of the law, must always be illusory, falls to the ground.[42] The new system is openly recognized to be as illusory as the old; it is being built because, as legal ideology, it has practical significance.

[41] This is also noted by Tuori 1988 p. 204, according to whom the models of alternative legal dogmatics only are statements in the general legal and social normative discourse, which are on the same starting-line as the other material systematization proposals.

[42] See also e.g. Joerges 1989 p. 639 f. on the disillusionment within Critical Legal Studies. From a deconstructivist perspective Dalton 1985, analysing American contract doctrine, stresses "the inevitable relevation that public cannot be separated from private, or form from substance, or objective manifestation from subjective intent", because we are basically incapable of knowing or controlling the boundary between self and other (p. 1113).

4. THE "LEGAL QUALITY" OF THE NEW GENERAL PRINCIPLES

Large sections of the general principles embraced by predominant forms of legal dogmatics are based on *tradition*. New legal dogmatics reproduces maxims embraced by previous legal dogmatics. Frequently there is not seen to be any need of special "verification", in the form of references to concrete legal cases or similar sources, of the validity of such principles. It stands above discussion that the tradition-based principles have the character of *legal* principles.

A legal dogmatics that strives to free itself from tradition needs a different ground for justifying why the system being presented lays claim to being called legal. A solution to this problem of justification was stated, in the introductory chapter, to lie in what has been called *symptomatic criticism* of law in force. One seeks *inside the law* reflections of the new social values one is attempting to promote. These points of attachment within the law are assumed to confer a legal character upon the conclusions.

The talk of a symptomatic criticism is another way of expressing the assertion made in several connections above in this chapter, that legal dogmatics should build up its general principles with the help of accessible "*concrete legal material*". If this building material does not suffice for erecting a building that matches the legal dogmatician's drawing, the drawing gives no possible *legal* building alternative. Granted, general principles that are entirely ungrounded in concrete legal material can form a beautiful whole, but this whole cannot in any generally accepted sense be called legal: it appears merely as some sort of social-philosophical moral code.

Of what, then, does this concrete legal material consist, that can confer legal quality upon the general principles? Can legal arguments really be distinguished from social-philosophical, political, moral, etc., arguments?[43] In part, such a demarcation line is of course impossible to draw: certain arguments definitely belong in *both* spheres. Yet there are also arguments that are typical only of legal discourse. This is well illustrated by the classification of legal sources in certain presentations of the doctrine of legal sources:[44] there are, on the one hand, *authoritative reasons* whose relevance follows not from their substantive content but primarily from the institutionalised importance of the legal source and, on the other hand, *substantial reasons*. What marks legal reasoning - as opposed from, for example, political reasoning - is the considerable relevance one accords certain authoritative reasons, chiefly of course law texts but also statements in *travaux préparatoires* and legal cases and, to some extent, dogmatic literature. It is these authoritative reasons that form the concrete legal material, that confer legal quality upon an edifice of general principles[45].

For juridical discourse to be possible at all one must, in other words, approve legal tradition to the extent that one accepts the binding force of legislation and grants legal practice a certain relevance as source material. This, however, does not imply that no changes may take place in the weight one places upon these traditional legal sources in relation to each other as well as in relation to other sources. A critical legal dogmatics can naturally call the traditional hierarchy of legal sources into question.[46]

The systematic relation of the concrete legal material used for critical purposes to the branch of law whose general principles are under discussion can vary depending on what kind of internal

---

[43] Cf. e.g. Rottleuthner 1973 p. 167: "Ich weiss nicht, woran man Argumenten ansehen könnte, ob sie politische oder rechtliche oder 'rechtsfremde' sind".

[44] See e.g. Aarnio 1987 p. 92 ff.

[45] Cf. also Esser 1964 p. 132 "*von wann ab* haben Rechtsprinzipien den Charakter positiven Rechts? Antwort: Sobald und soweit sie durch rechtsbildende Akte der Legislative, der Jurisprudenz oder des Rechtslebens institutionell verkörpert worden sind".

[46] Thus also Eriksson 1985 p. 93.

contradictions (see above 3.1 at points i-iii) are being employed in the analysis:

(i) Symptomatic criticism is obviously on strong ground when it can point to concrete legal material from the same branch of law in which alternative values have found expression. The traditional picture of a uniform set of general principles for the branch of law may be blown to pieces so to speak from within. Particularly if the new elements are many, one may state that an alternative principle is being created through a kind of "*legal induction*".[47] Tradition is called into question through new "induction". In the present work (Chapters V-VII), the main reasoning is precisely one of this kind.

(ii) One may also start with the value conflicts between different traditional branches of law. One may *question the classification* and attempt to cross the boundaries of the branches. One may attempt to introduce new values within one field which have been given legal quality in other fields.

This type of argumentation perhaps seems particularly convincing in cases where a division into separate branches of law has arisen just because traditional dogmatics has tried to *define out* new regulations from one field to protect tradition in this field from contamination by new ways of thinking. The separating of labour law into a special branch of law is a good example of this procedure. Increased, socially grounded regulation of the conditions of working life has in many countries led to this regulation being described as part of a special branch of law that no longer has any close connection with "general" private law. Critical legal dogmatics can query this systematization and attempt to draw labour-law values as alternative values into, for example, general contract law, too. This way of arguing is recommended by, e.g. *Udo Reifner*, who finds the new legal forms that contain alterna-

---

[47] The quotation marks stress that the "induction" is here a normative process where the choice of starting points is, as maintained above, openly value-bound.

tive principles particularly in labour law and the law of tenancy.[48]

The present work calls upon concrete material from the whole field of contract and tort law, including sections of labour law, in support of the development of new principles of contract law. For the rest, given the sufficiency of the "inductive" material, there has been no need to undertake comprehensive analyses of the value background to other branches of law than the one treated here. The exception is a brief overview of certain rules of family law and the law of succession.

(iii) Lastly it is possible to bring in hierarchically higher legal material in a vertical critique of private law. This has occurred in for example the West German debate on private law where there have been attempts to instate the Constitution as a new, central, authoritative source of law. The so-called *Sozialstaatsklausel* (social state clause) of the Constitution has been cited in support of development of the principles of private law: some scholars even maintain that the choice between the conflicting elements of private law *must* in the end be based on a social-state constitutional theory.[49] The notion of social state is perceived as giving legal support for developing the protection of the weaker party,[50] including for example consumer protection.[51] It is also natural that this constitutional notion may give certain guidance in applying the general clauses of private law.[52]

In Finnish and Nordic private law, however, such patterns of argument are not met with. The Constitution does not here offer such close points of support for a social reasoning in private law. Here, therefore, one must fall back on more traditional legal sources if the desire is to give new general principles legal anchorage. On the other hand these sources, in Finnish and Nordic law,

---

48 Reifner 1979 p. 92.

49 Reich 1977 p. 66. See also e.g. Brüggemeier 1980 p. 81.

50 See e.g. Esser - Schmidt 1984 p. 6.

51 Thus Reich 1977 p. 197.

52 See e.g. Henf 1978 p. 326 ff.

afford the legal dogmatician relatively large freedom of choice; in West German private law, dominated by the great codification (Bürgerliches Gesetzbuch), one probably has greater need of support from outside private law for an alternative doctrine.

In Finland the Constitution is often seen rather as an *obstacle* to regeneration. Against the development of a need-oriented law of contract that would take account of parties' economic and social position it would thus be conceivable to adduce the constitutional principle of the equality of Finnish citizens before the law. This *possible* way of arguing has not received any great weight in the present work since the need-oriented principles are here developed mainly "inductively" on the basis of, among other things, a concrete legislative material that has been checked for constitutionality. What is possible in, for example, the Act on Torts or the Act on Interest should also be possible in the general principles. And further, it is here a matter of stressing in private law ways of thinking that are accepted in social security law: nowhere is it written that the constitution should be given a different (stricter) content as regards private law than as regards social security law. And finally: increased need-orientation means merely an endeavour to take the premise of equality seriously, to give it a more material and a less formal content.

5. THE RELATIONSHIP OF THE GENERAL PRINCIPLES TO LEGAL CHANGE

In several contexts has been stressed how the general principles may fulfil various functions in legal change. If these principles are considered *from a selected starting point*, for example how the legal order meets the needs of weaker social groups, different general principles may be roughly and schematically placed in three groups:

(i) There are many examples of cases where the development towards the selected goal that has taken place in the concrete legal material, primarily in legislation and legal practice, has not been consciously reflected in the general principles. The concrete legal material affords a weakening basis for an overall generalization with the content embraced by the traditional general principles. The old principles live on largely by force of tradition without any longer having sufficient foundation in newer legal material. Those general principles that no longer correspond even to new concrete legal norms - which in their turn have of course arisen because of changes in social reality - act as *brakes on legal change*. The criticism levelled against the teachings of conceptual jurisprudence, that the old legal culture has unhappily been permitted to hold legislation in its grasp,[53] means just this.

(ii) The general principles may in some field or another be more or less *in step with legal change*: there is no evident conflict between the concrete legal material and the general principles. This does not, however, preclude an anomaly in the relationship between them and social change. The situation may be such that neither the majority of the concrete legal material nor the prevailing general principles provide solutions to social problems that may be considered satisfactory in the light of change in social conditions. The general principles do not reflect the *possibilities* of legal change that the developmental level of the society in question would offer.

(iii) The general principles may, however, very well function as *precursors* of the *legal development* striven for. In this case there is an attempt to generalize the concrete legal material so that the system of general principles points towards the future, runs one step ahead of legislation, which is always partly obsolete. When building general principles of this kind, the category of *the socially possible* assumes a central position.[54] To be practically relevant, the general principles should reflect the possibilities for change that are revealed by analysis of a society's economic and political level of development. The principles should at the same time, to be legal, build upon values which at least to some extent are expressed in the available concrete legal material (see above).

---

[53] Helin 1985 p. 89.

[54] See Eriksson 1979 p. 50 ff.

In other words, they should also be *legally possible*.

Historically, the notion of the general principles as precursors of legal change is not particularly remarkable. In earlier phases of legal development, legal science has often appeared as the chief motive force. Thus for example the starting points for the prevailing system of private law - freedom of contract and a general concept of ownership - have largely been formulated by legal science.[55]

A future-directed alternative legal dogmatics should, in other words, work within the framework of *the dialectic between the real and the possible*. Such a dogmatics should, adopting an objective that is socially desirable from the researcher's point of view - for example to improve the position of weaker social groups - develop general principles which, with regard to social conditions and the existing concrete legal material, are socially and legally possible.

Development of such future-directed general principles does not, however, take place "outside" this dialectic. The formulation of the new principles itself, through the legal-source function of legal dogmatics, contributes to *extending the limits of the legally possible*. The new principles constitute legal material and offer legitimation of changed practice for a critical decision-maker: via these principles the legally possible - in some time perspective or other - becomes legally real. The self-referential, circular nature of the law is employed to promote desired solutions.[56]

Much has been said here of alternative legal dogmatics as a *future-directed* dogmatics. There is reason to emphasize that this concept is not here understood in any deterministic way. The

---

[55] In the same way as there exist in the legislation "Möglichkeiten, die gesellschaftlichen Verhältnisse sowie die Ziele zu ihrer Bewahrung oder Veränderung mit unterschiedlichem Adäquatheitsgrad rechtsnormativ zum Ausdruck zu bringen", Mollnau 1986 p. 158, legal science can more or less adequately reflect such circumstances and goals.

[56] Teubner 1989, who analyses the circularity of the law, stresses that this should not, as in traditional legal science, be considered as a problem but as a fruitful and valuable insight (p. 407).

future is not something that may be extrapolated from earlier development. For this reason, as hinted in the introduction to this section, the general principles may be grouped in the way stated only from a *selected* normative starting point. If one chooses different desired futures one also understands the developmental levels of different principles in different ways.

A brief example may illustrate this. A scholar who bases his activity on the ideals of the welfare state and wishes to build future-directed general principles for, let us say, contract law, obviously tends to view various kinds of "social" elements in the concrete legal material as basic elements of his symptomatic critique;[57] while he would view emphasis on values connected to the principle of freedom of contract as brakes upon legal change. For a supporter of "the New Right", the picture is, at least partly, the opposite. For him, the latter values are at least in some respects representative of the future to which one is returning, or should return.[58] What is "braking", "in step with development" and "future-directed" for these two scholars obviously depends on the value system upon which they base their work.

The foregoing implies, if one does not wish to subsume under alternative legal dogmatics all forms of legal dogmatics that question *communis opinio* and strive for a refashioning of general principles with the stress on the legally and socially possible, that interest is focused upon the substantive *values* that support the alternative. What is of interest is ultimately *what one defines* as those *emancipatory ideals* that are typical of an alternative legal dogmatics (see above I.2.iv). This is without doubt the most central and at the same time the most difficult question in a discussion of the possibilities of developing an alternative legal dogmatics.

The aim of the present work is, within the framework of

---

[57] See e.g. the re-evaluation of English contract law in Collins 1986.

[58] The law of contract and "the New Right" have been analysed by Atiyah 1989, who also notes certain signs in legal practice of a development in the said direction (e.g. p. 20). In West German law the demands for a return to the ethic of formal freedom in private law has been formulated by e.g. Reuter 1989.

the socially and legally possible, to develop the general principles of private law in such ways that the needs of weaker social groups are better taken into account than heretofore. Why just this aim has been chosen and why it has been perceived as falling within the framework of the socially possible is explained in more detail in the next chapter.

6. CRITICISM AND LEGITIMATION

The notion of a future-directed legal dogmatics can be criticized, and has been criticized, for the fact that legal science of this kind takes on a legitimating function. As Roberto Mangabeira Unger claims, it can easily happen that "legal theories of substantive justice remain isolated in a politically inhospitable atmosphere so that, though sufficiently vital to help legitimate the social order, they may never become strong enough to help transform it".[59]

The criticism is basically just. By presenting the general principles as more emancipatory than what the actually observed principles are, one gives, on the normative, legal-scientific plane, an appearance that the social problems have been solved to a greater extent than is in fact the case. One can also say that all legal dogmatic activity has by definition a system-legitimating function: to be defined as legal dogmatics, the activity must accept at least certain elements of existing concrete legal material as a starting point. As against this, it can be maintained that a legal science that is endeavouring to create new general principles also always contributes tools for criticism of traditional learning. The critical legal dogmatician is in other words forced to choose his research strategy within the framework of a paradox that is not unknown within the rest of social debate either: *microcriticism* can lead to *macrolegitimation*.

Despite the risks mentioned, the issue treated in this work has been formulated on the basis of the assumption that an alternative legal dogmatics of the kind described here is both desirable

---

[59] Unger 1976 p. 213.

and possible. The formulation, in the general principles, of new ways of catering for weaker social groups is considered of sufficient practical significance (see below Chapter VIII) to merit the attempt.

CHAPTER III

GOALS: NEW ELEMENTS IN A CONTRACT LAW OF THE WELFARE STATE

1. THE IDEOLOGY OF THE WELFARE STATE AND PRIVATE LAW

There is a close interplay between the law and social ideology. *One* point of departure for assessing what is socially possible when developing the general principles must therefore be sought in the prevailing social ideology.

This link with the prevailing social ideology is also stressed by many of the representatives of alternative dogmatics presented earlier. We have seen how *Udo Reifner* emphasizes that one should start with the bourgeois ideals of freedom and equality codified in the Bürgerliches Gesetzbuch and give them a substantive interpretation, while *Lars D. Eriksson* prefers to take seriously the goal formulations characteristic of the late-capitalist legal order. The differences in reference points may be explained by differences between the prevailing Nordic and German social ideologies and by the continuing central position of the BGB in German discussion of private law.

Today's Nordic and Western European society is generally described using concepts such as "*welfare state*"[1], which do not

---

[1] In West German critical social science, the concept "social state" has from time to time been set as an emancipatory concept against "welfare state": see e.g. Joerges 1989 p. 613 ff. In this work the concept "welfare state" - as in Nordic usage - is perceived as more extensive,

only indicate certain traits supposed to predominate in social development but also contain an ideological legitimation of the society in question. The features which are supposed to be characteristic of this society are also presented as goals for developing society.

What marks the welfare state has been considered to be an endeavour to modify the effect of market forces in three respects:[2]

(1) to assure citizens a certain minimum subsistence,

(ii) to reduce the effects of life's uncertainty by creating protection against illness, unemployment and old age, and

(iii) by offering all citizens social services as far as available resources permit.

The first goal can naturally be interpreted in many different ways. The goal of assuring citizens a certain minimum subsistence may be considered to have been achieved when *absolute poverty* has largely been removed from society, i.e. when starvation and direct physical distress have been eliminated. But one can also have the goal of combatting more *relative poverty*, i.e. situations where some individuals' living standards are far below the general level for that society.[3] A goal of this kind has close links with the values of a distribution policy: endeavours to reduce differences in income and wealth and increase economic equality throughout a society are perceived as goals in themselves. Current welfare state ideology is obviously based on such more far-reaching notions of equality. Society is not perceived as "perfect" as soon as absolute poverty has been removed. Typical for the welfare state is "a distribution capable of assuring to every person a minimum not too far removed from the average level enjoyed in society".[4]

The goals of the welfare state as described above have not

---

also containing an emancipatory potential. "The welfare state" is taken seriously!

[2] Eräsaari 1984 p. 113.

[3] See e.g. Karisto - Takala - Haapola 1984 p. 103 ff.

[4] Vallauri 1985 p. 190.

been achieved. Absolute poverty is indeed no longer evident in the Nordic countries or in large parts of Western Europe, even though not even this evil has been entirely eliminated. Relative poverty, on the other hand, has not been removed in any significant sense. Income differences are still considerable and differences in consumption levels between social groups are now in many cases even more significant than what the information on income differences indicates.[5] The relative deprivation of the worst-affected groups is, we know, so great that such concepts as the "new poor" are commonly used. Growing average welfare does not necessarily imply, either, that the problems of relative poverty have become more marginal: paradoxically, it has been maintained that the importance of income differences has grown with the general raising of the standard of living,[6] in that the measure of success becomes one's own consumption standard. Nor is protection against life's uncertainty factors fully developed. Thus for example there are at present many unemployed persons in Europe in situations of evident relative poverty.[7] It is in other words obvious, and scarcely needs further justification here, that the goal of extending the welfare state is by no means obsolete. There are still weak groups in society - the unemployed, single providers etc. - who have just claims to special support from the legal order.

The ideology of the welfare state is of course to a high degree *mythical* in character.[8] This does not prevent legal discourse from choosing to take it seriously as an expression of primary social goals which should also find expression on the concrete legal level. Here one cannot *a priori* assume that private law, including the law of contract, should not be embraced by these goals. The contract law should not necessarily be infused

---

[5] Thus e.g. for Finland, Karisto - Takala - Haapola 1984 p. 107 f.

[6] See Karisto 1985 p. 40.

[7] Here it suffices to refer to the forthcoming report of the Hamburg Conference of 22-23.9.1989 on Unemployment and Consumer Debts in Europe.

[8] Eräsaari 1984 p. 116 f.

exclusively by an ideal of justice based on reciprocity: there is growing insight that its rules may also have links with different forms of distributive justice.[9] Contract law governs circumstances that may have direct effect on the living standard of affected parties, and it is consequently quite conceivable that the goals of the welfare state are to a greater degree than today taken account of in contract law.

That the norms for solving problems of contract law can be of practical significance in the endeavour to realize the goals of the welfare state is illustrated by the empirical data on payment delays, etc., reported below (see VI.6.3.1 and VII.2).[10] It is, however, obvious that the solutions of contract law - provided that one keeps within the framework of relationships that may conceivably be described with reasonable use of language as those of contract law - cannot offer any primary means for redistributing unevenly distributed welfare. In the law of contract and of obligations "they bake smaller loaves".[11]

In contract law the goals of the welfare state have often been considered to find expression through rules and principles relating to protection of the weaker party in a contractual relationship. Scrutinizing the characteristics of the welfare state given above, however, one easily sees that such regulations realize only certain aspects of the welfare-state goals. Through those regulations, an attempt is made above all to improve access to, and the quality of, the commercial services, in a very wide sense, offered to citizens (cf. welfare state goal iii): any citizen can when acting as a consumer, tenant, insured person etc. refer to these rules. The goal of *redistributing* (levelling out) *welfare* among different groups of citizens, which goal is also considered characteristic of the welfare state, has, however, received less attention in private

---

[9] See e.g. Unger 1976 p. 198 f., Köndgen 1981 p. 135 ff.

[10] Cf. also Groth 1986 p. 373: "Schuldnerberatung ist Sozialarbeit" (Counselling debtors is social work).

[11] Esser - Schmidt 1984 p. 6; "Im Schuldrecht werden "kleinere Brötchen gebacken"."

and contract law.[12] This goal is traditionally viewed as falling within the province of social security law. Now, a contract law of the welfare state could also take these redistributive goals seriously.

Typical of the law of the Welfare State is "the abandonment of the idea that the law ought to be the same for everyone".[13] Especially in social security law the economic and social position of a party constitutes a natural part of the sphere of application of many norms. Standard roles in the cast of social security law are delimited by using criteria of this type. When seeking to develop a corpus of contract law that is "welfare state" in the sense given above, one must ask whether such criteria are of use in this field, too.

In a contract law where the ideology of the welfare state is taken seriously, then, the possibilities should be examined, of course alongside other circumstances, of taking account of all three subgoals of the welfare state:

(i) Account of parties' need for a certain minimum subsistence *can* imply both reinforcement of such contract law rights which are important for a creditor's subsistence and a limitation of those obligations that threaten a debtor's standard of living (see in general Chapter VI).

(ii) Consideration of parties' need for protection when hit by special events such as illness, unemployment and old age can in private law be partly developed using the doctrine of *social force majeure* (see below Chapter VII).

(iii) Regulation of parties' needs for services can in private law result in rules on a duty to contract (see briefly on this point below VI.5.1).

---

[12] The discussion on the distributive effects of contract regulation mainly takes up the question of redistribution between the legal classes which the parties represent - "the class of sellers" v. "the class of buyers" or "landlords" v. "tenants" - see the impressive analysis by Kennedy 1982, esp. p. 609 ff. The focus here, however, is on the redistribution *within* those groups.

[13] Ewald 1986 p. 45. See also ibid. p. 46: "Social law is ... a law of positive discriminations".

2. TOWARDS A SUBSTANTIVE OR A "REFLEXIVE" JUSTICE?

2.1 The welfare state as an obsolete ideology?

A prominent theme in the socially oriented legal-theoretical international discussion during the last few years has been the issue of the development of different forms of legal rationality. The starting point has been taken from *Max Weber*'s well-known analysis of formal and antiformal elements in the development of law in capitalist society.

Perhaps the most noted contribution to this discussion has been that of *Gunther Teubner* (1983). This writer distinguishes three types of rationality which in his view have characterized the development of modern law:

(i) The original market economy is marked by a *formal rationality*. The law is justified by referring to the value of individualism and private autonomy. At the level of legal thinking this type emerges as rule-oriented: application of the law is understood as a deductive activity.

(ii) In step with the development of the welfare state, formal rationality has to a greater or lesser extent had to give ground to a *substantive (material) rationality*. Here, the law is justified on the basis of the need to regulate economic and social activity and to compensate for market inadequacies. Legal thinking becomes *purpose-oriented*: purposive programmes are implemented using general clauses, standards and principles.

(iii) Teubner does not, however, rest with the two types of rationality outlined but claims that a third type is emerging: *reflexive rationality*. The basis of justification of this lies in the ideal of self-regulation - Teubner's thinking has also, perhaps somewhat misleadingly, been described as a legal ideology for the Green movement.[14] The legal thinking in this rationality is *procedure-oriented*. The central goal of law becomes not to offer solutions regarding content, but only to guarantee the structural preconditions for genuinely reflexive, self-regulating processes.

Teubner is not alone in discussing new forms of rationality in modern law. That the theory of reflexive law obviously is anchored somewhere in reality is shown in the fact that many other similar theories regarding new features of the development of (private) law have recently been presented.

To mention a few examples:

- In private law there is reason to note *Eike Schmidt*'s[15] description of how the materialization phase of private law is shifting into a new phase, demonstrated with the help of the concept of "social autonomy". Social autonomy is marked by increasing opportunities for co-determination, i.e. for articulation of the concrete needs of affected parties. This articulation does not, however, take place individually - there is no idea of a return to formal private autonomy - but on the basis of solidarity. The development of social autonomy includes a phasing-out of the "yes/no rigour" of the law and permission for compromise solutions that are more adequate for the situation. The cooperation of those participating in the process is emphasized.

- Related lines of thought also underlie *Gert Brüggemeier*'s attempt to outline a new model for the relationship between state and economy in developed capitalist society. According to this writer development has run from the mediaeval status model via an original contract model (contract I) to the contract model of materialized private law (contract II). Now, however, the time is ripe to replace the contract models with a new paradigm, *organization*, which is characterized by, among other things, decision-making processes through decentralized organizations and the development of reflexive forms of interaction between the decen-

---

[14] Pöyhönen 1985.

[15] Schmidt 1980, especially p. 157 ff.

tralized centres of action and between the sub-systems of society.[16]

- Also showing a certain relationship with Teubner's reflexive elements is *Rudolf Wiethölter*'s "*proceduralization*".[17] "Modern" tendencies in the law are in this conceptual apparatus characterized by the fact that ""Formalisierungen" wie "Materialisierungen" werden in "Prozeduralisierungen" aufgehoben".[18] The idea is for the law to foster the learning capacity of social systems. Proceduralization "is the transformation of a social context of legal freedom ... in a system of justifications of ever-new social contexts of "ideas" and "interests"."[19] While it is unclear how far proceduralization and reflexive law are intended to cover the same phenomenon,[20] they are often used in discussion more or less as synonyms.[21] Teubner[22] himself maintains a considerable difference: while Wiethölter speaks of creating possibilities for discourse aiming at a *social* consensus, Teubner starts from a reflexion not at the level of the society as a whole but within individual social *subsystems*.

The theory that law is developing towards a new reflexive law has been criticized among other things for giving the impression of an evolution which the critics say has not actually taken place.[23] It has been claimed that the law always contains three

---

[16] Brüggemeier 1982 p. 69 f.

[17] See Wiethölter 1982, 1984, 1986 and 1989.

[18] Wiethölter 1982 p. 45.

[19] Wiethölter 1989 p. 509. Thus also Wiethölter 1986 p. 246.

[20] See e.g. Reich 1984 p. 280.

[21] Thus e.g. Hart 1984 p. 75.

[22] Teubner 1984 p. 91 f.

[23] See e.g. Reich 1984 p. 280f, Hydén 1984 p. 43 and Pöyhönen 1985 p. 134. See also Rottleuthner 1986 whose general criticism of theories of legal evolution is that, having too much of a selective empirical base, they simplify reality. "The price for the elegance of a model of evolution is a partial fade-out" (p. 226). Opposed to such a view is e.g. Dalberg-Larsen 1986 p. 13 f.

forms of rationality: form, content and procedure. It is also obvious that Teubner's three forms of rationality are not intended to be viewed as exclusive. Teubner himself also discusses in a later context the relationships between the procedural, formal and material elements in post-instrumental law.[24]

Despite criticism of the evolutionary aspect of the theory of reflexive law - which points at considerable problems and also seems to have led to a certain revision of the original theories[25] - it seems possible to maintain that development during this century has in general entailed an increase in the importance of the non-formal forms of rationality, at least in private law. No further comment is needed here on the evolutionary aspect of the theories summarized above. Here - when discussing the goals of a development of the general principles of private law - the *normative* side of the theories is of greater interest. Now the protagonists of a reflexive law maintain not only that this concept characterizes a new, emerging rationality: it is also seen as denoting a goal worthy of striving for. Teubner stresses, in meeting the criticism of his theory as an evolutionary one, that "theories" of the type he is presenting should not be viewed as scientific theories but as "strategic models of law", the main task of which is "to use the self-identity of law to produce criteria for its own transformation."[26] The theory contains normative criteria for a development of the law.

The theory of reflexive law and related theories are based on a critique of the pattern of regulation that is typical of the so-called welfare state.[27] Law in the good society should *not* according to this critique be marked primarily by a *material rationality* - the rationality of the welfare state - but by a reflexive rationality. In other words, when developing a future-directed dogmatics of

---

[24] Teubner 1986 p. 321.

[25] See also Tonner 1985 p. 118.

[26] Teubner 1986 p. 301.

[27] Reich 1984 p. 271.

private law, is it outdated to start - as is the case here - from the ideology that characterizes the welfare state? Is the supposedly future-directed legal dogmatics that is the subject of the present work based on a legal rationality that is becoming played out?[28]

Appraisal of this question presupposes a more detailed description of what in concrete terms can be meant by material and reflexive rationality, respectively, in private law. These concepts are in fact by no means unambiguous.

2.2 *On material rationality*

It will be clear even from the very brief presentation of material rationality in the previous section that two different elements are included, one of content and one of method. As to *content*, materialized law is characterized by the attempt, through its norms, not only to protect social positions but above all to allocate (realize) such positions,[29] to change given power structures[30] and in general to control socioeconomic development[31].

The *methodological* element in the definition of materialized law again means that instead of a deductive, rule-oriented, formal legal inference, there appears a goal-oriented argumentation based on general clauses, etc. In this sense assertions about shifts from a formal rationality towards a material rationality run parallel with the observations on changes in the structures of legal argu-

---

[28] The question is based on the popular assumption that the welfare state is undergoing a "crisis". A general assumption like this is questionable. In an extensive investigation of the challenges of the welfare state and the Nordic models, Pekka Kosonen (1989) has not found strong support for such an assertion of crisis (p. 323). The social problems that have arisen are connected with general problems of accumulation and capitalization, not with the welfare state as such. See also e.g. Friedman 1986, who links the welfare state with deep changes in legal culture and therefore perceives its core as "remarkably solid, remarkably hard to change" (p. 20).

[29] Wiethölter 1984 p. 32.

[30] Reich 1984 p. 283.

[31] Brüggemeier 1980 p. 72.

mentation that have been presented by many Nordic writers: here one need mention only *Lars D. Eriksson*'s[32] description of how the "subsumptional-logical model" is being forced out by "goal-rational" and "need-rational" models, or *Thomas Mathiesen*'s[33] analysis of the retreat of "legal security law" in favour of a "law of control" marked by the fact that the legal norms assume a less binding character and are applied with the help of legal sources of more recognized political nature.[34]

The two characteristics of materialized law described above do not necessarily belong together, either logically or historically. At least in the development of Nordic private law it appears - as also emerges from the description of the development of concepts given in Chapter IV - that *materialization as to content* represents an earlier phenomenon than does *methodological materialization*.

In the law of contract many varying types of regulations have been adduced as *examples* of a process of materialization. This becomes clearly evident in the classification produced by *Dieter Hart*[35] - who appears primarily to be analysing materialization as to content - of the regulations that affect "die Vertragsverfassung" (the constitution of contract) in West German Law:

(i) Control via *influence on conditions of competition* comprises:

- measures attempting to assure effective competition. This includes the attempt to improve information and advice to the purchasers on the market.[36] These measures exhibit at the same time a tendency towards a *re-formalization* of contract law,

- an interventionist law of competition in which, alongside goals of competition policy, account is also taken of the goals of

---

[32] Eriksson 1980 p. 108 f.

[33] Mathiesen 1985 p. 12 ff.

[34] See also Unger 1976 p. 199.

[35] Hart 1984 p. 72 ff.

[36] I.e. what Reich 1977 p. 198 calls "marktkomplementäre Konzeptionen eines Verbraucherrechtes".

economic, industrial, social and consumer policy.

(ii) Materialization through *regulation of fairness of contracts*, among other things through measures favouring consumer interests, comprises:

- new criteria for the creation of obligations (e.g. the binding nature of offers made in advertising),

- special social obligations such as those relating to information and counselling, intended to level out the imbalance between the parties. In developing these obligations there is a tendency towards *particularization*: a differentiation of the norms applying in different circumstances,

- a control of the reciprocity of contractual obligations. Binding orders of contract are laid down which cannot be amended by the parties.

2.3 On reflexive rationality

If, then, the concept of material rationality is unclear, so much more so is *reflexive* or procedural *rationality*. Reflexivity constitutes a portmanteau term for phenomena that are connected with organization and solidarity.[37] This concept, too, contains both an element of content and a methodological element.

As to content, reflexivity may be said to mean emphasis upon regulations "in terms of organization, procedure and competencies".[38] Reflexive law does not, for example, decide what is in the consumers' interest: it confines itself to defining who is competent to express such interests and to safeguarding their representation.[39] In other words, from the point of view of content, reflexive law is interested in regulation of self-regulating systems.

Methodologically, the *flexibility* of the law is stressed here as well. This makes possible legal reactions that are specific to the

---

[37] Brüggemeier 1983 p. 389.

[38] Teubner 1983 p. 275.

[39] Teubner 1983 p. 277.

situation in question, and that are future-oriented.[40] Methodologically, therefore, the differences between material rationality and reflexive rationality are not very easy to grasp. One may assume that the differences lie in the structure of argumentation when applying the flexible system of regulation; while in material argumentation definite *content goals* for social development are stressed, reflexive application is directed towards giving the parties (or perhaps more generally the interests affected) the possibility of *participating* in the process of norm formation.[41]

Because of the relatively open character of the concept of reflexive law, international discussion has been able to subsume many quite disparate phenomena under the heading reflexive law.[42] A traditional example is the regulation model of labour law (the collective agreement), another the new models in the field of consumer law such as, in West Germany, Stiftung-Warentest and, in Scandinavia, the Consumer Ombudsman negotiating with business organizations and enterprises on the basis of very open-ended general clauses and the more informal Nordic consumer complaint boards consisting partly of representatives of consumer and business interests.[43] In the field of public law different forms of institutional democracy have been mentioned in this context.[44] As many different kinds of tendencies have been dragged into the realm of reflexive law, the Utopia reflexive law offers us may be rather different depending on the preferences and specialties of the authors.

---

[40] Hart 1984 p. 75.

[41] See e.g. Hart 1984 p. 76.

[42] See on private law Teubner 1983 p. 276 ff.

[43] Blegvad 1988 p. 162 ff. has analysed the Danish consumer complaint board (Forbrugerklagenaevnet) as an example of reflexive law.

[44] See e.g. Eriksson 1986 p. 287.

2.4 *Material development as a precondition of reflexive justice*

We shall not yet discuss in any more detail the methodological aspect of these theories. The desired degree of flexibility in the law and the argumentational structures associated with this must wait for a later context (see section 4 below). Here, merely the aspects of the problems that concern *content* will be discussed: would the development of new general principles of *contract law* with an increased material rationality be considered outmoded; should one instead concentrate future-oriented activity upon reinforcement of the reflexive elements of legal development?

Without analysing in detail the arguments put forward by advocates of reflexive law for their normative position, one can indicate two main types of consideration that *could* be used as arguments for abandoning material rationality in favour of a new reflexive rationality. These two lines of criticism of welfare state law are as follows:

(i) Starting from the well-known work of *Jürgen Habermas*,[45] one can criticize materialized law for defining "from outside" what should be considered right for the actors in social subsystems, thus destroying traditional patterns of life. The law is effecting a "colonization of the life-world". In this sense, materialized law may be said to be *undemocratic*. From conservative points of view the same line of criticism has been distilled into the well known notion of a "*guardian society*" ("Big Brother society").

The great interest of progressive lawyers and social theorists in the theory of reflexive law is probably primarily explained by its potential to back up demands on new forms of direct democracy. The theory has, at least in the Nordic countries, brought new fuel to the democracy debate. The democracy concept is, however, not a goal in itself in Teubner's own theory. His notion of self-regulation is also founded on efficacy reasons, or, more specifically, on the endeavour to create a regulation which has the desired effects without being destructive. The law "seeks to identi-

---

[45] Habermas 1981. See also Habermas 1986.

fy opportunity structures that allow legal regulation to cope with social problems without, at the same time, irreversibly destroying valued patterns of social life".[46] In one connection, when describing examples of reflexive patterns in the law of private organizations, Teubner even states that the main goal of reflexive law "is neither power- equalization nor an increase of individual participation in the emphatic sense of "participatory democracy." Rather, it is the design of organizational structures which makes the institutions - corporations, semi-public associations, mass media, educational institutions - sensitive to the outside effects of their attempts to maximize internal rationality."[47]

When discussing the development of such material (welfare-state) norms of *contract law*, intended for application in disputes between individual parties, criticism based on the supposed negative effects of the "guardian society" hardly hits the mark. Not even mandatory contract legislation forces upon the parties solutions that neither desires: it merely *limits* one contracting party's possibilities of exploiting the state power apparatus to implement the contract *against the will of the other party* and, in other words, limits the possibilities of using this apparatus for antisocial purposes. If *both* parties wish to follow other norms during the whole period of the contractual relationship, legislation does not prevent them. Nobody compels the consumer to claim his rights under consumer protection legislation.[48] Nor does anybody compel a person offended by need-oriented emphasis on the poverty of the individual[49] to further a claim in contract law on such a ground.

---

[46] Teubner 1983 p. 274.

[47] Teubner 1983 p. 278: but cf. p. 275: "law must act at the Subsystem-specific level to install, correct, and redefine democratic self-regulatory mechanisms".

[48] See also Reifner 1980 p. 377.

[49] Cf. Habermas' (1986 p. 209) example of negative effects of a social-law colonization of the life-world: *individualization* such as "the individualizing definition of geriatric care ... has burdensome consequences for the self-image of the person concerned".

Disputes in contract law are in the majority of cases settled out of court. The function of the legislation is here to supply the foundation upon which the parties can negotiate a settlement. A legislation that supports a weaker party and takes account of his needs thereby strengthens his negotiating position. In this sense it can be said that a materialized law of contract is a *precondition* of a "reflexive" settlement of disputes.[50] Only against the background of materially balanced law can the parties in more equally-balanced negotiations settle their differences of opinion. The problem of distribution of power requires material solutions.[51]

This holds good at least for the rather short legal dogmatic time perspective adopted here. In a longer social-philosophical perspective one can naturally imagine a society where contractual relations have been completely restructured to equalize the negotiating power between the parties.[52] A genuinely reflexive law of contract obviously presupposes a thoroughgoing decentralization and democratization of the economic system.[53]

The type of criticism of the welfare state considered here can thus in the *short legal-dogmatic time perspective* of the present work hardly be raised against a development of material rationality in the general principles of contract law. On the contrary, there is an obvious need to let the material features of new legal material be reflected to a greater extent in the general principles which still are relatively formal. The question here is not whether material principles are needed; rather, *what* material elements are suited to

---

[50] See also Tonner 1985 p. 121.

[51] See e.g. Reich 1984 p. 283 f. and Graver 1988 p. 105 ff. Teubner is also aware of this. In his original contribution he touches upon the problem of power, albeit briefly. A kind of "simulation" of genuine reflexive processes is expressly recommended as a solution in cases where "social asymmetries of power and information can resist institutional attempts at equalization", see Teubner 1983 p. 277. See later also Teubner 1986 p. 317 f.

[52] As portrayed by certain of the advocates of reflexive law; see for example Hydén 1984 p. 42.

[53] See also Eriksson 1986 p. 286.

supporting the increased self-determination of one's own life-sphere that proponents of reflexive law present on good grounds as a positive goal of legal change. One possible answer is: those elements that most nearly relate to *the parties' concrete needs*.

(ii) But it is also asserted that materialized law has been *ineffective*, that, in practice, the use of legal regulations has not led to achievement of the social goals striven for.[54] Quite simply, society is so complex that such regulations cannot lead to the desired result. Yet it appears too early to conclude from this that material rationality should be abandoned. That material solutions have not "succeeded" may equally be because the legislators have not seriously attempted to realize the goals they say they are striving for. Criticism of the failure of law may be misdirected: the failure may just as well lie in the sphere of politics.

As for example *Dieter Hart*[55] correctly observes, what he terms proceduralizations may be used both to remove material regulations and to strengthen their efficiency. Reflexive elements in the legal order may help reduce problems of efficiency of material regulations, and thus the weight of criticism of materialized law.

In other words, a functioning social contract law presupposes measures based on both kinds of rationality. The material and the reflexive elements support each other: the material norms e.g. in Nordic consumer legislation would be far more ineffective without the procedural and organizational solutions the law provides; while the possibilities of action of the new consumer protection organs would be very limited if they lacked the support of a material regulation.

The endeavour of alternative legal dogmatics to develop the general principles of contract law aims at reinforcing this material support. The equally necessary development of new procedural and organizational elements is harder to realize with

---

[54] A key term here is "Rechtsversagen", see e.g. Reich 1984 p. 272 ff.

[55] Hart 1984 p. 77 ff.

legal-dogmatic means.[56] Arguing - even very critically - on the basis of the law in force, which has a fundamentally material content, can seldom lead to a realization of such new reflexive structures (cf. 3.2 below). Legal dogmatics cannot create a Consumer Ombudsman or a Consumer Complaints Board.

3. NEED-ORIENTATION AS A GOAL

3.1 Eriksson's need-rational argumentation

We have seen above how the ideology of the welfare state supports the notion of a development of rules of contract law which explicitly enable account to be taken of the individual economic and social needs of the parties involved. The Nordic discussion of an alternative legal dogmatics has also stressed the goal of taking the concrete needs of affected citizens into account. This view has found expression particularly in *Lars D. Eriksson*'s theory of need-rational argumentation.[57]

Eriksson's analysis of the development of need-rationality in law is organized in a way similar to Teubner's later presentation of the various "strategic models of law". Eriksson, too, who directs interest towards the development of *the models of legal argumentation* in the capitalist society, distinguishes three stages of development, the first two of which, at least, very closely resemble Teubner's corresponding models:

(i) The exchange value rationality of early capitalism forms the basis of the argumentation model of *subsumptional logic*. The legal norm itself is the starting point for the argumentation and the predictability of legal decisions is a central value.

(ii) In late capitalism, use-value rationality has attained a dominating position. This kind of rationality, however, forms the

---

[56] As Bayles 1987 p. 2 puts it: "Although legal decisions can sometimes lead to rather sweeping changes... courts do not have the power simply to institute a comprehensive no-fault accident insurance scheme."

[57] See Eriksson 1980 p. 108 ff. The same theory was presented, with a somewhat different terminology, in Eriksson 1979.

basis of two different models of legal argumentation. The first is the *goal-rational* model (or system-oriented goal-rational model), in which the social content of the legal decision comes to the fore. One starts from the goals of the legal regulations and evaluates the social consequences when making decisions. The decision-maker strives at getting socially balanced results which can contribute to the preserving of the system.

(iii) Use-value rationality also underlies the *need-rational* model (or need-oriented goal-rational model) of argumentation. The social content and consequences of a legal decision are emphasized in this model, too. The aim, however, is not to care for the needs of the system (its cohesion), but for the needs of the members of society. In evaluating the rationality of a decision the crucial question is what effects the decision has on the *concrete and real needs* of members of society.

This last stage is presented by Eriksson partly as a description of a new rationality structure which can already be seen in some elements of the law.[58] It is, however, in the same way as the theory of reflexive law also, and perhaps predominantly, a theory with a normative content, a legal Utopia.

Eriksson's analysis of the development of legal argumentation is naturally chiefly *methodological in character*: it touches upon the way in which legal inferences are made. At the same time, however, it also expresses *something about the content of these inferences*: the need-rational elements of the legal order gain importance, and this growth should also be promoted.

The increase of such a need-rationality must obviously, when the development is examined from the point of view of legal concepts, entail a raising of the status of need-oriented concepts in legal reasoning. Both a regulation system and a way of arguing that are directed at satisfying a party's individual needs presuppose

---

[58] Cf. also Unger 1976 p. 212: "In private law, substantive justice will be preoccupied with the elaboration of criteria for determining the equivalence of performances exchanged through contract and for allocating the losses arising from private disputes on the basis of both comparative fault and *relative need*" (italics mine).

some form of need-oriented concepts. The attempt to promote need-rational argumentation in private law presupposes development of need-oriented elements in the general principles of private law.

3.2 Need-orientation and reflexive law

Not even the third of Eriksson's development stages, the new normative ideal of need-rationality, is *necessarily* remote from the goals supported by the proponents of reflexive law. The doctrine of reflexive law can be interpreted in such a way as to place it close to the need-oriented reasoning here advocated.

This emerges already as one discusses at a general level *the goals* of reflexive law. In section 2.4.i above, we saw that reflexive law is not seen only as an instrument for achieving the self-determination of the individual, but also and perhaps primarily as a tool for coping effectively with social problems. Still, the way in which the problems are dealt with differs from the methods of substantive law: one should as far as possible increase the participation of the people concerned in the process where the problems are dealt with. This, however, will in turn mean that those involved gain greater possibilities of articulating their concrete and real needs and having them recognized as legally relevant. If one looks at reflexive law from this perspective its goals seem to lie rather close to those of the normative theory of need-rationality. This is confirmed by Teubner himself in a later work where, in connection with the question of how to differentiate between conservative and progressive forms of reflexive law, he stresses *responsiveness to human needs* as a central normative criterion for judging social institutions.[59]

In addition, closer study of the *material content* of the kind of law striven for shows clear parallels between reflexivity and need-rationality. Although reflexive law primarily emphasizes regulations in terms of organization, procedure and competencies,

---

[59] Teubner 1986 p. 318.

it has rather important material implications, too. The proponents of reflexive law talk of the possibilities of a "reflexive logic" within legal doctrine, a logic which implies a *simulation* of reflexive processes in cases where asymmetric power and information structures obstruct a genuine reflexivity. The tools for effecting this reflexive logic are certain general clauses which contain concepts such as "good faith" or "public policy". With the help of these general clauses one may reach "reflexive" norms with a material content.[60]

The differences and similarities between reflexive rationality and need-rationality, when one analyses the material content of their rules, thus depends to some extent on which kind of processes reflexive law is thought to "simulate".

The question of how such a simulation should be effected in practice is, however, left open by the theory on reflexive law. Different alternatives seem possible:

(i) One might take the idea of simulation seriously and try to investigate how all individuals and groups concerned *would* in fact *act* if they wished to solve the problem together in a completely democratic and equal bargaining situation. Such an analysis would, however, be rather fictional and out of touch with real life. In a world where the power structures are unequal and stronger groups may further their interests at the expense of weaker ones, arguments about the possible action of the parties concerned in quite a different, equal, world are not very convincing.

(ii) A more acceptable way of realizing the simulated reflexive process would be to connect the argumentation and decision explicitly to the *needs* and desires of the people *involved*. The reflexive solution would be the one which at this level would represent the optimal balance between the parties in any given

---

[60] In Teubner's, 1983 p. 277 f., words: "This means that, in the case of 'interaction deficiencies' between contracting parties, objective purposes and duties are defined authoritatively by virtue of law; in the case of 'market deficiencies', commercial customs are replaced by the judicial definition of market behavior rules; and in the case of 'political deficiencies' the judicial process defines standards of public policy."

case. This interpretation of reflexive law lies, however, quite near to the notion of need-rationality as a basis of critical legal doctrine. The theory of need-rationality expressly and directly states what is implicitly and indirectly contained in the simulated reflexive logic.

3.3 Need-orientation and person-related norms

Need-orientation is a diffuse concept. The goal of taking account of concrete and real needs of the members of society can in practice support a number of different strategies. These may conflict with each other but may also very well be imagined as being complementary.

The needs in question may be entirely general in a society or may exist at least in the great majority of its physical persons. Such needs are non-person-related. In argumentation based on non-person-related needs one refers, for example, to different kinds of physical and mental needs of "people in general", to consumers' "normal requirements"[61] etc. As the development of contract law in the welfare state - including the latest good example: consumer law - indicates, such satisfying of normal requirements by legal means is an important and indispensible element of the private law of a welfare state.[62] The principle of protection of the weaker party in contract law is perhaps the foremost expression of just this aspect of welfare-state contract law (see above, section 1).

However, this non-person-related aspect of the contract law of the welfare state, important though it may be, is not the

---

[61] See e.g. Köndgen 1981 pp. 135, 144.

[62] See also e.g. Peter Derleder 1982 p. 222 who, when establishing "Sozialiserung der Bedürfnisse" (socialization of needs) as a goal for the development of private law, uses "needs" in a relatively broad sense. For Derleder, socialization of needs consists of three elements: limiting the struggle for profit, internalizing general costs into private calculus and overcoming existing ghetto delimitations. Some of the needs mentioned by Derleder are, however, person-related. This is the case with the example concerning the obligation of the advocates to assist poor clients according to a lower social tariff (p. 223).

concern of the present work. The focus here is on that aspect of welfare-state thinking that has not hitherto been permitted to penetrate private law, viz. the concern with *person-related* needs (see above, section 1). By need-orientation is here meant the attaching of legal relevance to a party's actual needs arising from his poverty, low income, illness, unemployment etc. The question is whether such specific concrete and actual needs, of self-evident relevance in social security law, can be taken into account in contract law also.

Here some further justification for the above delimitation of the term need-orientation in this work should be given:

Private law has traditionally managed to preserve an appearance of consisting of a relatively "unpolitical" collection of norms. To this end it has used its abstract way of describing the persons to whom the norms are to be applied. The abstract personal concepts of "contracting party", "seller" and "buyer", "creditor" and "debtor" and so on determine the structure of private law (see above I. 3.2). General needs, which are not person-related, can often be made objects of law without giving up the use of such abstract person concepts. A more radical break with the traditional conceptual structure cannot occur until relevance is also attached to person-related needs. If one wishes to investigate the *limits of a need-oriented private law*, it is thus precisely person-related needs that should be the object of attention. In this way the outermost limits of the applicability of welfare-state ideology in private law can also be explored. As stated earlier, an alternative legal dogmatics should direct its attention precisely to the limits of what is legally possible (see above II. 5.).

It is true that various instances of more or less critical legal-dogmatic literature have noted in modern (private) law an increased concern with the person. This insight has, however, often been presented in very unanalytical terms. Here therefore we must first examine what this increased focussing on the person really implies and what aspects of this represent, in a need-oriented spirit, the radical break with tradition mentioned above. This central question merits a chapter of its own (IV).

In modern critical literature on contract law one often meets in the description of the contract law of the welfare state expressions such as "solidarity", "altruism", "community", "a fair distribution of wealth", etc.[63] These concepts, too, are vague and may be interpreted in many ways. It is obvious, however, that one of their aspects comprises observance of the concrete, person-related needs of individual parties.[64] The type example of an altruistic or solidarity-based action is the giving of a benefit to a person not because he has earned it but merely because it can contribute to meeting his needs.[65] "Community", too, is characterized by action that takes account of participants' personal needs.

In contract law one party's gain is always the other's loss. It can therefore be said that a need-oriented contract law in the meaning intended here expresses a kind of "Robin Hood morality": taking from the rich and giving to the poor. This endeavour has an old tradition in Western societies as a popularly cherished alternative-moral attitude. An alternative legal dogmatics with this perspective could function as a weapon of a modern *Robin Hood, J.*

A law of contract that stresses the parties' economic position, etc., could conceivably be criticised for *extreme individualism*, for breaking society down into private individuals with

---

[63] See in more detail e.g. Unger 1983 p. 616 ff., Collins 1986 p. 8 ff., Kennedy 1976 p. 1717 ff., Joerges 1989 p. 608 f., 622.

[64] The users of those concepts do not themselves necessarily interpret them in this way. See e.g. Kennedy 1982 p. 584 who points out that a change in a rule "in the direction of greater altruistic duty does not mean that the rule promotes more equal distribution between groups".

[65] Unger 1983 p. 638, in testing his vision on the law of mistake, expressly mentions as one of the criteria to be taken into account, "the relative ability of the parties to bear the loss." Or in the words of Collins 1986 p. 12: "In the modern law we look more closely at the *comparative wealth* and knowledge of the parties before we judge the legitimacy of the relation of power established between them." (present author's italics).

specific characteristics.[66] At first sight this may appear to be so, but the point is that conceptual change need not stop at the individual-centred concepts. From these, it is a short step to concepts at collective level that describe, for example, social classes. One can say that a breaking-down of the prevailing abstract conceptual structure in private law, using person-related concepts, is a condition for the development of relevant new collective concepts.

4. NEED-ORIENTATION AND FORMAL LEGAL SECURITY

The possibilities of taking account of the needs of a party are today often grounded, as we shall see, in general clauses that leave the courts a fairly wide discretion in evaluating the needs. Damages may be adjusted if the liability is found to be unreasonably burdensome, a contract term can be modified if it is unfair, and so on. The need-oriented principles discussed in the present work must to a great degree be abstracted from such fluid legal material.

Unbidden, the question presents itself of whether one should attempt to develop such abstractions at all. Does not a free assessment *in casu* always offer the greatest possibility of taking account of a party's concrete needs in a case? Does not any need-oriented principle again bind up the application of justice to a more abstract level where the party's "concrete, real needs" cannot be observed all the way? Does not a process of abstraction imply unacceptable methodological capitulation to an obsolete, formal, subsumptional-logical paradigm of legal argumentation (see above section 2.1.i and 3.1.i)? Should not an alternative legal dogmatics, starting as it does by stressing the wide discretion afforded legal decision-makers by the legal order (see above I.2.ii) strive as far

---

[66] This criticism has been given me by Udo Reifner in a very detailed letter as a response to an essay of mine presenting some of the main ideas of the present work (Wilhelmsson 1987b).

as possible to extend this discretion in the individual case?[67]

Such a view is argued for by e.g. *Gunther Teubner* even before he presented his theory of reflexive law. In an "alternative commentary" on the Bürgerliches Gesetzbuch he argued against the traditional notion that when applying the general clauses of private law, particularly BGB sec. 242, one should strive at increasing precision through what is called "*Fallgruppenbildung*" (case-group formation). In fact such a method is, to his mind, not compatible with the social function of the general clauses: as an expression of "a learning law" these should facilitate flexible legal reactions to social changes. For Teubner, the goal should be a drastic increase in the indefiniteness of the general clauses so as to develop, at a meta-level, "*programmes*" for how, with their help, one can adapt to social changes and intervene in social processes.[68]

Against this view can be set for example *Thomas Mathiesen*'s view of the significance of legal change leading from a law of legal security towards a law of control, from a closed method of regulation to a more open one (see above section 2.2). Mathiesen sees this development as primarily negative. In his view, the more the legal system is opened up the greater the possibilities powerful groups obtain of moving about within the legal system and exploiting it for their own ends. The law of control becomes an even more efficient means of suppressing weaker social groups than the law of legal security is.[69]

It is obvious that there is an element of truth in both the views represented here with Teubner's and Mathiesen's help.

On the one hand, adequate legal intervention in social

---

[67] That this discretion is not unlimited and may vary in extent will be explained in VIII.2.4.

[68] BGB-Kommentar p. 34 ff. See also Esser - Schmidt 1984 p. 11. In a later analysis Teubner sees the general clause as "a collision rule for intersystemic conflicts", which permits legal synchronization of the various demands placed upon a contract from the "interaction level", the "institutional level" and the "societal level": see Teubner 1989 p. 422 f.

[69] See Mathiesen 1985.

processes - one could here, slightly distorting Teubner, speak of a realization of a "needs programme" - presupposes a flexible and adaptable system of regulation. The more one seeks, in accordance with the ideal of reflexive rationality, to include the parties' views of their needs, the fewer opportunities one has of capturing need orientation in more abstract concepts.

It is possible to maintain, as *Roberto Mangabeira Unger* does, that there is a contradiction between formality and solidarity.[70] The question of how one should exercise power in accordance with solidarity cannot in fact, according to Unger, admit of a general answer: "Everything will depend on issues like the degree to which the other person has acted wrongly in the particular relationship and his ability to bear the loss that would result from the exercise of the power. These are not factors that can be made the basis of rules; instead, they are elements of the decision that bear on how one uses the rights allocated by existing rules".

On the other hand, there are naturally no guarantees that a flexible regulation would in practice favour the weaker groups whose needs should be met in the first instance. Considering the development of a need-oriented law of contract, over-emphasis on what is unique to the individual case, on the situation-specific character of the needs, may thus be risky in many respects:

- The actual use of a need-oriented legal protection would presumably be limited. The greater the procedural risk, the less the degree to which one can expect that the weaker groups, particularly, will use the possibilities offered by the legal order. The needs are not brought into the legal sphere.

- The power of the courts increases in a model that strongly stresses *in casu* solutions. However, there is nothing to say that need-oriented argumentation is widely accepted by the courts. The choice of need-oriented solutions is made difficult for uncertain judges who could potentially conceive of such alternatives, if there is no explicit body of doctrine. For this reason strong emphasis on

---

[70] Unger 1976 p. 206 ff. See also e.g. Broekman 1986 p. 87: "the dogmatic character of law could be rejected in favor of solidarity".

the unique can reduce the need-orientation of the system as a whole.

- This is significant on the level of legal policy, too. A development of need-oriented principles makes it easier to put through new need-oriented solutions in the legislation (see above II.2.3).

Thus it may be said that there are many *substantive reasons* for maintaining a certain degree of formal rationality.[71] The goal should be to develop a pattern of argumentation that as to content takes account of the values embedded in the need-oriented elements of contract law *and* methodologically takes, to the extent possible, account of the values expressed in the formal ideal of the rule of law, in the sense of *predictability*.[72] This can come about through a development of such need-oriented principles among the general principles of contract law, which on the one hand strengthen the formal rule of law by indicating main foci for legal argumentation and show the direction in which change in contract law should be encouraged, but which on the other hand are flexible enough to permit sufficient consideration of the parties' concrete needs.

In other words, what is needed is a process of abstraction of new need-oriented concepts. These can and should, however, in the majority of situations, not be perceived as formal concepts in the sense that they can be used as binding premises for subsumptional-logical inferences, but merely as *guideline concepts* and *degree concepts* (see below VI.5.3) that permit a modification of the abstract needs, articulated in the concepts, with reference to the concrete needs of the parties in the individual case.

On a more general level it could be said that once, employing the general clauses, development in legislation has been directed away from predictability towards fairness *in casu*, the task of the general principles becomes, with the observance and further

---

[71] See also Tuori 1988 p. 197 f. who sees the relationship between material and formal rationality in this way.

[72] See e.g. Bruun - Wilhelmsson 1983 p. 707 ff.

development of the new material values, to attempt within this framework to satisfy the predictability interest also. Or in other words: legal science can contribute to increased material justice in hard cases without at the same time sacrificing to an unreasonable extent the requirement for formal legal security, by developing new and, in relation to new values more adequate, general principles.

The legal security and predictability here in question do not, however, imply a better possibility of foreseeing the outcome of a specific case. An alternative systematization that extends the boundaries for what is legally possible can hardly have an effect like this, at least in the short term. Legal security increases, however, in the form of *enhanced transparency* in the law. By bringing out and making known such new ways of thinking as are already embedded, perhaps in a suppressed form, in concrete legal material, alternative legal dogmatics increases the possibility of foreseeing what kind of legal *argument may be considered acceptable*. At the same time the decision-maker is compelled to make an *open and conscious choice* among the different systematizations offered by traditional and alternative-dogmatic principles. When the choice of value base is explicit, the space available for a purely subjective, irrational discretionary decision shrinks.

CHAPTER IV

ON THE JURIDICAL ROLES OF CONTRACT LAW

1. ON JURIDICAL ROLES

When the problem was stated (above I.3.2) we saw how it has been asserted that the abstract "juridical roles" of private law can immunize private law against an explicitly value-bound alternative legal dogmatics. Private-law dogmatics of this kind therefore presupposes a critical re-valuation of the role concepts of private law.

This book has as its subject the role concepts of contract law. The relevant juridical "roles" will be discussed in many places. There is therefore reason to specify what is meant here by a role in contract law.

To speak of roles in connection with contract law is by no means a novelty. On the contrary, internationally speaking, it can be claimed that the concept of role is experiencing a boom in contract law.[1] But this is not to say that the content of this concept is clear and unambiguous. In the literature many very varying significations have been ascribed to the concept and there have also been warnings against the unreflecting use of such a vague concept.[2]

---

[1] Thus for West German law, Köndgen 1981 p. 192.

[2] Köndgen 1981 p. 193, see also e.g. Rottleuthner 1973 p. 135.

In legal studies relating to *the law of contract* the concept of role has been used at least with the following different connotations, which of course partly overlap:

(i) Starting with the role concepts of sociology, "social role" may be defined as a complex of *expectations* linked with a certain *social position*. Jurisprudence uses roles to summarize the norms of action that society has set for the occupant of such a position.[3]

(ii) In discussion of the development of consumer protection one speaks of the *economic role* in which a person acts on the market.[4]

(iii) The above, more elaborated, role concepts can be used for *specializing* the norms of contract law.[5] The concept of role is sometimes also used more generally to indicate the occurrence of norms which have become specialized in various ways. The opposite to "role" in this sense is the general term "person": as role concepts are named, for example, "merchant", "employee", "tenant" and even "seller" and "buyer".[6]

(iv) The concept of role can also be used simply to describe how, in traditional legal rules, one *disregards the parties' personal characteristics*. The opposite to the role concepts (e.g. "seller" and "buyer") is here concepts that contain a description of the characteristics of the party in question.[7]

In this work the concept of role is used in a way that cannot entirely be classified under any of the above points. As the goal is to analyse the development of the conceptual apparatus of contract law from more general towards more particular person-

---

[3] See e.g. Rehbinder 1968 p. 162 ff., Wüstmann 1972, Rebe 1978 p. 55 and Köndgen 1981 p. 193 ff.

[4] See e.g. Reich 1977 p. 191 f., Westermann 1983 p. 9.

[5] Thus e.g. Köndgen 1981 p. 198 "...ist Rolle primär ein Konzept der *Normdifferenzierung*".

[6] Thus e.g. - despite the theoretical connection with the sociological concept of role - Rehbinder 1968 p. 160 ff.

[7] Thus e.g. Zinke 1982 p. 168.

related concepts, it is not to the purpose to use a role concept that covers only a part of the alternatives under investigation. If one starts with the idea that only norms that are to some degree specialized can be the bearers of "roles" (above p.i - iii), one comes into fruitless discussions about where development has gone far enough for the role concept to be applicable; on the other hand if more person-related concepts are disqualified as "role concepts" (above p. iv), corresponding problems arise at the other end of the scale. The concept of role used here should embrace both the general "person" and detailed descriptions of a party's personal (economic and social) characteristics.

By *juridical role* is meant quite simply the way in which, *in a legal norm, the parties to whom the norm applies are described.* Such a role concept may lack reference to a party's personal characteristics (above p. iv) but may also be person-related; it may be general, but also specialized (above p. iii), for example regarding a party's social position (above p. i) or his function in the market (above p. ii).

In the latter cases, however, there is of course no idea of a direct taking-over of sociological and economic roles. Juridical role concepts are normative ones developed on the basis of the legal sources. Legal practice copies "artificially" the "natural" social process of role definition.[8] Consequently the role concept here does not correspond to the use of this concept in other social sciences. This is *not* a case of importing any sociological "*role theory*".

The foregoing also implies that the concept of role is used here *differently than in normal linguistic usage.* Typical of a "natural" role concept is clearly the ability of the actor in question to assume different roles in different contexts. The "role" is separate from the "person himself". The concept of juridical role in this work does, however, cover both cases where a party acts in an interchangeable (true) role and those where he to a greater or lesser degree "acts as himself". What makes the difference here

---

[8] BGB-Kommentar p. 63.

lies merely in what kind of description of parties is indicated by the legal norms as relevant for presentation on the legal stage.

Should one wish to describe the development here illustrated in terms of the concept of juridical roles - from formal roles to person-related roles - using a "natural" role concept of the type indicated above, the formula would run: *from "roles" to "real characteristics"*.

The role concept is thus not of itself necessary for describing the development which the alternative dogmatics in the present work has in mind. The concept has nevertheless, despite the risks of misunderstanding due to its partially deviant use in relation to general usage and to the usage of other social sciences, been found of use here. This is primarily because it links the analysis to the international discussion of contract law already touched upon. The use of the role concept may also be seen as a reaction against the idea that the roles of contract law as something necessarily unalterable could immunize this branch of law against alternative dogmatics.

2. THE MATERIALIZATION AND ROLE SPECIALIZATION OF CONTRACT LAW

The shifts in the structures of legal rationality that have taken place during this century have naturally been reflected in the juridical conceptual apparatus. The conceptual apparatus of formal law is inadequate for a materialized law of contract. Regulations based on material rationality presuppose new role concepts.

A contract law ruled by formal rationality is dominated by formal role concepts that entirely lack personal reference. In the traditional system of private law, the maxim of equality before the law is viewed as excluding all consideration of the parties' social positions and market functions. The entirely abstract description of the legal subjects is characterized as one of the fundamental ideas of the private law of a market economy.[9]

The formal role concepts are marked above all by the more or less unlimited *interchangeability* of the actors. The same rules are to apply regardless of what physical or legal person has assumed the juridical role in question. Equality is "a *pro forma* equality in which subjects become mutually interchangeable".[10] Only in certain definite special cases can the person's individual properties be of relevance: one example is the restricted legal competence of minors.

The *materialization* of contract law has been considered to entail a style of regulation that to a greater extent than formerly *differentiates between different parties*. This tendency has been described in various ways by various authors in different countries.

In West German legal writing *Manfred Rehbinder*[11] discusses the development of legal structure using the trichotome *Status-contract-role*.[12] While the central concept for the individualistic understanding of law (= formal law) was the legal concept "Person", which lacked individuality, the law of the social state differentiates people according to their status within the social system.[13] This law is in other words one that thinks in social

---

[9] The Finnish private law classic Robert Montgomery 1889 p. 311 f. stresses: "That the law should be the same for all is a tenet embedded in the very idea of law, which in no part of the legal system permits and demands a more complete performance than within general private law... Such difference in legal status as is in rank, occupation, dwelling within the boundaries of the state (country or town) etcetera, which has had its origin and correspondence essentially in public law, has gradually been levelled out by more recent legislation so that within private law ... little thereof remains" (translated here).

[10] Broekman 1986 p. 96.

[11] Rehbinder 1968 p. 161 f.

[12] "Role" is used here in the limited sense specified above in section 1 points i and iii.

[13] See also e.g. Preuss 1986 p. 166 who asserts that "the laws become evermore selective vis à vis different segments of the population and social situations and thus become concrete and special".

roles. An individual appears in the law no longer as an abstract person but as employer or employee, as worker, member of the staff or commercial representative, as occasional law-breaker or old lag, etc. The more differentiated social life becomes, the greater the number of such roles must be created.[14]

A corresponding general description of the structural change of private law is presented by e.g. *Bernd Rebe* when he traces development from "a universal picture of mankind to a segmented role expectation".[15]

The literature also contains more detailed discussion of special aspects of the growing differentiation between parties shown in the materialized norms. A much-discussed example is *Klaus Hopt*'s analysis of the growth of an "*occupational law*" as a concretization of the norms of private law. An "occupational liability" based on occupational roles is said to be growing up between and above the liability of contract and tort law.[16] Similar tendencies are mentioned by *Johannes Köndgen*:[17] role expectations render concrete the colourless "Werkunternehmer" of the law as architects, travel agents, dentists or opera singers.[18]

This development emerges also in legal practice concerning the general clauses of private law. It has even been asserted that thinking in social roles is becoming a predominant style of application of the general clause in sec. 242 of the Bürgerliches Gesetzbuch. This makes it possible, among other things, to define a basic notion such as "profession", "consumer" or economic function, as a help in interpretation.[19]

---

[14] Rehbinder 1968 p. 169.

[15] Rebe 1978 p. 54 ff.

[16] See Hopt 1983 p. 663 ff. Cf. also Ewald 1986 p. 53, whose "social law" is characterized among other things as "a law of occupational groupings".

[17] Köndgen 1981; see for occupational law generally p. 216 ff., 352 ff.

[18] Köndgen 1981 p. 203.

[19] BGB-Kommentar p. 63 f.

It should be noted in passing that not all West German authors are prepared either to see or to accept a development towards greater differentiation between parties. A considerable part of the theoretical discussion of this problem area has recently been pursued in connection with the question of whether a special consumer law (consumer role) should be developed. Some critics of this stress that the development of a special private law for consumers would entail fundamental changes in the system since it cannot be justified in agreement with the principles of the market economy and since it does not correspond with the systematics of general private law in force.[20]

The idea of a differentiation between parties in contract law is not found only in German legal writing. In English law for example, *Hugh Collins* has in a corresponding way characterized modern contract law as one which "is capable of discriminating between persons". Welfare state legislation identifies consumers, employees and tenants as categories which deserve special protection.[21]

On a more legal-scientific level, one of the creators of the discipline of woman's law in the Nordic countries, *Tove Stang Dahl*, has drawn attention to the growth of what she calls *person-directed disciplines* such as children's law, foreigners' law, prisoners' law, patients' law and consumer law as well as women's law.[22]

Reference may also be made to certain observations on the development of court procedure by *Kevät Nousiainen*. She notes that a process that concentrates only on a "legally relevant" part of reality and ignores the parties' past and future and social obligations, loses significance compared with a procedure in which the parties participate in a certain social character, e.g. as employer,

---

[20] Thus Dauner-Lieb 1983, e.g. p. 150.

[21] Collins 1986 p. 19.

[22] See Stang Dahl 1985 p. 29 ff., and also Eckhoff 1985 p. 84.

employee, consumer or merchant.[23]

If one is to believe what has been said in the excerpts from legal writing presented above, the materialization of private law - and hereby of contract law also - has thus entailed a growing differentiation of parties. From the perspective of juridical roles as defined above one could also say that this materialization has included a *specialization of roles*.

Yet no deeper understanding of what sorts of specialized role the development has produced is to be gained merely from the literature quoted. The descriptions of the increased differentiation of parties ("person-orientation", "role programming" etc.) are not particularly analytical. The examples of the tendency we are dealing with also vary from author to author. One writer may for instance mention "seller" and "buyer" or "landlord" and "tenant" directly as expressions of role specialization (in the sense intended here), while others may direct attention to the emergence of a consumer role or the development of specific occupational roles. Hence closer analysis is needed of the various types of role concept that the materialization of contract law has brought into being.[24]

The materialization of contract law, as is well known, has had a centre of gravity in the emergence of the principle of protection, of norms aiming to some extent to protect the weaker party in a contractual relationship. Of particular interest, therefore, is the way in which a party in need of protection has been defined in the norms of contract law. It seems possible to distinguish at least three types of "*weaker-party role*" as described below:

(i) formal roles,
(ii) function-related roles
(iii) person-related roles.

---

[23] Nousiainen 1985 p. 74.

[24] Following the terms of reference of this work, then, only person-related specialization is investigated here. Materialization of contract law has naturally also entailed other differentiations such as situation-related concepts.

The list also contains a certain time perspective. The formal roles appear earlier than many function-related and person-related ones. This does not mean that the formal roles of today have lost their significance. In the same way as formal legal rationality - to which in methodological respects the (material as to content) formal protective roles may be ascribed - continues to play an important part in law, so the formal role concepts of contract law today remain central. They have merely been partly supplemented and replaced by function-related and person-related role concepts.

3. FORMAL PROTECTIVE ROLES DESPITE MATERIAL RATIONALITY

The problems that the market economy and its formal legal rationality created - and which grew out of the conflict between legal private autonomy and economic and social inequality - early led to corrective legislative measures of different kinds. Even if the *content* of these measures was conditioned by a burgeoning *material legal rationality* there was long an attempt to maintain *formal rationality* on the *methodological* plane. This means among other things that the *conceptual apparatus of private law* was retained *at a formal level*. The weaker-party roles were described in terms of formal role concepts.

Within contract law this could be achieved by delimiting the material regulations introduced with the help of the division into *types of contract*. In the legislation were noted those contract types where the unsatisfactory state of things was generally evident in that the contracting parties' bargaining positions were for various reasons obviously unequal. As typical examples in many countries one may mention the first attempts at peremptory legislation regarding hire-purchase[25] and insurance contracts.

---

[25] For the sake of clarity it should be noted that Nordic hire-purchase law in its original form applied without distinction in favour of both consumers and enterprises. In this respect it differs from the German Gesetz betr. die Abzahlungsgeschäfte of 1894, which is not fully formal

In the protective legislation built upon formal role concepts, one party is able to call upon the protection offered by the rules regardless of whether he is, in the actual case, weaker than his counterpart and without consideration of whether he has entered the agreement as a private consumer or in connection with his business activity. The same cogent rules apply both to private home insurance and to large companies' fire insurance. The persons hiding behind the concept of "the insured" are *entirely interchangeable*.

These role concepts are in other words entirely "inside the law". The roles are determined exclusively by the *nature of the legal relationship*, without regard to outside circumstances. In this sense they may, in agreement with the demands of formal rationality, be said to be linked to *substance* and not to persons, even though the purpose, with regard to content, of the regulations has been to protect a definite group of persons. The formal protective roles do not yet express any person-directed law of contract in a real sense.

4. FUNCTION-RELATED ROLES

In recent years, new concepts of role, which are systematically cutting through the traditional roles built up around contract types, have penetrated the law of contract. In the legislation, weight has in certain cases been placed upon the *purpose* for which a party enters an agreement and on his market function (his "economic role"). Qualities and circumstances of these kinds, which fall "outside" the actual legal relationship, are being drawn into the delimitation of the sphere of application of the legal norms. A role that is based on such a delimitation is here termed function-related.

The most noted function-related, weaker-party role in both Nordic and international discussion of contract law is, as hinted earlier, the *consumer role*. Starting in the 1960s, the notion of

---

in that it does not apply to purchasers who are "merchants" (sec. 8).

consumer has become a central legal and legal-political concept in many developed countries with market economies. The more exact definition of this concept can of course vary from country to country, and even within the same country from act to act. By and large it means a non-commercial person "who buys goods or services for his own personal needs or for those of his family".[26] Consumer protection legislation is as a rule applied to the relationship between such a consumer and a merchant.

Introducing the consumer concept into contract law implies that the norms to be used in relation to one and the same formal-juridical contract type can vary, depending on what function-related roles the parties in the individual case have assumed, i.e. the purpose for which the utility in question has been procured. Different rules may be applied to consumer purchases and to commercial purchases, and so on.

It has sometimes been claimed that the idea of special rules for consumers has deeper roots than what at first sight appears to be the case. Long before the growth of consumer protection legislation the role of *merchant* (Kaufmann) - and thus its opposite, non-merchant - has had a certain significance in contract law. In Scandinavian sales law the distinction between commercial purchase and private purchase, built upon the use of this role figure, has been relevant.[27] The distinction stems from German law, where it has been a moot point whether the distinction can be viewed as some form of precursor of the lines of thought underlying the development of consumer law. Thus *Barbara Dauner-Lieb* maintains that the traditional distinction between merchant/non-

---

[26] Krämer 1986 p. 4 gives in this definition a summary of a number of definitions in various EEC Directives, Draft Directives and Conventions. However, he notes at the same time that "Community law has not yet developed a uniform term of 'consumer' suitable for general application" (p. 6). - For a negative evaluation of the need for a special consumer law, see, e.g., Reynolds 1982.

[27] See e.g. Hellner 1982 p. 37 ff. The development of special rules for consumer relationships has however led to abandonment of the distinction between private purchase and commercial purchase in the recent reform of sales law. See on this point e.g. NU 1984:5 p. 169 f.

merchant does not primarily have anything to do with the merchant's lesser need of protection, and therefore cannot be used for juridical legitimation of consumer-protective measures.[28] This position has, however, been criticized.[29]

In current Nordic law, the consumer concept enjoys a significance far beyond the issue of the scope of explicit consumer protection legislation. It is hardly necessary to point out to a Nordic lawyer that the concept can also be used as an aid when discussing many problems of private law that lie outside the scope of such specific legislation. The consumer role has become or is becoming a central systematic point of departure in the development of the general principles of contract law.

In West German discussion *Norbert Reich*, as early as in 1974, with the support of the theory of civil law of certain socialist countries, proposed a far-reaching reconstruction of West German property law into three sub-areas: enterprise law (Unternehmensrecht), which would concern the legal relationship between enterprises, consumer law (Verbraucherrecht) and citizen law (Bürgerrecht), which would regulate private legal relationships between citizens.[30] However, the proposal has not met with appreciable success.

The function-related consumer concept does not, as the formal role concepts do, completely detach the party from his social context. On the other hand it does not refer to the party's personal characteristics. The limits to the interchangeability of the concrete persons who may adopt the consumer role thus relate merely to the purpose of the *action* involved: when a person obtains goods for private consumption he cannot be replaced by a merchant. As the same person may play various function-related roles, now a consumer, now a merchant, there obtains on the *personal level* a more or less complete *exchangeability*. Any physical person can act as a consumer and is in this function

---

[28] Dauner-Lieb 1983 p. 46 ff.. See also e.g. Lieb 1983 p. 356 f.

[29] See e.g. Schuhmacher 1986.

[30] Reich 1974 p. 188.

exchangeable with any other person when the latter is performing a consumer function.

Only insofar as merely certain kinds of person can perform certain functions do the function-related role concepts have effects that are also person-related. Thus in many countries the consumer concept normally excludes legal persons, for example, from the circle of persons who can play the juridical role in question.[31]

Naturally, it is possible to define the consumer concept in a more person-related way so that certain, for example commercially experienced, physical persons always - regardless of the purpose of the action - fall outside the definition. Thus for example it has been proposed in West German discussion that businessmen, professional people and tradesmen, etc., should be excluded from the scope of certain consumer protection rules *even* when they are acting within the private sphere, since they can exploit their commercial experience here too.[32] As a rule, however, the starting point is in Germany, too, that the consumer corps is identical with the total population.[33]

In other words the consumer concept does not yet signal the advent of a social private law that particularly supports economically and socially weak social groups. For these groups, granted, the term "*risk consumer*" is used in the consumer literature. But no particular juridical role has (yet?) been developed in the Nordic countries, nor scarcely anywhere else, on the basis of this concept.

---

[31] See e.g. for Finnish law Reg.Prop. 8/1977 p. 15.

[32] Verhandlungen des 53. Deutschen Juristentages p. K 47 ff.

[33] Simitis 1976 p. 81, thus also e.g. Westermann 1983 p. 70, Esser - Schmidt 1984 p. 17.

5. PERSON-RELATED ROLES AND THEIR CLASSIFICATION

Furthest from the level of formal concept lie role concepts that relate to personal characteristics in the parties whose relations are to be judged. When applying these concepts, the *interchangeability is limited* to the class of persons exhibiting the same relevant characteristics. Criteria that could be used for delimiting person-related roles are, for example:

- technical knowledge
- trade or profession
- property status
- social class
- sex.

When one pays attention to the personal characteristics of people involved in contractual relationships, this may take place for different purposes. A certain characteristic of a person may be judged relevant because this gives the person particular skills - or, when considering weaker-party roles, lack of skills - that should be taken into account when assessing his action. In other cases a personal characteristic may be assigned significance because it reflects a particular need of the party concerned. The person-related role concepts of contract law can thus be divided into at least two sub-groups: (i) *ability-oriented person roles* and (ii) *need-oriented person roles*. To travesty a well-known Marx quotation, one could say that the former roles have a connection with the goals stated in the first element of the expression and the latter with the second: "From each according to his abilities, to each according to his needs".

6. ABILITY-ORIENTED PERSON ROLES

Criteria connected with the personal abilities of one party in a legal relationship can in many respects be of importance for the legal assessment of this relationship. Rules on legal competence are of course the traditional example of this. A description of ability-oriented elements in contract law in force need not, however, be limited to the role pair minor/of age, which indeed stems from the formal rational legal environment. The development of material rationality in contract law has generally increased opportunities of considering, in the legal assessment, the limitations to a party's abilities which may be a consequence both of, for example, *deficiencies in experience and knowledge* and of *an economic or other relationship of dependence* upon the other party.

Ability-oriented arguments have long had particular significance when assessing questions connected with *the making of a contract*. Diverse examples may be mentioned here:

- When one has to decide about the *validity of a contract*, the personal characteristics of one of the parties is significant over and above what follows from the rules on legal competence. The invalidity rules regarding coercion, fraud, usury and so on are based on criteria, the application of which to some extent presupposes consideration of the injured party's personal characteristics. In the usury rule in sec. 138 II of the Bürgerliches Gesetzbuch and in its Nordic copy in sec. 31 of the Contract Act, the more or less directly person-related criteria of distress, imprudence and irresponsibility are included in the actual legal text. It is also self-evident, in Nordic law for example, that it is a breach of faith and honour (sec. 33 of the Contract Act) to invoke an agreement where one party, for reasons of *age or illness*, has not been capable of correctly judging the significance of the agreement.[34]

- When assessing the question of the *binding effect of standard conditions*, the focus has often been upon the other party's personal ability. The more technically competent and well-endowed the other party is, the more easily can one accept that standard conditions become binding upon him;[35] if the other party

[34] See Wilhelmsson 1978 p. 61 ff.

[35] As an explicit example from Finnish legal practice may be mentioned HD 1977 II 103, where the Finnish Supreme Court expressly referred to the fact that the other party was a person with long experience of the car-hire business and the procurement of cars in connection with this.

is less well-endowed, higher demands are often placed on the information he should be given about the conditions if these are to become a part of the agreement.

- To the extent other types of *obligation to inform* in connection with the making of contracts *are developed*, this is also assumed to be more stringent in relation to inexperienced and ignorant parties. Thus in, for example, West German legal practice, in one case a contract-law obligation to inform has been expressly justified by referring to the requirement concerning honest dealing particularly with inexperienced persons belonging to the socially weaker stratum of the population.[36]

When assessing questions connected with the coming into being of a contract and also when specifying the parties' obligations during the period of the contractual relationship, the *role of expert* is of essential importance. More is demanded of an expert than of a person who lacks the corresponding expert knowledge:[37] a doctor, a lawyer and other similar professional people are judged more severely than persons who do not appear in this role. "The expert" may even be developed into a general role concept of private law: the concept has for example in Finland also been used in assessing, e.g., issues of good faith in property law[38] or problems of culpa in tort law.[39]

The opposite of the expert - the layman - may appear in a weaker-party role. The concept of expert is, however, used rather to stress the obligations of the stronger party in a legal relationship. Here, where the point of interest is different types of weaker-party role, there is no point in devoting much space to the expert as a private-law role figure, yet there is reason to observe that the role is not unambiguous. When one speaks of an expert's liability,

---

[36] BGH 27.2.1974, NJW 1974 p. 849 ff.

[37] See e.g. for German occupational liability section 2 above and, from Nordic law, Taxell 1972 p. 301.

[38] See e.g. HD 1980 II 39, where the term specialist is used in connection with trade in securities and housing shares.

[39] See e.g. Saxén 1975 p. 34 ff.

his good faith, etc., one is in fact slipping, often more or less unconsciously, between two planes of significance: sometimes the argumentation is based on the concrete, existing expert knowledge of the person involved, sometimes on the knowledge he may be presumed to (should) have. There are, in other words, two expert roles. *On the one hand* - and this is more common - the expert concept can be used in a way that resembles the sociological role concepts (see above, section 1 point i). One then starts with the idea that a certain degree of expert knowledge in connection with a certain activity may be *presumed*. This requirement as to expert knowledge forms the basis for the judgment irrespective of whether the person in question in the individual case has possessed such expert knowledge.[40] In cases where the expert concept is used in this way it is person-related only in the sense that it presupposes that the person in question is active within a certain sector or runs a certain type of activity.[41] *On the other hand* it is not excluded that a person's actual expert knowledge is considered.[42] In this case it is a matter of a more direct person-related judgment.

The possibility of considering personal ability is nothing new in private law.[43] Many of the concepts perceived as central in formally inclined private law, such as culpa, good faith, etc. presuppose in their concrete application that one considers the ability of the person whose action is to be judged. Consideration of personal ability is built into many abstract concepts and cannot

---

[40] As an illustration from Finnish law may be mentioned e.g. case HD 1980 II 49, where an entrepreneur could not plead, as a ground for exemption from liability, the circumstance that insufficient geotechnical knowledge was available, since it could be assumed that the company, as a business in the relevant sector, would possess this knowledge.

[41] Cf. the German "occupational roles"; see also Taxell 1972 p. 302, who points out that "Specialist characteristics by no means always attach to the debtor's person, but to the activity in which the debtor engages" (translated here).

[42] See e.g. Finnish case HD 1977 II 103, mentioned in footnote 35.

[43] Cf. also Hönn 1982 p. 134 ff.

be avoided when these are applied in an actual case. However, this consideration was not normally elevated to the conceptual level in classical private law. Particularly ability-oriented juridical roles - apart from that of "minor" - were seldom developed.

Today there is an increasing attempt to capture these ability-oriented elements of private law in more specific concepts. This has so far taken place chiefly on the basis of a party's special skills: both *the expert* and more *sector-specific role concepts*, as in West German "occupational law", are examples of this. The weaker-party roles are not yet equally well developed as regards concepts. The inexperienced, the sick, the elderly, etc. have not in the Nordic area, or hardly anywhere else either, more generally achieved the status of juridical roles.

7. NEED-ORIENTED PERSON ROLES: DEFINITIONS

The ability-oriented person roles relate to the assessment of a party's acts or omissions in connection with a legal relationship. It may happen, however, that when a party's need of legal protection is being examined such person-related criteria are granted a relevance which do not necessary have any connection with the party's ability or lack of ability. One might conceivably refer to a person's *wealth status*, and also to *illness*, *age*, etc., to indicate *a special need* of that party as an argument for his receiving protection in contract law.

As stated before the key concept in the present work is need-orientation. From the perspective of juridical roles, the goal of the presentation is *to investigate the occurrence of traces of need-oriented role concepts* and as far as possible *to develop these*. The forthcoming analysis will not be anticipated in this section and examples of need-orientation must therefore wait until later. Here certain concepts used later on will merely be briefly defined.

In this context there is first reason to note that a party's economic and social status can conceivably, in private law in the same way as in social law, be considered for various purposes. *On the one hand* the goal may be merely to compensate for various types of loss by granting the party benefits in relation to what he has earlier enjoyed, i.e. to maintain the *status quo*. *On the other hand*, one may strive to *redistribute* welfare benefits by giving more to the party who has the greater need. Private law has long known norms of the former type. A good example is the rules for calculating compensation for personal injury; the better the previous economic status of an injured party who has become unfit for work, the greater the compensation he is entitled to. When discussing the development of need-oriented private law it is naturally not this kind of "person-relation" that is of concern. Here the interest lies in the development of redistributive norms of the latter type.

By *need-oriented role concepts*, then, are meant concepts that recognize legal relevance in such circumstances connected to the person of a party as can give rise to particular needs for that party in the legal relationship in question. Circumstances of this kind may be poverty, low income, illness, unemployment, that one is female, etc. Thus in other words, need-oriented concepts, as we have already seen, are here defined as concepts which refer to *person-related* needs. By *need-oriented regulation* and *need-oriented argumentation* is meant, correspondingly, a system of regulation and a way of arguing that grant legal relevance to such person-related needs.

The particular needs that might be found relevant in a need-oriented judgment may be of various kinds. Disputes in contract law often concern economic relations between the parties. We shall also see later on that the traces of need-orientation that may be found in the concrete legal material are linked predominantly to a party's *economic needs*. In certain cases, however, attention has been paid to needs that are perhaps not directly economic, such as the need of somewhere to live, the special needs of an ill person, etc. For this reason the somewhat imprecise expression *economic and social needs* will be used.

Against role concepts that express particular needs must, logically, be set concepts that express not-need. Special rules for a party who is out of work cannot be applied to a party who is not out of work, and an argumentation that stresses the poverty of a party cannot be called upon in favour of a non-poor party. As long as the delimitation is made on the basis of a party's particular needs, it is naturally a less interesting - but, considering its potential in argumentation, not entirely uninteresting - question whether role concepts have been formulated in positive or in negative terms. However, one can also conceive of role concepts that express a *marked lack* of a certain *need*, such as the concept 'wealthy'. If the limit for the application of such a concept is drawn "high", so that the majority of citizens are excluded, its opposite, e.g. 'not-wealthy', becomes only weakly need-oriented. For this reason such concepts are considered here only to a more limited extent. The centre of gravity, as already stated, lies in concepts that express particular needs.

A role concept that expresses the marked lack of a need is not always easy to distinguish from an ability-oriented role concept. The ratio of the concept is not always clear; should, for example, the stricter requirements placed on a person of means always be justified with reference to his considerable ability or do they sometimes stand in relation to his small needs? An example would be a role concept that is recurring with increasing frequency in many countries, viz. "bank", credit institute or similar. It is often to some extent possible to apply different principles of assessment to banks than to non-professional givers and receivers of credit: this is obviously primarily connected with a bank's presumed expertise, but perhaps also to some extent with the bank's limited economic need seen in relation to the individual contract.

Parties in a legal relationship of contract law have as a rule both rights and duties towards each other. Each party appears both in the character of creditor (entitled) and debtor (obliged) in relation to the other. The outcome of need-oriented argumentation naturally varies depending on the character in which a party pleads his special needs. On this basis, two types of need-oriented person role can be differentiated:

- To the extent one considers the creditor's needs, for

example the need of an injured party for compensation, in specifying his rights, one can speak of a *need-oriented creditor role*. The need of one party to receive a performance or increased performance from the other party is here given relevance.

- To the extent one considers the debtor's needs, for example a hire-purchaser's need to postpone payment, in specifying his obligations, it is a matter of a *need-oriented debtor role*. In other words, one considers here the party's need to escape from or to reduce his obligation to perform.

CHAPTER V

THE CONCRETE LEGAL MATERIAL - A FINNISH EXAMPLE

1. INTRODUCTION

A concept that is central to the model of alternative legal dogmatics proffered here is *symptomatic criticism*. Alternatives are developed on the basis of a kind of "legal induction" from those elements in the concrete legal material that express a new and desirable legal thinking. In this chapter symptoms of a person-related need-orientation in Finnish law are presented.

As the chief purpose of this section is to exemplify the type of grounds on which need-oriented principles can be built, *no* overall picture of the general principles of Finnish and Nordic contract law is given. Suffice it to say that the *starting points* for Nordic contract law and its juridical roles are *parallel with those of other developed market economies*. The doctrine of contract law rests primarily on formal role concepts, supplemented with function-related and ability-related concepts of the kind described in the previous chapter. The individual needs of contracting parties are not considered: the principle that each person is responsible for his ability to pay is central in Nordic law, too (see 7.1 below). In the Nordic countries as elsewhere, development of need-oriented principles implies a break with the traditional systematization of contract law.

The symptomatic criticism, which provides the building blocks for the alternative principles, is based, as explained earlier, on the traditional legal sources: chiefly legislation, *travaux préparatoires*, legal practice and legal writing. The *developmental perspective* that marks the presentation has naturally guided the selection of these building blocks. As the work concentrates on the growth of need-oriented elements in the legal source material and the aim is not to give a complete picture of all the questions treated here, the emphasis, for example in the analysis of practice concerning the rules on adjustment of damages and contract terms, is on those legal cases in which adjustment has been effected on the basis of need-oriented argumentation. Cases where a claim for adjustment has been rejected or where adjustment has been justified on other grounds are of less interest in the present connection, even though they would of course be relevant in a general analysis of the institution of adjustment. The legal cases - as well as other authoritative material - treated here express the legal *possibilities* for need-oriented decisions that are available. These possibilities are not eliminated by the fact that in some other cases need-oriented views have been denied relevance.

Concerning the legal cases there is reason to repeat that they have been analysed only as legal sources. Interest is directed towards their usefulness in justifying need-oriented general principles. For this reason, only decisions are described in which more or less explicitly need-oriented arguments have been used. Only decisions of this kind can be adduced as expressions of the fact that need-oriented arguments are considered legitimate in law. The question whether the courts in other cases have covertly - referring to other arguments - taken the needs of the parties into account cannot and need not be touched upon here.

From the present English version of the work, which of course cannot function in the same way as the original as a contribution to national and Nordic discussion of dogmatics, a considerable quantity of concrete legal material and detailed analyses judged to lack interest for international readers has been excluded. For these readers the concrete sections are intended to act merely as exemplification.

2. NEED-ORIENTATION IN FAMILY LAW AND THE LAW OF SUCCESSION

The social elements do not penetrate private law only, and hardly even primarily, via the law of contracts and torts. Need-oriented roles are part of and are being introduced into the scripts of family law and the law of succession also.

The issue of private-law role structure represents a whole. Conceptual changes within one part of private law often reflect changes in the general way of approaching problems of private law. Although the present work concentrates on the need-oriented roles of contract law, the corresponding formation of concepts in other parts of private law cannot be entirely overlooked. A description of need-orientation in family and inheritance legislation and practice can provide impulses for the formation of concepts within the law of contracts and torts.

The status of need-oriented elements varies among different parts of private law. Depending on the questions regulated and the value traditionally placed upon social views within each branch of law, there exists a varying degree of receptivity towards need-oriented thinking.

Family law (in a limited sense) is that part of private law that can be said to lie nearest to social security law. This is true particularly of the regulation of the obligation of maintenance, which indeed has the character of a kind of private social law. One may therefore assume that need-oriented considerations here mark the resolution of many questions. Family law represents, thus far at least, the channel along which need-oriented viewpoints can most easily be expected to navigate into private law.

The Finnish legal rules in force concerning the maintenance obligation in family law are also *doubly* marked by need-oriented thinking. On the one hand it is fairly self-evident that one point of departure is the *need of maintenance* of the party entitled to maintenance: on the other the liable party's ability to maintain, i.e. the *debtor's economic needs*. This applies both to child maintenance and to maintenance payable to a former spouse after divorce.[1]

Although family law is not very closely related to contract and tort law, it cannot be ruled out that the need-oriented solutions of family law may be used as *one* model when developing the general principles of contract and tort law.[2] A good example is found in the principles concerning adjustment of repayment of unjust enrichment, developed on the pattern of problem cases in family law (see section 6 below).

The *law of succession*, as a regulator of more "pure" relations of property, is nearer to contract and tort law, even though its social security function has sometimes been given more pronounced emphasis.[3]

In the development of the law of succession the need has been discussed of safeguarding the positions both of lineal descendants and of surviving spouses. Regulation has, however, usually focused only on the relationship of the party in question to the deceased, without consideration of his individual needs. The lawful portion of a lineal descendant is independent of his financial position and need of the inheritance, and so on. Yet certain rules that are need-oriented in the sense intended here can be found in the inheritance law material, too.

Firstly, not all property in the estate shall of necessity be divided in accordance with the formal division rules in the law of succession. Parties to the estate with special economic needs, e.g. for upbringing and education, may be allowed the right to contributions from the estate to meet these needs. The deceased's children, and parents with the right to inherit, may also, if as a

---

[1] See Child Maintenance Act sec. 1-2 and Marriage Act sec. 48 (as amended 411/87).

[2] Cf. Unger 1983 p. 618 ff. who constructs one of the counter-principles to freedom of contract, viz. community, on the basis of, *inter alia*, the regulation of family relations.

[3] See especially Kangas 1982.

result of *illness* or for other similar reasons they are incapable of maintaining themselves, be granted the right to contributions from a beneficiary.[4]

Secondly, in the development of the protection of widows in the law of succession, regulations have also been used that partly include need-oriented roles. According to Ch. 3, sec. 1a of the Code of Inheritance, a surviving spouse may as a rule keep undivided a dwelling that has been used as the spouses' common home, if the survivor's property does not include a dwelling that is suitable as a home. The surviving spouse may in other words achieve a better position in the law of succession if he/she does not own a dwelling that may be considered suitable as a home. One could speak of the particular inheritance-law role of *non-owner of dwelling*.

3. NEED-ORIENTED PERSON ROLES IN CONTRACT AND TORT LAW. SYSTEMATICS

In contract and tort law, obligations have traditionally been assumed to arise in three different ways:

- through contracts and other undertakings,
- through the infliction of damage (tort) and
- through unjust enrichment.

The concrete legal material from which the new person roles can be extracted has come into being bound to a large extent by this systematics. The important general clause in sec. 36 of the Contract Act, and the special provisions on hire-purchase and consumer credit, are within the realm of contract law, while the general clause in the Act on Torts stressed below applies formally merely to non-contractual liability in damages. The material under examination could, for this reason, be discussed on the basis of the traditional division into contract law, tort law and repayment of unjust enrichment. A study that focuses on need-orientation in the

---

[4] See for more detail the need-oriented rules of the Code of Inheritance, Ch. 8, sec. 1-4, 6.

law of contract would here concentrate chiefly on the legal material from just this branch of law.

However, with regard to the development of the new person roles, keeping strictly to the traditional division is problematical in many respects. The division does not reflect the fact that the different branches of the law of obligations do not develop in isolated spheres. The re-shaping of contract law affects tort law and vice-versa, and each can also of course affect the institution of repayment of unjust enrichment, which is one of less practical significance. If one is attempting to illustrate the connections between different concrete person roles, a more functionally and temporally suitable systematics should therefore be used.

In addition, a three-part systematics of the conventional type can easily lead to one's overlooking interesting issues concerning the possibilities of calling, directly or by analogy, upon more general principles developed within, e.g., tort law when discussing contractual issues. And, what is even worse, the systematic solution may itself offer seeming arguments against such generalizations.

There is also reason to note that international discussion has begun to query the material correctness of the tripartite division of the grounds for legal obligations, and has suggested new bases for the assessment of, particularly, the binding nature of more or less contractual obligations.[5]

What follows is a description of a number of need-oriented person roles in the law of obligations, starting with those regulations that, as to content, lie *"close" to social security law* and that therefore offer natural points at which these roles can break into contract and tort law. The presentation will then proceed to increasingly "central" and "traditional" areas of the law of obligations. This "natural" exposition parallels very largely - but by no means completely - the development in time of need-orientation in Finnish law.

---

[5] See e.g. Atiyah 1979.

4. NEED OF HOUSING, ETC., IN TENANCY LAW

The guarantee of reasonable housing for members of society is - or at least should be - a fundamental aim of social security law. The private-law regulation of the right to housing - tenancy law - has a close relationship to such social security law. It is not surprising, therefore, that features of a social private law where a party's economic and social needs are considered in the settlement of individual disputes can be found precisely in tenancy law. Such features were to be found in the 1961 Rent Act (82/61) and have of course also been included in the new Rent Act of 1987.

In any discussion of need-orientation in tenancy law, interest must obviously be directed primarily at the tenant's *protection against eviction*. For social reasons the landlord's opportunities of terminating the tenancy have been severely limited. The concepts used for introducing these limitations are partly formal and partly function-related.[6] It has been possible to start with the notion that a tenant hiring a flat to live in always has an "existential interest"[7] in the rented dwelling. To meet this need to be able to remain in the dwelling, which all tenants are assumed to have, no rules differentiating between person groups are required.

In certain respects, however, explicit account is taken of the concrete economic and social needs of the parties involved. The best example of this - there are many - is found in the rules on the postponement of moving day.

According to the Rent Act the landlord can terminate a rental agreement for an apartment in certain cases, among others where he himself or his family needs the dwelling.[8] Even where

---

[6] Here the legal distinction between renting an apartment and renting commercial premises is referred to.

[7] Dauner-Lieb 1983 p. 50.

[8] This need-orientation has not been noted particularly here since it is a kind of "stronger-party" need, which supersedes the weaker party's protection against eviction.

there are grounds for termination of this kind, consideration of the tenant's interest may nevertheless entail postponement of the effects of notice to quit. The tenant's moving day can be postponed by a year at most, on account of his specific, concrete needs, which are specified by law (sec. 67 of the Rent Act). Postponement of moving day is also under certain circumstances possible in the case of commercial premises (sec. 122 of the Rent Act).

For an apartment tenant, moving day can be postponed if the tenant has appreciable difficulties in finding somewhere else to live before the moving day. A commercial tenant, again, can use the provisions on postponement of moving day if the acquisition of other premises and the cessation of the activity for which the premises are used would lead to his opportunities of subsistence becoming unreasonably circumscribed. An attempt has been made with these provisions, roughly speaking, to consider the needs of the *presumptively homeless tenant* and the *presumptively straitened tenant*. Moving day may, however, not be postponed if the landlord or other person is caused considerable inconvenience or damage thereby. The landlord's needs and those of others - for example the new tenant or the neighbours[9] - can thus, if adjudged considerable, be given precedence over the tenant's needs.

Since termination of the relationship basically means that the landlord withdraws his obligation to make the apartment available to the tenant, while the tenant is deprived of his claim to occupy it, it may be said that the landlord, in connection with the termination, acts as an (in natura) debtor while the tenant is in the position of an (in natura) creditor. The presumptively homeless or straitened tenant can thus be spoken of as one of the few examples of need-oriented *creditor roles*.

---

[9] Reg.prop. 127/1984 p. 58.

5. LIABILITY IN DAMAGES AND THE NEEDS OF THE PARTIES

5.1 Introduction. Need for maintenance

When computing compensation in tort law it is assumed that the injured party is to be indemnified for the whole of the economic loss inflicted upon him through the damaging action. The application of this formal and abstract norm, determination of the damage suffered, must necessarily, particularly in personal injury cases, depend on the injured party's economic and other personal circumstances. A person with a high income who becomes incapable of work suffers greater economic loss than does one with a low income. In relation to the development of social private law, this relating of the calculation of compensation to the person is naturally of no interest: it is but a traditional example of a regulation that maintains the *status quo* (see IV.7 above). This does not prevent discussion of the amount of damages from sometimes taking a certain need-rational tone.[10]

Tort law also contains, however, provisions that appear to link legal consequences to the needs of weak injured parties: this kind of need-orientation has, in the Nordic countries, traditionally appeared in the rules governing the right of a person entitled to maintenance to receive compensation when the person obliged to maintain him has been killed. In Ch. 5, sec. 4 of the Finnish Act on Torts now in force it is provided that a person entitled to maintenance, primarily a spouse or a child[11], left unprovided for because the person liable for their maintenance has been killed,

---

[10] See as an example taken at random the case HD 1972 II 82: as a result of a traffic accident, a person's mobility had been impaired to such a degree that he was unable to manage his former occupation. As he was, in view of his *age*, no longer able to obtain suitable work in his home area and had thus lost his possibilities of income, he was awarded a full invalidity pension from his traffic insurance, even though his degree of invalidity was medically defined as less than 100%.

[11] See Saxén 1975 p. 300 ff. and 1983 p. 444.

shall, with due consideration of the tortfeasor's assets and circumstances, be awarded in damages what she requires until she is able to support herself. Departing from the principle of full compensation, it is stated here that the compensation shall be computed on the basis of a *means test*. The needs of the creditor become legally relevant.

The rules on survivors' right to compensation for maintenance are closely linked to the family-law rules on maintenance.[12] What has been said above on the proximity of family-law maintenance regulations and social security law thus has a certain validity here, too. In other words, from this point of view it is not surprising that we find a need-oriented regulation just here. The regulation has a long history, too: a similar provision was part of Finnish law as early as in the 19th century.[13]

The provisions under discussion are need-oriented not only in relation to the survivors (the creditors). They also contain a reference to the tortfeasor's assets and circumstances. This is intended to empower the courts to reduce the liability of tortfeasors with limited assets. The poor tortfeasor is in a better position than the rich one. It is interesting to note that also this rule, which is oriented against the debtor's needs, was included in the 1889 law and has its roots in the debate on the construction of tort law that had taken place earlier in the century. Even then it was generally accepted that when fixing compensation for survivors the amount should be related to the ability of the liable person to pay.[14] The explanation of why "need-rationality" thinking appeared so early might be found in the close link, already mentioned, with ways of thinking in family law.

The old rule on compensation for maintenance, taking account of both the *creditor's* and the *debtor's* needs, may in this way be explained by its connection to family law. In modern

[12] Kangas 1982 p. 242 f. even considers that the preconditions for compensation and maintenance respectively are basically the same.

[13] See Ch. 9, sec. 3 of the Criminal Code of 1889.

[14] See Kivivuori 1969 p. 242 ff.

Nordic tort law, however, need-orientation has made more thorough inroads through new statutes according to which compensation shall be established after a test of fairness, or may be adjusted. In the need-orientation appearing here, the emphasis is upon the tortfeasor's (debtor's) need to avoid liability, though the other party's needs are also accorded a certain legal relevance. These rules, which with regard to the development of a need-oriented law of contract are extremely important, are treated in detail in what follows.

5.2 *Adjustment of damages, etc.*

5.2.1 Introduction

The main principle in tort law in the Nordic countries as elsewhere has been the *principle of full compensation*. Far into the twentieth century it was considered unthinkable - except in the special case, treated above, of maintenance to survivors - to depart from this principle on any ground of need-orientation. Only with the new Act on Torts of 1974 - which has a direct counterpart in e.g. Swedish law - was there a change in this respect. One of the most widely discussed innovations of the 1974 Act was in fact the provision, in Ch. 2, sec. 1.2 (and also Ch. 3, sec. 6), on the possibility of *adjustment* of damages. Also connected with this provision are those empowering courts to fix damages on the basis of a *test of fairness* where the damage has been caused by children (Ch. 2, sec. 2), persons of unsound mind (Ch. 2, sec. 3) or employees (Ch. 4, sec. 1).

There is no express delimitation of the circumstances to be taken into account in this adjustment and reasonableness testing. All the provisions mentioned above are *open-ended general clauses* that empower the courts to take into consideration both the criteria stated in the provisions and "other circumstances". Scrutiny of the circumstances particularly stressed in the law nevertheless shows that the chief weight has been placed differently in the different provisions. In the general rule on adjustment in Ch. 2, sec 1.2, only *the tortfeasor's and the injured party's economic circumstances* are expressly specified as grounds that should be considered when making adjustments, while, for example, the relevance of the degree of fault that can be ascribed to the tortfeasor emerges only from the *travaux préparatoires* to the Act;[15] for malicious mischief, however, there is a special rule. In the other provisions concerning fixing damages on the basis of fairness testing, several criteria for assessment are indicated, including the age and development of the child and the nature of the action. Regard to the situation of the parties and to their needs appears here as only one of many circumstances of equal relevance.

The present work is concerned with those criteria of judgment that have to do with a party's economic and social needs. Consequently we shall here examine how just these criteria have been made concrete, while the other criteria shall largely be overlooked. The purpose is to find out what kind of need-oriented person roles can be used in this connection. In view of the emphasis upon this kind of circumstance in the wording of the general adjustment rule, one can expect to find that much material for our discussion is associated with this rule, and it will therefore be examined first. The other rules of discretion will then be shortly touched upon, for in them - given the multiplicity of the criteria - it is harder to draw, from the actual decisions, firm conclusions about the significance of the need-oriented roles.

In all the provisions mentioned, attention is paid both to the tortfeasor's and the injured party's needs: these provisions can generate both need-oriented debtor roles and need-oriented creditor roles. Since we are concerned with a departure from the time-honoured tort-law principle of full compensation, though, it is natural to concentrate first on the arguments for reduction of liability, i.e. normally on arguments that bear upon the tortfeasor's (debtor's) needs.

With this in mind, it would appear natural first to analyse the relevant debtor roles in association with each provision, before

---

[15] Reg.prop. 187/1973 p. 13.

presenting together certain views on the creditor roles. Yet in the application of the provisions it is of course impossible to judge each party thus detached one from the other. The role concepts described here are *typical guideline concepts*, which indicate circumstances that are relevant in an overall assessment where the needs of each party must be weighed together. The greater the need of adjustment on the debtor's side, the greater the need the creditor must be able to show if he is to be able to prevent adjustment, and vice-versa.

5.2.2 The general adjustment rule in the Act on Torts

Under Ch. 2, sec. 1.2 of the Finnish Act on Torts, damages may be adjusted if the liability is found unreasonably burdensome with regard to the tortfeasor's and the injured party's economic situation and other circumstances.

According to the wording of the Act, a condition for adjustment is that the liability is "unreasonably burdensome" for the person liable to pay. The word "burdensome" can be taken to mean that the adjustment hurdle should be placed high: that the liable person has to cut down his standard of living in some way should not of itself be sufficient reason for adjustment. The *travaux préparatoires* to the Act on Torts also indicate such a view of the issue: it is stated that it would be unreasonable that an individual's and his family's income should be *entirely ruined* by a liability that he has incurred through negligence.[16]

This purpose of the provision - to protect against ruinous claims for damages - has not, however, been maintained in legal practice. The Supreme Court has not yielded to such a strict interpretation of the expression "unreasonably burdensome" as the *travaux préparatoires* could give cause for. Damages have in fact also been adjusted in cases where the amounts in question are so small that the tortfeasor's economy could hardly have been endangered or ruined by full compensation. As the following summary

---

[16] Reg.prop. 187/1973 p. 13.

of Supreme Court cases where damages have been adjusted under Ch.2, sec. 1.2 of the Act on Torts shows, the adjustment has often involved, in absolute terms, fairly insignificant amounts.

Supreme Court adjustment with (direct or analogous) support of Ch.2, sec. 1.2 of the Act on Torts

	Full compensation/ FIM	Adjusted (awarded) amount/FIM
HD 1979 II 14	6,409.01	3,204.50
HD 1980 II 50	62,248.62	10,000.-[a]
HD 1981 II 10	10,000.-	4,000.-[b]
HD 1981 II 23	93,250.-	62,167.-
HD 1981 II 102	11,572.77	4,000.-
HD 1981 II 124	6,000.-+750.-[c]/month	3,000.-+250.-/month
HD 1982 II 103	15,782.-	2,000.- / 5000.-[d]
HD 1982 II 107	35,000.-[e]	12,000.-
HD 1984 II 47	2,057,396.84	500,000.-/300,000.-[d]
HD 1984 II 182	7,577.35	3,788.65[f]
HD 1985 II 51	220,000.-	120,000.-
HD 1985 II 82	1,055,181.34	527,590.67
HD 1985 II 154	149,472.49	50,000.-[g]
HD 1987:26	90,597.-	20,000.-

a Adjustment both due to the general adjustment rule and to contributory negligence
b Three jointly liable tortfeasors
c Claimed amount
d One of the jointly liable tortfeasors was ordered to pay the higher amount
e Already adjusted for contributory negligence
f No express reference to Ch.2, sec 1.2 of the Act on Torts
g Reason unclear, possibly also contributory negligence, consent

During the period given, 1000.-FIM (Finnish Marks) corresponded to about 150-270 USD.[17]

[17] During the period in question the value in FIM of the American dollar and the British pound varied as follows:

	1 $	1 £
2.1.1979	3.908	8.026
2.1.1980	3.705	8.245

It emerges clearly from the summary that the Supreme Court has not perceived the general clause of the Act on Torts as a provision that could be adduced merely for extraordinarily high amounts of damages which would obviously ruin the tortfeasor's economy. On the contrary, in the majority of cases the adjusted amounts have been relatively moderate. It can therefore be said that Ch. 2, sec. 1.2 of the Act on Torts has, in Supreme Court practice, been developed into a *more general principle of fairness* with the help of which the court may award damages which it finds suitable with consideration to the degree of fault, the needs of the parties, etc. Seen against the background of the decisions of the Supreme Court, therefore, the general clause in this way also offers a good basis for developing the need-oriented person roles that are the subject of this work. Adjustment may take place not only where compensation is so large that it would appear burdensome for most people, but, in a need-oriented spirit, account can also be taken of less economically advantaged tortfeasors' needs for even smaller amounts to be adjusted.[18]

In rough and general terms - and using a need-oriented terminology the Supreme Court naturally does not use itself - it

---

2.1.1981	3.850	9.206
4.1.1982	4.325	8.383
2.1.1983	5.282	8.583
2.1.1984	5.825	8.444
2.1.1985	6.615	7.591
2.1.1986	5.391	7.877
2.1.1987	4.765	7.085
2.1.1988	3.930	7.363
2.1.1989	4.154	7.521
2.1.1990	4.041	6.572

[18] The fact that the Supreme Court has not apparently set up strict conditions for the use of Ch.2, sec. 1.2 of the Act on Torts does not of course necessarily mean that the provision is of central importance in lower court practice. In a survey of lower court practice in cases of compensation for personal injury, carried out at the National Research Institute of Legal Policy, the 128 cases from 1982 of which the material consisted contained only one case where compensation had been adjusted because of the tortfeasor's poor economic circumstances and low ability to pay: See Mäkipää 1984 p. 35.

can be said that Ch. 2, sec. 1.2 of the Act on Torts as understood in the Supreme Court particularly protects the "*poor debtor*" in a broad sense. The more detailed content of this concept is, however, determined by the situation. Assessment of when a tortfeasor's economy is so poor that he should not have full liability placed upon him naturally depends - even when one leaves aside the demand that paying compensation should ruin his economy - on the extent of the damage, etc.: the greater the damage the easier it is for full compensation to become unreasonable even for a person in easy circumstances.

When assessing the tortfeasor's economic situation to which full compensation is to be related, the following circumstances, among others, can be considered:

(i) *The tortfeasor's wealth and income*. If the tortfeasor lacks assets and income, this is a good argument in favour of adjustment even of a relatively small compensation amount. *The debtor without means and the low-income debtor* are role figures that merit the sympathy of those who apply the law.[19]

Any assessment of the tortfeasor's means should not take account merely of the total value of his property: different types of property should, according to views expressed in legal literature, be valued in different ways.[20] It is particularly worth noting that here, as in many other areas of private law, special attempts have

---

[19] As an illustrative example reference can be made to HD 1981 II 102, where, as an argument for adjustment, reference was made expressly to the tortfeasor's lack of means and small income as an argument for reducing the relatively small amount of FIM 11,572.77 (about USD 3,000) to FIM 4,000. In favour of the adjustment was obviously the fact in this case that the other party was an insurance company which exercized its right of subrogation. The case is a good example of adjustment based on a tortfeasor's economic circumstances insofar as there could hardly be a question of adjustment on the grounds of low degree of fault: the tortfeasor was guilty of drunken driving.

[20] See Bengtsson 1982 p. 261.

been made to safeguard a party's right to *housing*, etc.[21]

Closer study of the documents in cases where small compensation amounts have been reduced, and where details of tortfeasors' incomes are included, shows that these really have been low-income people:

	income/FIM	adjustment/FIM
HD 1979 II 14	1,800 - 2,800.- /month	6,409.01 --> 3,204.50
HD 1981 II 23	1,872.66 /month	93,250.- -->62,167.-
HD 1981 II 102	no present income, studies being financed under invalid care legislation; living free at home	11,572.77 --> 4,000.-
HD 1981 II 124	1,700.-/month (husband) and no income (wife)	6,000,- + 750.- /month--> 3,000,- + 250.- /month (same adjustment for husband as for wife)

During this period FIM 1,000 corresponded to about USD 260.

(ii) *The tortfeasor's family circumstances and maintenance liability*. When assessing whether compensation should be considered burdensome it is natural to consider not only the tortfeasor himself but also the needs of his family. The tortfeasor's maintenance liability should be taken into account in the assessment of reasonability.[22] The *debtor with considerable maintenance liabilities* should receive the support of those applying the law.[23]

---

[21] In the *travaux préparatoires* to the corresponding adjustment rule in Sweden it is expressly stated that it may be considered unreasonable to compel the liable person to sell an ordinary residence or an agricultural holding he has long occupied and farmed: Sv.Prop. 1975:12 p. 177.

[22] Thus Bengtsson 1982 p. 257, Saxén 1975 p. 163.

[23] An illustrative example is Supreme Court case HD 1979 II 14, in which the creditor had *four children*. A small amount of damages was here adjusted with express reference to the tortfeasor's small income and his maintenance obligation. In this case, too, the creditor was an insurance company; nor could the adjustment be justified with reference to the

5.2.3 The employer's liability

In Finnish and Nordic law an employer carries a vicarious liability for damage caused by an employee through negligence at work. This vicarious liability may, however, under a special adjustment rule of the Act on Torts (Ch. 3, sec. 6), be adjusted if it appears unreasonable.

As in the cases mentioned above (5.2.2), the financial standing of the liable person is of central importance in the application of this adjustment rule. This is because, when assessing whether the liability may be considered clearly unreasonable, one should according to the *travaux préparatoires* to the Act consider both the amount of full compensation and the liable party's economic circumstances; one should consider his "economic strength".[24] In other words the adjustment rule should be used primarily to attempt to protect the *small enterprise of limited financial strength.*[25]

In certain more recent labour legislation, rules of fairness have also been introduced that empower the courts to take account of, *inter alia*, the employer's financial position when fixing the amount of compensation. Here may be mentioned the provision on compensation for unjustified dismissal of employees in the Act on Procedure for Termination of Contracts of Employment and the provision on the employer's obligation to indemnify in cases of sex discrimination under the Act on Equality between Women and Men, sec. 11. In both cases, account can be taken of the employer's financial position as a circumstance that may lead to reduc-

---

degree of fault: at the same trial the tortfeasor received a prison sentence for dangerous driving and infliction of bodily injury.

[24] Reg.prop. 187/1973 p. 19.

[25] See also HD 1985 II 23, where the compensation was adjusted in favour of a housing company.

tion.[26] These statutes, too, thus express the notion of the small enterprise of limited financial strength as a particular need-oriented debtor role.

A severe liability in damages imposed upon a small company may adversely affect not only the employer but also the employees. The company may run into economic difficulties and fold up, with the consequence that these employees lose their jobs. It may be wondered whether such concern for employment could be taken into account when considering adjustment of the employer's liability. Turning to the general adjustment rule in Swedish law, it has been argued that circumstances may probably be so fraught for the employees that it sometimes becomes hard to disregard the situation in which they may be placed.[27] Returning to Finland, in connection with the passing of the Act on Procedure for Termination of Contracts of Employment, mentioned above, the legislator has clearly decided to allow consideration of the effect of compensation upon employment.[28]

The statements are interesting in that it has here been considered possible for social reasons to depart from the traditional private-law fixation on the parties and to include consideration of the needs of third parties when assessing a relationship in private law. In a dispute over damages between an employer and an injured party one can observe not only the employer's needs and those of the injured party but also the employer's *employees' need to be able to retain their jobs*.

---

[26] See for more detail the *travaux préparatoires* in Reg.prop. 205/1983 p. 21 and Reg.prop. 57/1985 p. 25, respectively. In 1991 the Act on Procedure for Termination of Contracts of Employment has been substituted by a chapter on this subject in the Labour Contracts Act. The provision on indemnification in the new chapter (art. 47 f) contains a reference to the employer's position, too.

[27] Bengtsson 1982 p. 260 f.

[28] Reg.prop. 205/1983 p. 21.

5.2.4 The employee's liability

A central innovation in the Act on Torts was the limitation of an employee's personal liability for damage caused by him in the course of his work. According to Ch. 4, sec. 1 of the Act, an employee's liability for such damage depends primarily on the *degree of fault*:

(i) For slight negligence the employee is free of liability.

(ii) If the negligence of the employee is more grave, he is liable insofar as, considering the extent of the damage, the nature of the action, his position, the interest of the injured party and other circumstances, this is found to be reasonable.

(iii) If the damage has been caused deliberately, full liability shall be imposed unless a reduction is found reasonable because of special circumstances.

Considering the theme of this work - the influence of a party's economic and social position upon a decision in private law - it is primarily the effect of the rule under point (ii) that is of interest. This empowers the courts to use a number of criteria when fixing a reasonable amount of damages. One such criterion is the "tortfeasor's position", by which is meant, according to the *travaux préparatoires*, not only the employee's position in the employer's organisation but also the former's emoluments.[29]

In the discussions preceding the advent of the Act on Torts the question of the employee's personal liability was a central one. There was a desire in union quarters to link this liability expressly to the employee's *income from work*. The Confederation of Finnish Trade Unions several times proposed a ceiling on compensation which would amount to, for example, the employee's salary for one month.[30] This proposal as such met with no response. As - somewhat slight - compensation, however, a statement was included in the Government bill to the effect that interpretation of

---

[29] Kom.bet. 1965:A4 p. 38.

[30] See e.g. the Confederation's statement to the Ministry of Justice, 7.11.1972 p. 9.

the provision should pay special attention to the employee's and his family's ability to provide for themselves and to their living conditions, and that the amount of damages should not be permitted to rise unreasonably with regard to the employee's income from work.[31] The new rule was to give *the low-income earner* better protection than the highly-paid.[32]

5.2.5 The liability of children and others

The Act on Torts was also innovative regarding children's and young persons' liability. According to Ch. 2, sec. 2 of the Act, which has a correspondence in Swedish law, a person under eighteen years of age who has caused damage shall pay damages for this to the extent found reasonable with regard to his age and development, the nature of the action, the tortfeasor's and the injured party's economic circumstances and other circumstances. A similar rule - but one in which the reference to the tortfeasor's "age" is replaced by reference to his "condition" - applies to the mentally ill, the mentally retarded and to persons of unsound mind (Ch. 2, sec. 3).

These rules, too, are *fairness rules* giving the courts almost unlimited discretion. Consideration of the parties' needs represents *merely one of many* criteria of assessment mentioned in the relevant sections.

Supreme Court practice appears to have placed considerable weight upon the tortfeasor's current economic circumstances in the application of the relevant provisions. This emerges plainly when in the light of statements in the *travaux préparatoires* to the Act one examines some legal cases concerning damage caused by persons aged between 15 and 17 years. In the bill preceding the

---

[31] Reg.prop. 187/1973 p. 21.

[32] From legal practice one case may be particularly mentioned in which a temporary worker (a student of theology) in the Tampere Evangelical-Lutheran parishes had caused damage valued at FIM 4,008 (approx. USD 1,040), which relatively insignificant amount was reduced to FIM 2,000 (HD 1981 II 54).

Act on Torts it is explicitly stated that reduction of liability can seldom be considered for reasons other than economic in cases concerning a young person who has passed his fifteenth birthday.[33] The Supreme Court has nevertheless often avoided imposing full compensation in cases where the tortfeasor has been of this age.[34]

Consideration of the tortfeasor's economic standing emerges even more clearly from a case concerning damage caused by a person of unsound mind. In this case, HD 1980 II 67, a person had rendered himself guilty of arson, for which he was sentenced to prison for an act committed while not in full possession of his faculties. Even though it has often been considered that full compensation should be imposed for "deliberate" acts, the compensation was reduced in this case from FIM 21,338.- to FIM 14,260.- with reference to, among other things, the tortfeasor's ability to pay and his economic standing. The description of these speaks volumes: the documents were understood to say that the tortfeasor lived at home on his farm with his mother and brother in a remote area and under primitive conditions. A better example of a social justification of a private-law decision is hard to find. What is indicated here is an explicit attempt to *support a down-and-out debtor*.

Even where the tortfeasor may have certain property, this does not exclude reduction of liability on economic grounds. One may recall here the attempt to safeguard a person's right to *hous-*

---

[33] Reg.prop. 187/1983 p. 14.

[34] Reference may be made here to HD 1978 II 149, where the amount of compensation was reduced from FIM 13,208.75 to FIM 3,000.-, HD 1981 II 124, where FIM 6,000.- + FIM 750.- /month was reduced to FIM 3,000,- + FIM 250,- /month, and HD 1982 II 140, where FIM 15,490.- was reduced to FIM 7,745.- (FIM 1,000 = approx. USD 230-270 during this period). These cases are also good examples of a reduction of liability for financial reasons, insofar as the tortfeasor's guilt in all these cases was relatively large (in all three cases the tortfeasor received a penal sentence) and the degree of fault could thus hardly be adduced in favour of a mild decision.

ing, etc.[35]

5.2.6 The needs of the injured party

Both when adjusting the amount of damages under the general adjustment rule and in a discretionary fixing of reasonable compensation under the provisions on the liability of children, of the mentally unsound and of employees, account should be taken not only of the tortfeasor's needs but also of the injured party's need of compensation. The wording of the Act explicitly states that attention should also be paid to the injured party's economic circumstances (Ch. 2, sec. 1.2, 2 and 3) or to his interests (Ch. 4, sec. 1). In the *travaux préparatoires* to the general adjustment rule the importance is also stressed of such a balancing of interests, and it is explicitly stated that if the injured party's need of compensation is so great that adjustment would be unreasonable from his point of view, no adjustment shall be undertaken.[36]

Consideration of the injured party's needs appears here as a final argument:[37] (i) the starting point is full compensation - (ii) if the tortfeasor's needs so require, there may be adjustment - (iii) consideration for the injured party's needs may, however, in such a case, entail there being no adjustment, or adjustment by a smaller amount. If the structure of justification is understood in

---

[35] Such ways of thinking obviously underly a relatively recent decision in which the significance of the parties' economic circumstances was explicitly discussed. In this case (HD 1984 II 93), two seven-year-old children playing with matches had lighted a fire which caused damage valued at about FIM 250,000. One of the children had no assets of his own while the other owned a share in his father's estate, which consisted of a plot of land cultivated by his family. The damage had not unduly worsened the injured party's possibilities of subsistence or other circumstances. On these grounds, and with regard to the children's age and development, they were ordered jointly to pay compensation for the damage to an amount of FIM 20,000. The share of one of the tortfeasors in the plot of land cultivated by his family was consequently not adjudged a ground for increasing his liability.

[36] Reg.prop. 187/1973 p. 13.

[37] Thus also e.g. Hellner 1985 p. 326.

this way, it is natural that legal practice has reason to note the tortfeasor's need more frequently than the injured party's: if at phase (ii) it has already been established that there will be no adjustment, there is no need to touch upon phase (iii) at all. It is therefore not surprising that it is hard to find cases in for example Supreme Court practice where the refusal of adjustment has been justified by reference to the needs of the injured party.[38]

Consideration of the injured party's economic standing frequently seems in practice to emerge in an opposite form: the injured party's *non-needs* constitute an *argument for adjustment* or reduction. In such a case, the structure of argument is actually no longer that given above, since consideration of the injured party's economic standing - and this time of his sound economic standing - is understood as a *prima facie* argument for departing from the full compensation principle. The reference to the injured party's non-needs thus has the same position in the structure of argumentation as the reference to the tortfeasor's needs.[39]

Many of the cases where there has been adjustment or reduction of relatively small compensation amounts have involved recourse by an *insurance company*. One may presume here that the fact that the other party has been an insurance company rather than something else has rendered the Supreme Court more inclined to reduce the compensation, even where this circumstance has not been adduced explicitly.[40] In legal writing this practice has also

---

[38] But see HD 1981 II 39.

[39] In the *discretionary assessment* to be made when liability is imposed on a child, it is natural to adduce such non-needs as arguments for reduction. A good example is case HD 1984 II 93 (see note 35 above) where a large reduction - for fire damage of FIM 250,000 (approx. USD 43,000) FIM 20,000 was fixed as damages - was justified with, *inter alia*, the argument that the damage had not unreasonably impaired the injured party's subsistence possibilities or other circumstances. The *well-to-do injured party* has to bear a large reduction.

[40] See e.g HD 1978 II 149, HD 1979 II 14, HD 1980 II 50, HD 1980 II 64, HD 1981 II 102 and HD 1982 II 140. In HD 1989:70 the court, however, expressly maintained that the existence of insurance and the property status of the insurance company cannot *alone* (without other supporting arguments) constitute grounds for adjustment of damages.

been considered correct: when damage has through insurance been split up to be borne collectively, one should try and avoid re-concentrating it upon one person, the tortfeasor.[41]

5.2.7 Summary

The foregoing analysis of legal practice concerning the general adjustment rule shows that the provision is by no means used merely as a "safety valve" that permits reduction of extreme amounts of damages. Rather, it functions as a more general rule of fairness which even in ordinary cases allows the courts to consider the parties' economic circumstances when awarding damages. The difference between the general adjustment rule and the special rules of fairness covering the liability of minors and the mentally unsound, and that of employees, consequently appears smaller in practice than in theory. All in all, these provisions today afford the courts great possibilities of taking need-oriented person roles into account in tort cases. The role concepts of interest here must, however, for natural reasons have the character of *guideline concepts*.

In practice there more often appears to be reason (see above, 5.2.6) to consider explicitly the needs of the tortfeasor (the debtor). Analysis of the tort law material reveals many relevant *need-oriented debtor roles*:

- the *debtor without means* or, more broadly, the *debtor with limited means*; sometimes perhaps the most telling description is a debtor with no other assets than *somewhere to live*,

- the *low-income debtor*; the extreme case, calling for special goodwill from those who apply the law, is the *down-and-out debtor*,

- the *debtor with considerable maintenance liabilities*, and

- the *small-enterprise debtor of limited financial strength*; here the debtor's employees' *need of jobs* can also be taken into consideration.

---

[41] See Saxén 1983 p. 403, 413.

5.2.8 Adjustment within contractual relationships

The Act on Torts does not apply, unless specially provided otherwise, to liability in damages based upon contract (Ch. 1, sec. 1). This rigid delimitation of the scope of the Act, the extensive criticism of which hardly needs repeating here, raises in this context the question: can liability in damages within a contractual relation be adjusted e.g. with the support of an analogy from the Act on Torts? Or, as a more concrete follow-up question: can a court awarding damages in a contractual relationship consider the liable party's and the injured party's economic standing (their needs)? In other words, are the role concepts sketched above relevant also within contractual relationships?

In some cases the position is already quite clear from the legislation. A situation of practical importance is where an employee inflicts damage upon his contractual partner, the employer. According to an explicit provision in sec. 51 of the Labour Contracts Act, compensation shall here be determined under the Act on Torts. What has been said above about discretionary assessment of the employee's liability applies also when the damage has been inflicted upon the employer. Some of the cases cited in the section mentioned concern precisely damage inflicted upon an employer.[42]

As to liability in damages under contract law in general, the situation was long unclear.[43] Now, however, it has become more clear as the Supreme Court has explicitly shown itself prepared to adjust damages within contractual relationships also. In addition, in the new Sale of Goods Act (sec. 70) there is a provision which codifies the possibility to adjust damages within contractual relationships.

In particular, the Supreme Court has also clearly considered it possible to adjust contractual liability in damages with

---

[42] HD 1980 II 64, 1981 II 54.

[43] See as examples of different views in the doctrine Godenhielm 1975 and Saxén 1983 p. 383.

regard to *the parties' economic circumstances*.[44] The need-oriented debtor roles described above (5.2.7) are thus also relevant within contractual relationships.

6. ADJUSTMENT OF REPAYMENT OF UNJUST ENRICHMENT

The doctrine of repayment of unjust enrichment, which has not been codified by legislation in the Nordic countries, regulates a repayment debtor's obligation to return a sum which he has received for some reason without any right thereto. The doctrine is based upon the notion that the whole sum wrongfully acquired should be repaid. Naturally, such an obligation to repay may sometimes appear unreasonable, particularly in cases where the repayment debtor becomes obliged to repay means that he has perhaps used to cover his living costs. It is therefore not surprising that, within the doctrine of repayment of unjust enrichment, scholars have begun to discuss possibilities of adjusting an unreasonable claim for repayment. This discussion will not be reported in detail here but, as a starting point, it may be noted that both in the literature and in more recent legal practice the possibility of adjusting repayment claims without explicit support in legislation has been accepted.[45]

The present interest is to examine how far it has been felt

---

[44] See HD 1985 II 51, where compensation to be granted a builder in consequence of breach of contract by the designer of a factory unit was adjusted. The town court, whose justification in this part was upheld by the Supreme Court, adjusted the compensation, taking into account the designer's fee for the commission (FIM 8,000), compared with the amount of the damage (the court put this at FIM 150,000), *the plaintiff's and the defendant's economic circumstances* and the absence of malicious intent. - In the doctrine, adjustment of contractual liability for reasons of parties' economic circumstances has earlier been advocated by Godenhielm 1975 p. 410 f., who maintains that small workshops and entrepreneurs should be protected from claims for damages that would hit them too hard.

[45] See Aurejärvi 1988 p. 250 ff. and e.g. HD 1972 I 1, 1983 II 174 and 1986 II 126.

possible to consider the parties' needs when adjusting claims for repayment. Can the economic needs of the repayment debtor be used as an argument in support of adjustment, and, if so, can the repayment creditor's needs be used as a counter-argument?

It has already been frequently noted that need-oriented roles have often gained admission to private law via areas that are adjacent to social security law. One example has been the rules of *maintenance in family law*. It is therefore not surprising that these roles have gained entrance into the doctrine of repayment of unjust enrichment in the same way: the problem of adjustment of such repayment has been particularly acute in cases of repayment of maintenance contributions following the setting aside of a decision on a maintenance liability or of an agreement on such a liability. In the first legal case where adjustment of a repayment obligation was clearly approved without support in legislation, the claim for repayment of a relatively small sum was rejected since the child's mother had in good faith received maintenance contributions which were used for the child's maintenance and upbringing, and since repayment of the maintenance contributions, *considering the mother's and the child's economic standing on the one hand and that of the party who had been held liable for maintenance on the other*, could not reasonably be considered as required.[46]

Legal practice has since, in parallel with certain statements of position in the doctrine,[47] embraced the notion that the repayment liability may also be adjusted to take account of parties' economic circumstances where the claim is for performances other than maintenance contributions under family law. A typical example is adjustment of an employer's demand for repayment of excessively large amounts paid out by him on the basis of the

---

[46] HD 1972 I 1: the repayment claim amounted to FIM 2,228.89. The same line is followed in HD 1978 II 133 and 1979 II 55. The principle expounded in the case has since been developed in sec. 12 of the Child Maintenance Act.

[47] See Aurejärvi 1988 p. 252, and also the earlier Hakulinen 1962 p. 390.

labour relationship.[48]

The cases touch upon demands for repayment of expenses and daily allowances paid periodically in the same way as salaries. For natural reasons, repayment of such performances often seems unreasonable since the monies paid, in accordance with their purpose, have gone to cover the repayment debtor's living expenses and hence are no longer available to him. The grounds mentioned in the Supreme Court decision in HD 1983 II 174, however, do not necessarily limit the scope of the possibility to adjust a repayment liability with reference to the parties' economic circumstances in such a way that it would apply only to repayment of periodic performances like salary and maintenance.

In adjustment of repayment of unjust enrichment, as in tort law, there has in practice primarily been reason to concentrate on the need-oriented *debtor roles*. If a claim for repayment becomes unreasonable for the debtor without means or with limited means, the low-income debtor or the one who is burdened with considerable maintenance liabilities, it is obvious that adjustment seems the natural solution. For this to be adopted it is obviously not required that the liability must be *extremely burdensome*. Here, as in the legal practice concerning the Act on Torts, adjustment has also been used for relatively modest claims.

---

[48] See in particular HD 1983 II 174. In this case a state employer had for more than four years paid unjustified travel expenses and a daily allowance to a person in its employ. It had not been shown that the employee had supplied incorrect details of where he had stayed during this time. He had even, with regard to the payment period and the fact that the provisions on the grounds for payment of travel expenses and daily allowance gave scope for interpretation, been able to rely on the employer's having in due order examined the grounds and its obligation to pay travel expenses and daily allowances. For these reasons, and *with regard to the employee's economic standing*, it was considered reasonable for the employee to repay only a portion (FIM 10,000) of the unjust enrichment (totally FIM 39,205.90, i.e. about USD 7,400) that he had received. -- In a similar case before the Helsinki Court of Appeal (11.12.1985/751), clearly in observance of the Supreme Court decision, the Court adjusted a claim for repayment of remuneration for evening and Sunday work.

7. CONSEQUENCES OF DELAYS IN PAYMENT

7.1 Introduction

A debtor who does not pay his debt on time may incur various kinds of consequences resulting from the delay. The traditional starting point in private law when assessing the prerequisites of sanctions for delays in payment in the Nordic countries, as elsewhere, has been the thesis that *each person is responsible for his ability to pay*. The same thesis has sometimes been formulated with more acerbity: "you've got to have money".[49] The circumstance that the debtor is in financial difficulty or is even quite unable to pay has not been viewed as an excuse that would enable the debtor to escape the consequences. Not even where the difficulties have arisen through no fault of the debtor - he has fallen ill, become unemployed, etc. - have these been considered as grounds for exemption from liability.[50]

More recently, however, rules have been incorporated in several different acts which mitigate the consequences for a monetary debtor who, because of illness, unemployment or similar circumstances is suffering payment difficulties and who for this reason has not managed to pay in time. These regulations follow such a consistent pattern that this is perhaps the area that offers the most obvious arguments for the "switching of principles" typical of alternative dogmatics. In what follows, a number of such regulations will be described in more detail.

Several of these regulations also have their counterparts in

---

[49] Medicus 1988.

[50] See e.g. Hakulinen 1962 p. 75, who stresses that a debtor, regardless of subjective guilt, is, where his obligation is not fulfilled within the appointed time, obliged to compensate his creditor for the damage caused by his inadequate financial ability to perform; and Taxell 1972 p. 118 who similarly maintains that a debtor himself carries the risk of not having financial resources to fulfil contracts entered into, and that the reason for his lacking financial resources has not been accorded significance.

the other Nordic countries.[51]

7.2 *The development of the legislation*

7.2.1 Hire-purchase and consumer credit

As early as 1966 the Act on Hire-Purchase of that year incorporated some rules expressly attempting to mitigate the consequences of delays in payment, over and above the mitigation afforded by the general rules in the Act, in cases where the hire-purchaser has run into payment difficulties through no fault of his own.

The Act regulates among other things the conditions under which a hire-purchase seller may repossess goods sold, or implement other sanctions provided in the contract, because of delay in payment. As a supplement to the general conditions for repossession the Act includes a provision (sec. 2.2) granting further relief for a buyer who as a result of illness or unemployment, or for other special reasons, has got into payment difficulties through no fault of his own. If because of the buyer's predicament it would be unreasonable to implement a contractual sanction on a delay in payment and the buyer pays the outstanding instalment together with interest and costs before the goods are repossessed, the sanction may not be implemented. In addition, where the seller has sought the assistance of the bailiff to effect repossession, the bailiff can grant the buyer a stay of execution of up to four months if the cause of delay is clearly that the buyer because of illness, unemployment or for some other special reason through no fault of his own is having payment difficulties which may be assumed to be temporary, and if the seller's rights are not unreasonably set aside thereby (sec. 11).

As far as consumer credits are concerned the Act on Hire-

---

[51] See for more detail Wilhelmsson 1990. See now also Bärlund 1990, who shows that in Denmark there has been obvious restraint in this area.

Purchase has since been replaced by new provisions in Ch. 7 of the Consumer Protection Act. During the drafting of these provisions a much more far-reaching regulation was proposed. According to this, a consumer should have the right to postponement of the due date for an instalment if his performance was delayed because of unemployment, illness or a comparable cause.[52] In the newly-adopted legislation on consumer credits, however, there had been a return to a system closer to that of the Act on Hire-Purchase. According to Ch. 7, sec. 16.2 of the Consumer Protection Act, the creditor shall not have the right to enforce repossession of the goods, claim an instalment that has not otherwise fallen due, or enforce any other special sanction agreed upon by the parties, if the delay is due to the illness or unemployment of the consumer or to a similar factor that is not the fault of the consumer, unless the length of the delay and other circumstances would clearly make this unreasonable for the creditor.

7.2.2 Interest on delayed payments

Where payment is delayed the debtor is as a rule obliged to pay penal interest. In Finland, this obligation is regulated in the Act on Interest.

With support from sec. 11 of the Act, the debtor may also be entirely or partially freed from this sanction on social grounds. In other words, the provision has extended the area of social mitigation of sanctions, from applying merely to sanctions agreed upon in the contract as in the consumer credit legislation to covering the most central *statutory* sanction for delay in payment, penal interest.

Under this provision a consumer, a purchaser of a dwelling or a tenant may claim adjustment of his liability to pay such interest if the delay was caused by payment difficulties which he has encountered mainly through no fault of his own in consequence of illness, unemployment or some other special cause. The

---

[52] See KM 1977:30, sec. 13 and OLJ 8/1982, sec. 20.

provision gives the court wide discretion: the interest *may* be adjusted, and the adjustment may be effected by a lowering of the interest rate or a postponement of the date from which interest should be paid, or both.[53]

7.2.3 Registration of delayed payments

The obstacles to due payment referred to in this section may be taken into account in the regulation of credit information registers as well. In the Finnish Registration of Persons Decree, there is a provision which - according to the *travaux préparatoires*[54] - is intended to prevent registration of some (temporary) defaults caused by illness, unemployment or other special factors. In this way, one may try to protect the credit-worthiness of debtors hit by temporary difficulties.

7.2.4 Payment of insurance premiums

In insurance law very severe sanctions have traditionally been associated with delays in payment on the part of the insured. A delayed premium payment can lead to the insured losing his cover according to the insurance contract. One might therefore expect there to be special reasons in this branch of law for asking whether mitigation of sanctions should be considered on social grounds, among others. This has already happened in Swedish law[55] and similar proposals for legislation have long been in the

---

[53] Wilhelmsson - Sevón p. 146 f.

[54] Reg.prop. 49/1986 p. 31.

[55] According to sec. 25 of the Swedish Consumer Insurance Act (Konsumentförsäkringslag, 38/80), an insurance contract does not cease on the basis of the general rules on delayed payment of premiums if the delay was caused by severe illness of the policyholder, by his loss of liberty, by the fact that he has not received his pension or salary, or by some other similar unexpected event. In this provision, the effects of physical as well as economic obstacles to payment are regulated. In the leading commentary to the Act, it is clearly stated that the policyholder in these situations should primarily use his available means to finance the

drafting in Finland. In the Finnish proposals, in accordance with the rules mentioned earlier, illness and unemployment have been referred to as grounds for limiting sanctions for delay. The presence of such a circumstance shall for a certain period prevent the insurer from terminating the insurance contract for reasons of delay in paying premiums.[56]

7.2.5 Current proposed legislation

The line of thought underlying the provisions mentioned above has also found expression in certain more recent proposed legislation that has yet to be implemented.

In 1988 a Working Group appointed by the Ministry of Justice published a proposal concerning new rules on consumer sales and some consumer services (new Chapters 5 and 8 of the Consumer Protection Act). According to the proposal, a supplier would be entitled to compensation for special costs incurred by him in the making, performance and termination of the contract as well as to reasonable compensation for other losses when he declares the contract avoided because of delay in payment by the consumer or when the consumer cancels the contract (which he would be entitled to do). However, if the delay in payment or cancellation is caused by the consumer's illness, unemployment or some other special occurrence for which the consumer is not to blame, the latter would be obliged to pay compensation only for the above special costs; he would bear no liability for other losses such as loss of profit.[57] A government bill is being prepared on the basis of this proposal and is expected to be laid before Parliament in the near future.

---

basic needs of himself and his family; one should not demand payment of an insurance premium before such necessary expenses. See Nilsson - Strömbäck 1984 p. 105 f.

[56] See the proposed bill for an act on the insurance of persons, in OLJ 16/1985, Ch. 5, sec. 2.2 and the proposed bill for an act on insurance of property in OLJ 3/1988, Ch. 5, sec. 2.2.

[57] See OLJ 9/1988, Ch. 5, sec. 21 and Ch. 8, sec. 24.

Recently a legislative committee has made a proposal for an act on the purchase of dwellings which contains corresponding rules. According to this proposal also, illness, unemployment or a similar event adversely affecting the purchaser is to limit the purchaser's liability to pay damages in cases of delay in payment and in the event of cancellation of the purchase.[58]

7.3 Summary

In Finnish law several regulations and proposals can be found that grant a debtor the right to mitigation of sanctions when delays in payment have been caused by social factors. The conditions for such mitigation have in these provisions been specified in a strikingly uniform manner. It is therefore possible to make a common analysis of the prerequisites for mitigation of sanctions enumerated in the relevant legislation:

(i) The delay should be a consequence of the debtor having run into *payment difficulties*.[59] That the debtor has fallen ill or become unemployed is irrelevant as long as the illness or unemployment has not resulted in payment difficulties. This means that the debtor, to claim mitigation of sanctions, should have *limited means*. The regulation is need-oriented, in the sense intended here.

(ii) The difficulties or the delay in payment should have been caused by certain particular occurrences. In all cases, illness and unemployment are mentioned directly in the wording of the acts as circumstances that should be taken into account. In addition, other circumstances of a similar nature may be relevant. As examples may be mentioned other unanticipated reduction of income,[60] reduction of economic support from a relation,[61]

---

[58] See KM 1989:47, Ch. 4, sec. 34 and Ch. 6, sec. 24.

[59] The payment difficulties need not be so dire that one may speak of inability to pay. In the *travaux préparatoires* to the Act on Interest it is clearly stressed that adjustment may take place as soon as payment cannot be effected in time without jeopardising the debtor's reasonable housing and other living conditions. See Reg.prop. 109/1981 p. 23.

[60] See e.g. SOU 1985:11 p. 182 and OLJ 16/1985 p. 212 f.

homelessness,[62] and other increases in costs.[63]

(iii) The provisions under discussion are based on the notion that the debtor should have "run into" payment difficulties. The possibilities of mitigation of sanctions are therefore affected by the point at which the payment difficulties or obstacle occurred, and also by the debtor's possibilities of *foreseeing* them. If the debtor has anticipated the obstacle and its effect on his ability to pay, mitigation is scarcely possible.[64]

(iv) The debtor should have got into payment difficulties *chiefly through no fault of his own*. If the difficulties are entirely or predominantly self-inflicted, there is no question of mitigation of sanctions.

As the rules on mitigation of sanctions are very similar, one is tempted to ask whether these regulations could be considered to express a more *general principle* that is in course of development. This question is discussed in more detail in Chapter VII. There is already reason to note here, however, that there exists a need to discuss a generalization of the rules on mitigation of sanctions in many different respects:

- The provisions mentioned often apply only to certain types of debtor (primarily consumers). The question is thus how far one can overlook the tendency to confine the mitigation rules to consumer relations and similar and grant application of similar

---

[61] See e.g. Eklund - Nordström 1957 p. 111 and SOU 1985:11 p. 182.

[62] See e.g. Hakulinen - Raninen 1968 p. 80 and OLJ 16/1985 p. 212.

[63] Various examples may be found of causes of a debtor's costs rising so that he gets into payment difficulties. SOU 1985:11 p. 182 mentions the debtor's divorce, which naturally, because of increased living costs, can radically worsen his ability to pay, while Hakulinen - Raninen 1968 p. 80 mention the accident of a family member, where the difficulties are a consequence of the help one feels one ought to give the person in question.

[64] See e.g. OLJ 16/1985 p. 212. In the *travaux préparatoires* to the consumer credit legislation the only circumstance considered is whether the debtor was "aware" that the obstacle would arise. See Reg.prop. 88/1985 p. 32.

principles outside this area as well, to the extent relevant social reasons exist.

- The rules on mitigation of sanctions cover only certain types of sanction. One may ask whether other sanctions that may be relevant to payment delay - e.g. recovery of the debt, avoidance of the contract, etc. - should be affected by a possible general principle on mitigation of sanctions.

- The rules treated here cover only delays in payment. Hence one may ask whether and how far a possible general principle on mitigation of sanctions ought also to include other kinds of breach of contract.

No attempt to answer the questions raised can yet be made at this stage of the work. The considerations presented in Chapters VI and VII below are intended to form a bridge to these very issues, among others. To conclude this section, we shall merely introduce a concept which is to be found in certain parts of the source material associated with the issues under discussion and which in itself hints that the presented rules could be considered as exponents of a more generally valid principle. The concept is *social force majeure*. This very general concept, which is also used in connection with other regulations, has been chosen to describe, among other things, the rules on mitigation of sanctions presented here (see below Chapter VII).

8. GENERAL CLAUSES ON THE FAIRNESS OF CONTRACTS

8.1 The legislation

8.1.1 Adjustment of unfair contract terms

During this century the possibilities of adjusting unfair contract terms have continually increased. The process has been a long one: as early as in, for example, sec. 34 of the Insurance Contracts Act (1933) and in sec. 8 of the Promissory Notes Act (1947), provisions were included that empowered courts to adjust contractual conditions that were apparently unfair. Since corresponding provisions were subsequently incorporated in legislation on other types of contract, it is natural to see them increasingly as expressions of a general principle.[65] The current position of legislative development was reached in 1982[66], when, in the same way as in the other Nordic countries, a *general adjustment rule* was incorporated as a general clause in sec. 36 of the Contract Act. According to this rule, a contract term which is unfair, or whose application would lead to an unfair result, may be adjusted or disregarded.

Application of the adjustment rules has always been intended to take place *in casu*, with observance of all circumstances affecting the case. A circumstance directly stated in the general clause as one that should be considered is "the standing of the parties". This expression is intended above all to stress one of the central purposes of the adjustment rule, the endeavour to *protect the weaker* party in a contractual relationship.[67] This does not necessarily imply a wish to stress the significance of need-oriented judicial application. As we have seen, different types of person-related roles can be differentiated in contract law: particularly noted have been ability-oriented person roles on the one hand and need-oriented person roles on the other. It is obvious that, when stressing the importance of the parties' standing and the protection of the weaker party in connection with the adjustment rules, it is chiefly the former type of role that has been in mind. The adjustment rules are directed mainly against an imbalance in contractual relationships that follows from a party's *lack of ability* (inadequate financial strength, poor specialist knowledge, poor bargaining position in other respects) to look after his rights when a contract is being concluded.[68]

---

[65] See on this development e.g. Aro 1974.

[66] Act 956/82.

[67] See in the *travaux préparatoires* e.g. Reg.prop. 247/1981 p. 3.

[68] See e.g. Reg.prop. 247/1981 p. 14.

The foregoing does not, however, prevent the reference to the parties' standing from being understood as covering need-oriented person roles *as well*. A curious early example from the *travaux préparatoires* to a corresponding older general clause in the legislation on tenancy[69] shows that this way of thinking was not felt to be foreign. In legal practice the adjustment rule has also in some cases been applied in a clearly need-oriented manner. These cases will be described in more detail below.

8.1.2 Regulation of unfair contract terms

The adjustment rules of contract law shall apply in disputes between two parties. Alongside these there exist in Finnish and Nordic law certain forms of *collective* regulation of contract terms. The most important is, in Finland, Ch. 3 of the Consumer Protection Act, which empowers the consumer authorities - the Consumer Ombudsman and the Market Court - to intervene and issue injunctions against the use of contract terms that should be viewed as unfair towards the consumer. This machinery is used primarily to monitor the fairness of standard conditions used by enterprises.

Interventions by the Consumer Ombudsman and the Market Court do not directly affect the validity of individual contractual relationships. They are nevertheless considered to weigh very heavily as arguments in decisions regarding the need to adjust individual contracts. They are therefore by no means irrelevant to a discussion of the general principles of contract law applied in the general courts. The assessment of fairness at the collective level can act as a *model* for such an assessment in the application of the general clauses of contract law.[70] For this reason, aspects of practice from this level will also be mentioned below.

---

[69] See KM 1957:8 p. 25 which, as an example of the type of situation the proposed adjustment rule is to cover, mentions that a contract term that forbids a tenant to keep a dog in the rented apartment shall not apply if the tenant becomes blind during the tenancy.

[70] Reg.prop. 8/1977 p. 40.

8.2 *Need-oriented assessment of fairness in practice*

In the practice of courts and consumer authorities one can find some examples of decisions where attention has been paid *expressis verbis* to the debtor's need of limitations to his liability.

Several of these decisions have interesting connections with the need-oriented regulations in the law of contracts and torts, and elsewhere in private law, treated earlier in this chapter. Need-orientation in the adjustment of wages paid to a brother may, for example, be linked with lines of thought in family law; certain decisions have clear points of contact with tenancy law rules on protecting a party's need of housing and, in other cases, the decision has a connection with the rules on adjustment of damages. Lastly, some decisions express considerations of *social force majeure* with a clear link to the provisions on mitigation of sanctions.

(i) *Wages paid within a family*. When work is performed within a family or among relations, the parties often assume that wages or full wages will not be paid. However, collective agreement rules may lead to a different result, and here a general clause affords a possibility of adjusting the collective agreement, particularly in cases where the family member acting as employer has a *weak economic position*. The Finnish Supreme Court has proceeded thus in a case concerning farm work performed by a person for his brother. The person in question was in theory entitled to payment according to the generally binding agricultural labour collective agreement. As however the parties, according to what had come out in the case, had had no clear understanding of the person's position in labour law, and as retroactive application of the collective agreement would have led to a *result that would have been unreasonable considering the brother's economic position*, the payment was adjusted.[71]

(ii) *Need of housing*. In a case before the Helsinki Court of Appeal the *landlord's physical condition* (age and health) was

[71] HD 1986 II 144.

expressly noted as a decisive argument in favour of adjustment. As the landlord *needed his apartment* because of these special circumstances, a time limit was set on his obligation to keep his apartment available to his tenant. In this case, A had on 18.9.1976 rented his apartment to B and C, among other things on condition that the tenancy should cease on 1.1.1980. A, who wished to move into the apartment himself, claimed that he should be able to terminate the tenancy earlier. The Court of Appeal found that A - who was born in 1896 - could not adapt to, or be comfortable in, his one-room sublet in a family with four children under ten years of age. According to a medical certificate, living there involved danger to A's health, for which reason he urgently needed housing where he could be in peace. For this reason the tenancy agreement was adjusted so that the last day of each calendar month after judgment had been given should be the day of notice of termination.[72]

(iii) *Adjustment of damages.* An unreasonably heavy liability to pay damages may, as we have seen, be adjusted within a contractual relationship. It is thus self-evident that *agreements* on liability may be adjusted with the support of a contract-law adjustment rule. In such adjustment it is naturally a short step to considering, in the decision, the strong need-orientation that marks the practice of tort law. Thus it is not particularly surprising that, regarding adjustment of agreed liability, one meets a case where there is express reference to the *debtor's poor ability to pay* as a ground for reducing her obligation. In this case an employee working as manageress of a cooperative shop caused damage to her employer, the shop. When her employment had ceased, employer and employee had agreed that she would recompense the shop for the damage in the amount of FIM 44,067 (about USD 7,600). The Supreme Court adjusted the compensation to FIM 28,000, referring *inter alia* to the fact that, even after termination of her employment, she was in a substantially weaker position in relation to the cooperative shop, she had little opportunity of

[72] Helsinki Court of Appeal 29.6.1977/81.

examining its accounts and her *ability to manage the agreed obligation to pay was uncertain.*[73]

(iv) *Social force majeure.* As we have seen, a debtor may in certain cases claim mitigation of sanctions if he, for reasons of illness, unemployment or similar circumstance, has run into payment difficulties. Such consideration of what is termed social force majeure has found clear expression in the practice of the consumer authorities. First, the Market Court has considered the Act on Hire-Purchase when assessing the fairness of the leasing conditions used in some consumer relationships: the lessor may not reserve a wider right of cancellation e.g. in the event of social force majeure, than the hire-purchase seller has.[74] Secondly - and this is more interesting - the Consumer Ombudsman has also employed social force majeure reasoning in cases where there has been no question of mitigation of sanctions. The possibility of considering the debtor's *illness, unemployment*, etc. has been extended by the Consumer Ombudsman to regulation of the *binding nature of contracts*. The Consumer Ombudsman has been of the opinion that fairness presupposes that in the conditions for certain kinds of contract the debtor is given the right to withdraw from the contact in the event of social force majeure. As an example may be mentioned the case in which the Consumer Ombudsman intervened against a supplier who sold pewter chessmen on long-term contracts according to which the consumer had to buy one piece every month at a price of FIM 145 (about USD 25). In his negotiations with the supplier, the Consumer Ombudsman demanded, *inter alia* that a clause be inserted in the standard contract according to which the consumer would have the right to terminate the contract (with a small compensation for costs) if fulfillment would be unreasonably burdensome for him because of illness, unemployment or other such occurrence. As justification for this require-

---

[73] HD 1984 I 1. Also in HD 1985 II 171 the Court adjusted an agreed compensation liability with reference *inter alia* to the *debtor's economic situation.*

[74] See MD 1986:6.

ment the Consumer Ombudsman expressly referred to a developing principle of social force majeure which, among other things, was claimed to give the consumer the right to terminate a long-term contract upon payment of fair compensation.[75]

8.3 Summary. General principles of interpretation, etc.

In application of the adjustment rules it is naturally possible to consider both the debtor's need of limitation of his obligations and the creditor's need of extended rights. However, in the cases associated with these rules, where need-oriented decisions have been made more explicitly, it has been chiefly the debtor's needs that have been in view. In the explicitly need-oriented decisions, only need-oriented *debtor roles* have been accorded relevance. These roles appear to be chiefly the same as those indicated in connection with the other provisions mentioned in this chapter. Here, too, one can come upon the *low-income debtor*, the *debtor with limited means*, straitened circumstances and poor ability to pay, the debtor *in need of housing* and the *ill* debtor.

It is also interesting to see how need-oriented practice regarding the fairness rules of contract law described in this work are linked, as to situation, with the need-oriented regulations discussed earlier in this chapter. One might say that an important function of the general clauses of contract law has been to offer a juridically tenable basis for a more general consideration of developmental tendencies that, legislatively, have come into view in more particular contexts. The general clauses have been able to act as *gateways* into contract law for need-oriented reasoning which has been established outside this branch of law (chiefly in tort law, and also in family law) and as a basis for *generalization* of particular need-oriented contract-law regulations with limited scope (social force majeure).

---

[75] Consumer Ombudsman 84/40/3689. As other similar decisions may be mentioned Consumer Ombudsman 80/42/440 and 82/40/1166.

In addition to this, it is indeed possible in practice on the basis of the general clauses more *freely to take into account need-oriented viewpoints*. Both the wording of the law and the *travaux préparatoires* to the general clause give the judge (and the legal scientist) wide scope for developing new need-oriented person roles.

Lastly, there is reason to note that the general clauses of contract law do not necessarily represent the only conceivable gateways through which need-oriented argumentation can be introduced into the general principles of contract law. In *interpretation* and *supplementation* of contracts, too, one can conceive of paying explicit attention to the needs of the parties. Legal practice contains such cases, in which the grounds for decision have expressly considered the parties' economic situation[76] or the debtor's age, illness and poverty.[77] If one is endeavouring to

---

[76] See HD 1981 II 140. The case concerned an annuity condition linked to the purchase of a property, whereby the purchaser would, upon purchase, grant to his then 29-year-old sister, whose working capacity was impaired, "living accommodation and care during her lifetime". At the age of 67 she moved to a municipal home to be looked after there. Her guardian claimed that the granter of the annuity should, instead of giving the annuity in kind in the home, be obliged to pay compensation in money. The district court, considering the directives of the Tax Board, awarded FIM 8,541.63 (about USD 2,200) for time already elapsed and also obliged the granter of the annuity to pay, in future, half the municipal home care charges, or FIM 6 per day. The appeal court did not change the decision. The Supreme Court found, *with due consideration to the income, property and standard of living of the granter, the beneficiary's old age pension* and other circumstances, together with the changes occurring in them since the purchase, that it was right and reasonable to require the granter of the annuity to pay FIM 4,000 for the aforesaid elapsed time, and subsequently FIM 90/month.

[77] See HD 1980 II 42. The contractual relationship between house owner A and tenant B was considered, on the basis of a practice of many years' standing, to imply that each tenant was responsible for snow-ploughing and sanding the roads around the house where they felt this was called for. For this reason, B's action against A for damages because B had injured himself through falling on an unsanded and slippery road was rejected. In the justification of why the practice that had arisen concerning sanding should be considered binding, the Supreme Court referred expressly to the fact that A, because of his *age, illness* and *poverty* had been unable to take care of the snowploughing and sanding.

legitimate need-oriented general principles, these cases can be put forward as a sign that a certain degree of explicit need-orientation, at least, is beginning to permeate the whole of contract law.

CHAPTER VI

TOWARDS NEED-ORIENTED GENERAL PRINCIPLES

1. INTRODUCTION

In the law of obligations the parties in a legal relationship have traditionally been defined using abstract and formal role concepts. These concepts have to some extent, as we saw in Chapter IV, been supplemented with function-related concepts such as 'consumer' and with ability-oriented concepts such as 'expert'. The cases within the law of obligations where it has been possible to consider a party's concrete economic and social needs have until now been viewed as somewhat isolated exceptions.

However, the previous chapter's examination of the concrete legal material from Finnish law affords a chance of adopting a new perspective on the law of obligations in the latter respect. Need-oriented roles can be found in many different contexts within all sections of the law of obligations. The possibilities of making need-oriented assessments also appear to be clearly on the increase. The concrete legal material under discussion has come into being during a relatively short space of time. With few exceptions, the material presented in Chapter V is from the 1970s and to an even larger extent the 1980s. Finnish law of obligations, and as a part thereof contract law, thus seems to be developing rapidly towards a position where it appears meaningful to raise the question of a possible "*switching of principles*". Should need-oriented roles continue to be seen as exceptions, or is there reason to attempt, using available material, to work out more general principles of need-orientation?

The growing need-orientation in Finnish law of obligations has an obvious connection with the comprehensive changes towards a welfare state that took place in Finnish society and the legal system in general particularly during the 1970s and the latter half of the 1960s. The need-oriented elements are elements of the law in a welfare state. Even though *what is legally possible* in developing need-oriented principles is analysed on the basis of symptomatic criticism of Finnish law, the perspective of this chapter is more general. What is *socially possible* in Finland may be assumed to be so in other "welfare states" also.

2. NEED-ORIENTED PRINCIPLES AS AIDS AND AS INDEPENDENT NORMS

In more legalistically inclined legal cultures the possibility of formally establishing new ways of thought in existing legislation is of crucial importance when assessing whether such ways may be considered to fall within the framework of what is legally possible. Access to suitable anchorage points in legislation for an overtly need-oriented approach naturally varies from country to country, from branch of law to branch of law and from problem to problem.

In Finnish law, the legal possibilities of need-oriented decisions are most evident within tort law. Both the general adjustment rule and other fairness rules in the Act on Torts give the courts more or less unlimited powers to consider openly the parties', predominantly the tortfeasors', needs when imposing damages. Consequently, Finnish tort law requires no new principles that would form an independent basis for need-oriented decisions: need-oriented general principles are required here only as *aids* to the application of the need-oriented rules of the Act on Torts. Access to such aids may naturally, in its turn, lead to greater use of the possibilities for need-oriented decisions that the act affords.

In contract law, too, it is possible in Finland to establish a need-oriented decision firmly in the legislation. Here may be mentioned - in addition to the rules on mitigation of sanctions where need-orientation has statutory confirmation - the generally approved possibility of applying the adjustment rule of the Act on Torts by analogy to contract-based damages, and, above all, the general adjustment rule on unfair contract terms in sec. 36 of the Contract Act. The general adjustment rule empowers a court, basing its action on, *inter alia*, need-oriented thinking, to intervene in all kinds of contractual undertaking, and legal practice contains examples where this power has been used. In other words, if in legal practice one seeks legislative support for a need-oriented decision, one can in the majority of cases *establish* the decision in a reference to the general clause of contract law. Here also, then, need-oriented general principles may be understood as *aids* to the application of the general clause. As, however, sec. 36 of the Contract Act is not clearly need-oriented in its wording, such general principles represent at the same time a clear *development* of the conditions for application of the provision. The further such a development goes in practice, the greater reason there is to consider the relevant general principles more as an *independent legal ground* for the decision than merely as an aid to application of sec. 36 of the Contract Act. Developmentally, one may say that the general clause can function as a *gateway* through which new general principles, need-oriented and otherwise, may pass to gradual independence.

In West German law a similar view of general clauses has been stressed by *Udo Reifner*, who claims that they offer an opportunity of developing more adequate legal forms out of existing ones.[1] In West German doctrine there also occur characterizations of general clauses as break-in points[2] and as starting points for further development.[3]

---

[1] Reifner 1979 p. 76 f.

[2] Esser - Schmidt 1984 p. 17.

[3] Esser - Schmidt 1984 p. 146.

But the possibilities of grounding need-oriented contract-law decisions in a general clause by no means cover all cases, either in Finnish law or hardly anywhere else. The Finnish general clause, for example, applies merely to adjustment of contract terms, and thus not to supplementation of contracts. Where a need-oriented assessment is desired here, it must be on *independent grounds*. The need-oriented principles adduced in a situation of this kind cannot be given any legislative grounding: they act as material, directly applicable principles of law.

This is the case in Finland in the third main area of the law of obligations, the doctrine of repayment of unjust enrichment. This doctrine has not been regulated by statute, nor is it covered by any general clause. Here the need-oriented principles developed in legal practice must be understood as *independent* principles which intervene in the other principles governing the repayment.

As to the possibilities of grounding need-oriented decisions in the legislation, then, one can distinguish between two different situations: cases where need-oriented principles are brought in as *aids* (arguments) in the application of some general clause, and cases where they appear as *independent norms*. In the former cases the limit to what is legally possible is obviously broader: in the light of the material presented in Chapter V above it is easy to describe need-oriented principles in such cases as legally possible in Finnish law. More is required to show that there might also exist a legal potential for need-oriented principles of the latter, independent, kind. Even if the concrete legal material is not equally convincing here, it appears reasonable to maintain, on the basis of legal practice, that there exists in Finland a legal *possibility*, which *can* be realized, of actually developing such principles. While it is naturally impossible to state that there would be any general tendency in legal practice to argue "*in dubio pro paupere*",[4] the material shows that those applying the law are *sometimes* prepared, without support from any general clause, to

---

[4] "In doubtful cases, (decide) for the poor (party)"; the expression is taken from BGB-Kommentar p. 23.

take into account the needs of one party, perhaps primarily a debtor's economic needs. This suffices for alternative dogmatics to indicate a legal possibility.

The relationships of influence between the legislation on the one hand and the general principles on the other are not one-sided. Even though the legislation constitutes an important producer of the building blocks used to help create general principles, these, in turn, naturally influence the way the legislation is interpreted. As we have seen, the general principles may represent aids to legal interpretation. The need-oriented principles, created among other ways on the basis of certain more or less explicitly need-oriented statutory provisions and the practice associated with them, affect in their turn the interpretation of these provisions. Such influence, however, is also possible regarding other statutes than the explicitly need-oriented. Schematically, this influence may look like this:

Need-oriented legislation

a ↓ generalization ↑ interpretation

Need-oriented principles

b ↓ interpretation

Other legislation

It is obvious that the possibilities of bringing in need-oriented principles as aids in the interpretation of the legislation must vary depending on the question to be regulated, the design of the relevant statute, etc. For this reason the question of the significance of need-oriented arguments in the interpretation of contract-law legislation cannot be illustrated in all its breadth, but must be referred to specialized works on the relevant legislation. The problems touched upon here relate chiefly to level a) in the figure above.

3. RELEVANT NEEDS

3.1 Needs of parties

In a rather more concrete attempt to analyse in what situations need-oriented application of the law appears possible, one meets first the problem of identifying the needs that are relevant. Expressed in role terminology, the question can be formulated as follows: what need-oriented juridical roles may be included in the cast of characters of contract law? The legal answer must of course be sought primarily on the basis of national symptomatic criticism.

In connection with the presentation of the application of the general adjustment rules in Finnish practice, it was claimed that the need-oriented decisions which may be found here have concerned a debtor's need of limitations to his liability; while concrete examples of contract adjustment based on the creditor's needs are absent. This tendency in the development of need-oriented person roles appears in the whole of the material treated in the previous chapter. The material contains many examples of need-oriented debtor roles, while corresponding creditor roles occur more sparsely, being found chiefly in the area of tenancy and tort law. In the tenancy-law rules on postponement of moving day the *presumptively homeless tenant* and the *presumptively straitened tenant* are protected (see Ch. V.4.). When a survivor's right to damages is being assessed the basis is that person's need of maintenance, and when adjusting damages the injured party's needs should, in principle, also be considered.

On the debtor side, a more complete need-oriented cast can be found. In the statutory provisions of tort and contract law and in the practice regarding them, the following kinds of role, among others, have been accorded relevance:

(i) *The debtor with limited means*, straitened living conditions, poor ability to pay, etc. (see V.5.2.7., V.7.3.i. and V.8.3.).

(ii) The *debtor in need of housing*. Need of housing has been adduced as a ground for adjustment of contract (see

V.8.2.ii.); payment difficulties influenced by homelessness may also lead to mitigation of sanctions (see V.7.3.ii). If so desired, one may view role ii as a sub-group of role i; but homelessness can easily appear as a relatively independent element in the assessment.

(iii) *The low-income debtor* (see V.5.2.7. and V.8.3.) This role most often comprises also the more specific roles iv and v; these may also, however, in certain cases, gain more or less independent significance.

(iv) The *unemployed* debtor (see V.5.2.7, V.7.3.ii and V.8.2.iv.).

(v) The *ill debtor* and the elderly debtor (see V.5.2.7., V.7.3.ii, V.8.2.ii, iv and V.8.3. at the end). Even though the relevance of this concept often has connections with the ill debtor's impaired earning capacity, it has been possible in its application to pay direct attention to such needs as do not directly have to do with the debtor's economic standing.

(vi) The *debtor burdened with considerable maintenance liabilities* (see V.5.2.7.).

(vii) *The small-enterprise debtor of limited financial strength* (see V.5.2.7.). The reason for noting this role particularly and not, for example, under role i is that it is thought possible in its application to consider to some extent third-party, i.e. employee, needs as well (see below for more detail).

In view of a central issue in recent discussion of the development of person-related elements in the legal system, there is reason to point out that *woman* is absent from the cast of characters presented above. In the Finnish law of obligations there is no concrete legal material to show that a party's gender has been accorded relevance in need-oriented reasoning. Even if this is the case, it should nevertheless be noted that *increased need-orientation* in the system of private law also *increases the possibilities* (what is legally possible) *of a women's-rights orientation.*

3.2 *The needs of the work force*

In welfare-state ideology the individual citizen's welfare stands at the centre of interest. In the concrete legal material described in Chapter V, in which a party's economic standing has been accorded relevance in assessment, attention has been paid mainly to the standing of individual persons. In some need-oriented material, the endeavour has nevertheless also been to safeguard the small enterprise of limited financial strength. From the welfare-state perspective this may be natural since the needs of a small business often coincide to some extent with those of the small businessman. The finances of the business and those of the businessman may in fact - even legally in the case of more undeveloped enterprise forms - appear as one unit.

The foregoing would not, however, justify the special attention paid to the small enterprise in the present context: the point is one of social considerations similar to those concerning other private citizens. Yet the question of the position of the small enterprise becomes a special one in that decisions concerning the enterprise also affect the needs of a third party, *the work force*. As we have seen, unemployment is a main cause of relative deprivation in society today. A prime task of the welfare state is therefore seen as being to counteract not only the economic and the social consequences of unemployment but also unemployment as such. Measures that attempt to prevent small enterprises active in, for example, sensitive areas of employment policy from having to close down may be called for by the prevailing ideology. The problem can also be examined from the perspective of regional policy: special weight is placed upon the role of the small enterprise as an employer in economically vulnerable areas.

In view of the above it is not surprising that in the concrete legal material from the law of obligations it has been thought possible to consider to some extent small-business employees' need to be able to retain their jobs. It must be stressed, however, that the needs of the work force are met only indirectly, and with considerable uncertainty, by solutions in the law of obligations that favour the small enterprise in question. From the welfare-state point of view such solutions must appear secondary in relation to the attempt at direct support of citizens at risk. The theoretical fixation of the law of obligations on the two parties also renders it more difficult to legitimate decisions that are grounded upon the needs of third parties. For these reasons it appears neither desirable nor realistic to accord consideration for the needs of the work force any central part in the development of need-oriented principles in the law of contract. The concern for jobs should be viewed rather as a *supplementary argument* supporting observance of the needs of a small enterprise in situations where the businessman's own needs appear worthy of consideration. This implies above all that larger companies with more diffuse ownership profiles and limited owner liability should not be permitted to call upon employment policy arguments.

4. "FINANCERS" OF SOCIAL PROTECTION IN THE LAW OF OBLIGATIONS

4.1 Introduction

The fact that there are such economic needs among the citizens of a society which ought to be met within the framework of the welfare state may justify extension of the social-legal responsibility of the public sector. On the other hand the existence of economic needs among citizens is not itself sufficient argument for need-oriented solutions within the party relationship of the law of obligations. Consideration of the needs of one private party is here always taking place at the expense of the other party. Hence one must be able to justify further why the needs of one party should be met in whole or in part by the other. Upon what grounds may one party be obliged to act as "financer" of the other party's social security?

In the light of the material presented earlier, the following grounds, at least, appear possible:

(i) enterprises' (etc.) social responsibility,

(ii) owner's social responsibility,
(iii) solidarity in the event of accidents, and
(iv) social community.

4.2 Enterprises', etc., social responsibility

A fact hardly needing support here is that economic power has continually been concentrated. The market is dominated increasingly by large companies which, in relation to the citizen, appear as impersonal, bureaucratic institutions at the same level as public institutions. It is thus but a short step to assume a certain social responsibility on the part of such enterprises. Power begets responsibility. This view has often been extended to include *industry and commerce* at large, and such a view appears, partly at least, to be justified: with economic profit one can also imagine linking a certain social responsibility towards the citizens from which the profit is gained. Even accepting on this ground the notion that all enterprises carry a social responsibility, it is nevertheless obvious that the argument bears upon different kinds of enterprise with differing weight. The greater the assets a enterprise has at its disposal and the more dominant it is, the more its social responsibility can be stressed.[5]

To some extent, the social responsibility of an enterprise can also be justified with reference to the fact that it, through its marketing and other measures, has contributed to creating the social problems one is striving to solve. A concrete example from consumer law may illustrate this: when a company markets consumer capital goods with a strong emphasis on credit facilities, hence encouraging the consumer to incur a burden of expenses he is unable to bear, it is plausible to argue that that company should also carry the social consequences of this. Where the expansion of the credit card market leads to excessive indebtedness on the part

---

[5] In this context reference should be made to the comprehensive international discussion on "Corporate Social Responsibility": see e.g. Dübeck 1989.

of consumers, it may also be argued that the credit card companies that have made the indebtedness possible should help mitigate its social consequences.

The introduction of the concept of *merchant* (enterprise) into the conceptual world of private law, through the development of consumer law, has also been seen as introducing new opportunities for *collectivized* argumentation in contract law. The merchant is actually a contracting party who *per definitionem* enters into many contracts and who can therefore be used as a means of channelling and fragmenting risks. By being able to direct attention to the merchant's whole stock of contracts and not only to the individual contract, one can observe his possibilities of using the price mechanism to spread risks among all his customers. Strict liability for the merchant has been justified through reference to his opportunities for fragmenting the risks his liability involves via third party liability insurance and, ultimately, prices. This way of arguing can equally well be extended beyond the issue of risk-spreading, to be used in theory to justify a need-oriented social responsibility for the enterprise, as long as this affects a relatively limited proportion of its customers. The economic needs of individual customers that the enterprise can be forced to meet may be channelled via the price mechanism so as to be borne by its whole clientele. The more dominant the enterprise is and the weaker the competition in the area, the greater its opportunities of fragmenting economic needs in this way.

The social responsibility of the enterprise also appears, in the light of the concrete legal material already presented, as the most important ground for imposing upon one party to a legal relationship under the law of obligations the duty to consider to some extent the needs of the other party. This follows from many regulations:

- The majority of the statutory provisions and decisions concerning mitigation of sanctions in cases of social force majeure cover only cases where the counter-party to the one adversely affected is a merchant.

- The limitation of the employee's personal liability in tort law is based largely on the notion that the employer, in the majority of cases an enterprise, is the one to bear the costs of the damage.

- The adjustment rules of tort law are generally much influenced by insurance thinking. In many contexts the starting point is that the existence of insurance on either side will affect the decision. Even if the decision in such cases formally concerns the liability of the individual party, and does not directly regulate the insurance relationship, it is assumed that it is possible through a suitable tort law decision to channel as large as possible a portion of the damage so as to be borne by an insurer, that is, an enterprise that has specialized in carrying risks. The same tendency to channel damages to insurers naturally appears also in cases where the insurer himself is a party, e.g. in subrogation proceedings. Here there has often been a tendency to pay great attention to the counter-party's economic needs.

To the extent public bodies enter into relationships of private law, one can naturally, *mutatis mutandis*, bring in the same considerations as when discussing the responsibility of enterprises. The reasoning also bears, at least partly, upon such non-entrepreneurial private organizations whose size or activity enables them to function as risk- and need-fragmenters.

4.3 The owner's social responsibility

Property, too, is said to entail responsibility. It is reasonable for owners of socially important types of property to have to accept that social obligations attach to such property.

Examples of this way of thinking may be found in tenancy law in many countries. In Finland, as we have seen, the *owner of a dwelling* has a certain need-oriented social responsibility towards his tenant.

4.4 *Solidarity in the case of accidents*

Disputes over extra-contractual liability in damages are most frequently based, insofar as there is no question of deliberately caused damage, on events that appear unfortunate for each party. Neither the person causing the damage nor the injured party have wished the event to occur.

The adjustment rules of tort law appear to be based on this notion, that damage to property or persons is to some degree an undesirable occurrence for both parties involved. In such situations one can call for a certain solidarity between the parties, each of whom is adversely affected in his own way by the accident. An injured party in good economic circumstances may through adjustment of damages be charged to consider to some extent the tortfeasor's need to be relieved of full liability.

In a case of deliberate damage, the above justification is not practicable: the damage no longer appears as an accident suffered by each party. Consequently, there has been a very restrictive attitude towards the possibilities of adjusting compensation for damage of this kind.

Where adjustment can take account of the needs of the work force, special relations of solidarity may be considered. Thus rules that allow adjustment of an employer's liability in damages in cases of wrongful dismissal where full compensation would jeopardise his conditions of activity appear to be based on the notion that a dismissed employee has to show a certain solidarity with his former co-workers.

4.5 *Social community*

In alternative private-law jurisprudence the model-forming significance of the structures that control activities in a community such as the family has been stressed.[6] It also seems easy to accept, from an ethical point of view, the idea that the parties in a

---

[6] See e.g. Unger 1983 p. 618 ff.

social community may have a social responsibility with a need-oriented tinge towards each other. In the field of private law such lines of thought normally occur in family law. The rules on maintenance usually have a strongly need-oriented character.

In the concrete legal material from the area of the law of obligations, however, few signs can be found that a need-oriented social responsibility has been imposed on anyone on this ground. Yet this may depend more on the limited occurrence of cases of this nature than on doubt over the theoretical possibility of taking particular account of the existence of a social community. However, one case of adjustment of wages (see V.8.2.i) can be mentioned in this connection.

4.6 Need-orientation in different types of relationships

Against the background of the above it is possible to rank schematically the relationships in which one could argue for need-oriented decisions in contract law:

(i) *Individual citizens versus enterprises, organizations and public bodies*. On the above analysis this relation appears as the one in which the hurdle for need-oriented solutions may be set lowest. Both in consumer relationships and in others between individuals and enterprises, good grounds can be given for why one should also consider the individual citizen's needs in contract-law deliberations. In the development of need-oriented general principles in contract law, the starting point can therefore be that the model relationship in which the principles of need-orientation must be applied as broadly as possible is that between an individual citizen whose need is in question and an enterprise, a fairly large private organization or a public body.

(ii) *Small enterprises of limited financial strength versus large enterprises*, and comparable organizations and bodies. The role of a small enterprise of limited financial strength has already been noted in several connections. To the extent this role is perceived as relevant, it is natural for it to be considered primarily in relation to a larger company or corresponding organization or body. At least from a Nordic angle, this appears possible since one can refer to the lively discussion of protection of small enterprises during recent years, which has among other things led to viewing contracts between small and large companies as a special category where the adjustment threshold should be low.[7]

(iii) *Individual citizens versus individual citizens.* In the relationship between private persons one should normally, for a need-oriented solution to be considered, assume that there exists e.g. a particular link between the parties in question - a social community - or that one party may be considered to bear a particular responsibility, for example as owner of socially important property. When apportioning the costs of unfortunate occurrences, however, one can also conceive of a more far-reaching solidarity between individual citizens.

5. NEED-ORIENTED LAW AND THE MARKET

5.1 The problem

A main principle of the private-law system in a market society is the notion that each market actor shall have the right to decide himself whether or not to conclude contracts, and with whom. To the extent one maintains this principle, however, one subjects the legal order at the same time to important limitations regarding the possibilities available for regulating the content of the contractual relationships to the end desired. Strong protection of the weaker party in a contractual relationship may lead to the other party not wishing to conclude the contract at all.[8] It has, for

---

[7] See e.g. Aurejärvi 1979.

[8] Eidemüller 1989 p. 40 argues on a more general level against Unger's "solidarity rights" precisely because he considers them to have corresponding counterproductive side-effects. Such rights would in his opinion lead to a person who may be adversely affected by them being "careful to avoid situations in which he runs the risk of being confronted with solidarity claims. He might even be careful to avoid other people altogether."

example, been claimed - and it is unnecessary to decide here whether there is any ground for the claim - that the reduction in the supply of rental housing would be a consequence of the protection of the tenant through tenancy law.

It is clear that such side-effects may be very probable if an attempt should be made through the legal system to protect a special, socially vulnerable group of persons. A protection that is not limited in this way but is to cover, e.g., all consumers must obviously be extremely far-reaching if it is to affect the supply directly, at least as regards utilities intended chiefly for private consumption: since all or the large majority of consumers belong to the protected group, the enterprise which wishes to remain in the market at all must conclude contracts with protected persons. But if the protection is confined to a limited group such as the unemployed, the enterprise can more easily, through a discriminatory contract policy, avoid the burdens the protection may entail. If the law grants relief for unemployed persons in the repayment of credit, this may have the effect that even less credit is granted to the unemployed than heretofore. Such a result is of course not what is being sought through a need-oriented law of contract.

It is self-evident that need-oriented regulations may have undesirable consequences of this type only if the "financing" party can influence the emergence of the legal relationship. If a kind of "relationship of coercion" arises, into which the party in question enters independently of his own will, he cannot avoid parties who may possibly obtain the protection of a need-oriented regulation. For this reason one has not witnessed any such troubles in connection with the need-oriented regulations of, e.g., the law of succession and tort law.[9]

---

[9] Another negative side-effect of a need-oriented tort law is naturally conceivable: if the prospective, economically weak tortfeasor is aware that his own need to avoid liability is given considerable weight in the legal assessment, this may possibly lead to a reduction of the preventive effect of damages. In discussion of tort law, however, opinions have always diverged strongly regarding whether and how far liability in damages has a preventive effect at all. As long as opportunities for need-oriented solutions are relatively limited in cases of deliberate damage and

The negative side-effects described in the introductory section can be assumed, then, to arise chiefly within the *law of contract*. It is here that need-oriented regulations can lead to the groups intended for support experiencing difficulties when they attempt to enter desirable legal relationships. The law of contract in a market economy is in this sense to some degree "immune" to need-oriented solutions.

Only as far as contract law departs from the premise that each person shall have the right to decide whether and with whom he will enter a contract, and limits the effect of market forces using rules on *duty to contract*, do the relationships of contract law assume the character of such relationships of coercion as on the above showing would make more far-reaching need-orientation possible. A more general extension of the scope of the duty to contract[10] (which does not itself have to be need-oriented but can embrace all presumptive customers) is a precondition for a law of contract that would be more thoroughly need-oriented. Referring to the social responsibility of enterprises one could well argue for the duty to contract being extended under certain conditions to include not only monopolies but also other - at least larger - enterprises which regularly conclude contracts with private persons. An extension of this kind would accord with the welfare-state goal of offering all citizens social services within the framework of available resources. Continued and deeper discussion of the possibilities for a social private law must give considerable weight to this problem area.

The issue of the duty to contract will not be analysed

---

the assumption is not that consideration of the tortfeasor's needs will normally lead to the liability disappearing entirely, one can obviously disregard the risk that need-orientation would weaken the preventive effects of tort law.

[10] The position today in Finland is that only public institutions such as the post office and the state railways, together with companies in a monopoly position and comparable companies, are obliged to conclude contracts with any person who is prepared to supply his counter-performance; see Kivimäki - Ylöstalo 1981 p. 263. In for example German law the development seems to have gone further, see e.g. Kilian 1980.

further here since, as a more general one, it falls outside the need-oriented theme of this work. A well-founded analysis of the efficiency and effects of such a general duty would also rapidly fill an additional volume.

The focus is thus upon the question of where need-oriented solutions are possible in a law of contract from which there has been no attempt to withdraw market forces in the ways mentioned. Such solutions are conceivable only in certain situations or under certain conditions:

(i) the need-orientation refers to "subsequent needs",

(ii) the need-orientation is implemented using "unpredictable" regulations (concepts of degree and guideline), or

(iii) the need-orientation refers to less significant side-issues.

5.2 "Subsequent" needs

When need-oriented rules are applied it is sometimes, but not always, important *when* the need of the party in question has arisen. Considering this temporal aspect, the concrete need-oriented material in Chapter V can thus be divided into two main groups:

(i) The cases where it is of no essential importance when the need has arisen. Assessments of the reasonableness of a tortfeasor's liability in damages in Nordic law here constitute a type example: if the tortfeasor at the time the dispute is decided has limited means, is a low-income earner, etc., this indicates adjustment more or less regardless of when he came into this condition. In addition, many of the cases regarding assessment of the fairness of contracts are of this type.

(ii) The case is different when we are dealing with rules that come under the heading of *social force majeure*. Here it is assumed that the need arose only after conclusion of the contract in question. In these cases only *subsequent needs* are accorded relevance.

The parties must make their decision regarding the setting

up of a contractual relationship on the basis of the information available at the time when the contract is concluded. Later occurrences which could not be foreseen at the time of concluding the contract cannot affect the decision. The risk of such side-effects of need-oriented principles as those described above is therefore clearly less when the needs met are subsequent ones. Hence there has in Finnish law been no worry concerning these effects when rules have been introduced to mitigate the consequences of a delay of payment caused by unemployment or illness arising after conclusion of the contract.

For the reason given, the question of possibly recognizing the relevance of subsequent needs in certain cases is clearly the one in which the analysis of need-oriented general principles can be made most concrete. The legal figure that here comes to the fore, the doctrine of *social force majeure*, will therefore be treated specially below in Chapter VII.

5.3 Degree and guideline concepts

The undesired side-effects of a need-oriented regulation in the law of contract are presumably greatest in cases where the rules are intended to favour (a) a relatively limited group of persons who (b) are easy to delimit from other person groups, and this favouring takes place (c) with the help of rules where the legal consequences are fairly unambiguously framed. In such a case the "financing" party can clearly foresee the negative consequences of entering into contracts with persons belonging to the group in question and often also has a realistic possibility of refusing to make contracts with such persons. The more unclear the delimitation of the group is and the more unpredictable the coming into effect of the particular legal consequences, the more difficult it is for the "financing" party to avoid contractual relationships where there is a possibility that the law will be applied in a need-oriented manner.

A need-oriented regulation that aims not merely at allowing subsequent needs to be taken into account is therefore possible in the law of contract in the form of provisions, more or less of the nature of general clauses, whose scope and sanctions are determined on the basis of an *overall assessment* in each particular case. In this way the content of the regulation may be left open in one or the other of the following respects:

(i) The scope of the need-oriented assessment can be established using *degree concepts*. Instead of referring to qualities which in a particular case are either present or absent, one can refer to qualities that may be present to a greater or a lesser degree. The type example is a reference to financial strength: there exist no clearly defined groups of "poor" and "rich" (or e.g. "poor", "of average means" and "rich"); rather there is a sliding scale, at one end of which one finds persons entirely without income and assets and at the other the large capital owners.

The need-oriented role concepts in the cases concerning application of the general clauses of contract law are also usually of the type mentioned. They are mainly on the *scale of economic strength*. This applies both to low-income debtors and to debtors with limited means; even if reference is made only to *some* circumstance affecting the debtor's economic position, such as income, property or maintenance obligation, one must naturally in an overall assessment *in casu* theoretically note everything that affects the debtor's economic strength.[11]

The foregoing implies that concepts such as *unemployment*, which cover qualities that are either present or not present, cannot as a rule be used generally within contract law. At least, attaching specific legal consequences to unemployment appears unthinkable considering the effect this would have on the unemployed person's possibilities of making contracts; it is only in connection with the rules on the effect of subsequent needs that such attachment could

---

[11] An exception from the tendency in contract law - except for cases of subsequent needs - to operate with need-oriented degree concepts is, in Finnish law as in many other systems, the reference to the need of housing in tenancy law. That it has been possible here to employ such a concept is presumably linked with the size of the group indicated as meriting protection: most tenants can be assumed to have no housing other than where they have been given notice to quit.

be considered. It is quite another matter that unemployment can be brought in to demonstrate that the person in question has limited economic strength. One can conceivably erect a *presumption* that an unemployed person is in such a vulnerable position. Then, however, the term unemployed is used merely as an aid for placing the party on the scale described above.

Using concepts of degree of the type mentioned implies that the legal assessment can in theory vary over an infinite number of different relationships. Instead of, for example, the formal relationship between buyer and seller in general sale-of-goods law which, on the advent of consumer law, was divided into relationships between a) merchant and merchant, b) merchant-seller and consumer, c) individual seller and merchant-buyer and d) individual and individual, the following type of pattern of relationships emerges:

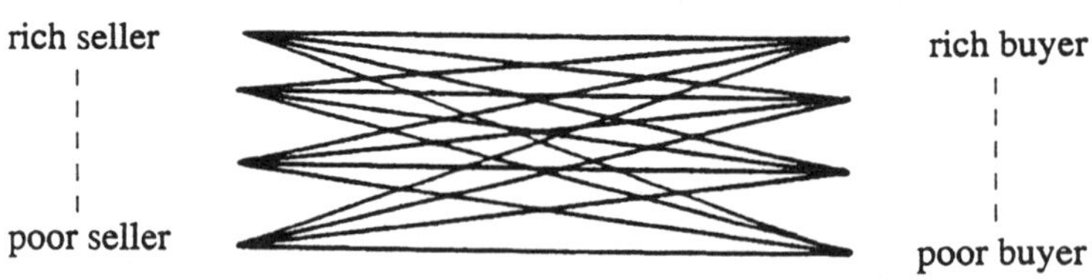

(ii) The need-oriented role concepts can also be *guideline concepts*. Legal consequences associated with such concepts are established on the basis of balancing need-oriented arguments with other arguments. This means that the use of the concepts becomes to a high degree *situation-bound*: the centre of gravity in the assessment is shifted from roles to situations.

In other words, the distinction between rule concept and guideline concept, as employed here, concerns the question of how the concepts may be used in juridical problem-solving. If a rule concept is applied, the appropriate legal consequence should follow if the facts of the case can be subsumed under this concept. A guideline concept, on the other hand, can be applicable without the legal consequence needing to follow of normative necessity: even if the party is without means, there may perhaps be no adjustment because other considerations speak against adjustment.

In the need-oriented case examples within contract law, the role concepts under consideration have precisely this character of guideline concepts. When contracts are being adjusted, there must be an overall assessment where the need-oriented arguments can always be met by counter-arguments. Regard for a party's needs is merely *one* element in the decision.

Many of the need-oriented concepts analysed in Chapter V are *combinations* of degree concepts and guideline concepts. When applying one of these combinations, one imagines that the significance of the need and of the counter-argument can somehow be weighed against each other: the greater the needs, i.e. the higher up the need scale a party is, the heavier the counter-argument must be for the needs to remain unconsidered. A type example is the need-oriented concepts of tort law: they are degree concepts through which reference is made primarily to the economic strength of the parties *and* guideline concepts without normatively necessary legal consequences. Hence, analogous application of these concepts in the field of contract law has not been seen as causing problems of the kind analysed in this section.

What has been said in this section implies that the goal of greater predictability in the application of need-oriented approaches (see above III.4) in contract law can only be reached to a very limited extent. Regard to the undesirable side-effects of the need-oriented regulations entails that, rather, the unpredictability and the importance of the decision *in casu* must be stressed. At the same time, however, this means that, as indicated in section III.4 just mentioned, one limits the actual importance of the need-oriented regulations. Without considerable reassessments of the principle of the freedom of a party to choose a contractual partner, however, it seems impossible to go further in the direction of more precise norms except as regards subsequent needs.

5.4 Side issues

What has just been said of the possibilities of developing more precise need-oriented norms must not be understood too categorically. The possible undesirable side effects of a need-oriented regulation must obviously in practice depend also upon the weight of the issue being regulated.

Rules implying, for example, that a certain party's main obligation would be limited on the basis of his needs must certainly as a rule lead to attempts from possible counter-parties to avoid contracts with this particular party. As against this, it is not equally certain that need-oriented rules directed at generally less important questions, which may be expected to come up only in a limited number of situations, will have such side-effects. The "financing" contracting party's interest in the contract may be so great that he is prepared to enter it despite these rules. In cases of contracts concluded by enterprises and others with a comprehensive portfolio of contracts, the possibilities of fragmenting "social risks" may lead to this result: if the risk of situations where a need-oriented judgment may be made is relatively limited, it may be more rational to calculate this risk as a cost rather than to attempt to avoid all contracting parties in relation to whom the risk *may* become manifest.

The importance of a question may depend on many circumstances. Hence it is impossible to analyse in detail what questions are open in this way to a more precise need-oriented regulation that is not limited merely to subsequent needs.

6. DEVELOPMENT OF THE NEW PRINCIPLES USING CONSTRUCTED EXAMPLES

6.1 Introduction

Starting from the symptomatic criticism in Chapter V, the analysis above has shown how one could argue for more general need-oriented principles. It has emerged that such principles - as long as one is not discussing subsequent needs - must of necessity be very loose so as not to lead to undesirable side effects. They must be elastic in content, for example using degree concepts and guideline concepts.

Such flexible principles can in practice gain limited significance, particularly if they are formulated merely on a very abstract level. An alternative legal dogmatics that is attempting to introduce such new ways of thinking into practical legal life should therefore not stop at the abstract presentation of the new, loose, principles. Concrete demonstration of the principles through constructed examples may increase the actual force of the ideas.

In what follows, some examples of imaginary situations are presented where need-oriented reasoning may appear natural.

6.2 Need-oriented protection of creditors

6.2.1 General

We have earlier seen that relatively few examples of need-oriented creditor roles can be met with in the concrete legal material in Finland. Those that are found appear more seldom as independent reasons for increasing the creditor's rights. Most often they have to a greater or lesser degree the character of *reasons against* a need-oriented assessment on the debtor side. This is particularly clear in the application of the adjustment rules of tort law, where pleading the creditor's needs becomes relevant only where it is first established that the debtor's needs indicate adjustment.

The concrete legal material shows, then, that it can obviously be seen as more acceptable to *limit the needy party's obligations*, and hence also the "financer's" rights, than to *increase the needy party's rights* and the "financer's" obligations. This appears understandable in the light of a general traditional restraint in prescribing new obligations for a contracting party on grounds of fairness. In Finnish doctrine, for example, caution has been advocated in adjusting contracts "upwards".[12]

For an alternative dogmatics, such traditional restraint should not of course be of decisive importance. Since there are no formal obstacles to "upward" adjustment, there is nothing to prevent one from developing need-oriented protection for the creditor, based on e.g. the general clauses of contract law. The conceivable situations where such creditor protection would come in may be assumed to vary greatly in character. In the light of the analysis earlier in this chapter, just a few situations will be indicated here where need-oriented reasoning in favour of the creditor in an existing contractual relationship should be understood as legally possible.

Naturally, it is sometime difficult to make any clear distinction between need-oriented protection of the creditor and corresponding protection of the debtor, where a party's rights and obligations can appear as different sides of the same coin: even if postponement of moving day can be understood primarily as increasing the tenant's right to occupy the apartment, the measure can naturally also be seen as a limitation on his obligation to move.

6.2.2 Satisfaction of need of compensation

One fact emerging from the concrete legal material is that it has appeared possible to consider to some extent the creditor's

---

[12] Very great restraint is evident in Taxell 1972 p. 158 f.: "Can adjustment be 'upwards', e.g. so that a party is enjoined to pay a greater sum than agreed when this, because of other circumstances, has become unreasonably low from the opposite party's point of view? In theory this should be ruled out. There is cause to be restrictive in heaping upon a party obligations over and above those he may be considered to have undertaken" (translated here). Statements with the same burden can also be found in other "older" doctrine: see e.g. Portin 1974 p. 334. While it is today clear that adjustment may also be "upwards", see e.g. Wilhelmsson 1984 p. 77 and references there, one can assume that there still obtains a certain scepticism about imposing increased obligations upon a party in a contract-law relationship on the basis of considerations of fairness.

(the injured party's) concrete needs particularly within tort law. Specially when assessing survivors' right to compensation, but also when applying the adjustment and fairness rules of tort law, these needs have been taken into account. It therefore seems plausible to consider the concrete needs of the party entitled to compensation in contract-law decisions regarding the obligation to indemnify as well.

It appears specially natural to adjust agreed compensation "upwards" on the basis of the injured party's needs in disputes regarding application of *insurance contracts*. Studies of *ex gratia* payments of insurance companies show that, in practice, insurers consider such needs to some extent.[13] This "extra-legal" practice can be inserted into the legal assessment via the general clauses. Insurance companies belong to the type of company that should, according to what has been said earlier, bear a certain social responsibility. When dealing with insurance contracts it should therefore be possible to use as an argument for adjustment in the insured's favour his poor economic position and similar circumstances.

Within the law of compensation, the importance of special protection for sufferers of personal injury has often been emphasized.[14] One could therefore claim on good grounds that the social arguments should be accorded particularly great weight in the regulation of such injury; but this is not to say that they should be denied importance in cases of damage to property.

Yet one can hardly imagine imposing a duty to pay compensation to an unlimited extent on the basis of a need-oriented

---

[13] In an empirical study of the practice of some Swedish insurance companies for settling compensation, in which it was attempted to map whether and how far compensation is granted in cases where there is no strict juridical obligation, Eva Lindell-Frantz and Carl Martin Roos (1985 p. 52 f., 64) noted cases of generous application of contracts not only in relation to important clients and those of long standing but also towards clients in socially vulnerable circumstances.

[14] In Finland this has found expression in, among other places, the discussion on the consequences of contributory negligence: see e.g. Saxén 1975 p. 127 and 1983 p. 407.

assessment. It seems obvious that there is often an upper limit for what the injured party can obtain, namely the size of the damage (which naturally cannot always be unambiguously established in practice). Even where the injured party has a very great need of further subsistence over and above the sum corresponding to the damage he has suffered, it appears hard to justify decisions that would charge the "financer" to meet such needs also. Of course the rather arbitrary ways of measuring especially immaterial losses, such as pain and suffering etc., give the courts wide discretion even if this theoretical limitation is accepted.

The principles just stated, according to which one must as a rule operate along the scale no compensation/part compensation/full compensation, imply that need-oriented reasoning is in practice relevant chiefly when various kinds of *limitation of liability* are being addressed. Such limitations are also common in other types of contract than insurance contracts: the considerations given can be adduced more generally when one has to assess contract terms that limit in some way the liability of a party, especially of an enterprise. Typical subjects for the application of general clauses in contract law are various kinds of clauses limiting liability, clauses on notification of claims, etc. In the adjustment of such clauses it should be possible to adduce in favour of the party claiming damages his poor economic position and similar circumstances.

6.2.3 Satisfaction of housing needs

At many points in the concrete legal material, a party's need of housing has been noted. The presumptively homeless tenant and the presumptively straitened tenant are two of the few need-oriented creditor roles found in the Finnish material.

It should obviously be possible to consider these role concepts outside tenancy law, too. A readily accessible example of a contract in which such concepts could possibly be given relevance is *contracts on purchase of dwellings*. In the application, e.g. adjustment and interpretation, of a contract of this kind it should be possible to consider each contracting party's need of housing. Reasoning of this kind could be relevant for example with respect to transfer of possession, possible cancellation or avoidance of the purchase, etc.

6.3 Need-oriented protection of debtors

6.3.1 Introduction

Deficiencies in a person's economic position normally become visible on the level of contract law in that the person cannot meet the contract-law obligations for which he is liable. From the perspective of those applying the law - examining only the problems placed before the legal machinery - the issue of developing a more need-oriented law of contract is therefore often the same as that of the growth of need-oriented protection of debtors. As we have seen, this is also evident from the concrete legal material presented in Chapter V. The majority of the regulations and decisions in which a party's economic needs have been expressly taken into account have concerned mitigation of the party's obligations as a debtor in a legal relationship.

The growing social importance of developing such protection for debtors is also evident. In the majority of market-economy countries the numbers of overindebted households increased strongly during the 1980s. Comprehensive groups of persons and households would today be in need of need-oriented debtor protection. The numbers of people suffering from problems of over-indebtedness can be counted in hundreds of thousands, if not millions, in many countries.[15] It can also be noted that persons belonging (in a broad sense) to underprivileged population groups

---

[15] In 1987 for example over 2 million households in Great Britain were stated to be unable to repay credits. In France the over-indebted households at the end of the eighties were about 200,000. The figures are mentioned in the preliminary General Report from the conference on Unemployment and Consumer Debts in Europe, 22-23.9.1989 in Hamburg.

are clearly overrepresented among the debtors who have difficulty in repaying private debts and are affected by legal measures as a consequence of this. Detailed studies in various countries show parallel features: low-income earners, persons with heavy maintenance burdens, manual workers and the uneducated figure disproportionately largely among debtors affected by legal consequences because of payment difficulties.[16]

The comprehensive nature of the concrete legal material, in which there has been a departure from the traditional principle that each person shall be responsible without limitation for his ability to pay, affords a good basis for need-oriented generalizations at this point. Here the step to a "switching of principles" is shorter. The information just presented also shows the need for a more general need-oriented protection of debtors. With the help of such a protection one can bring out problems on the level of contract law whose existence the legislator has long recognized but has attempted to solve through regulation of the execution phase using rules on exceptions from distraint (see below).

One could try to formulate a kind of *main principle*: in the application (adjustment, interpretation and supplementation) of contracts one should take into account the poor economic situation and other concrete needs of the debtor as *one* argument for restricting his obligations, especially in relationships between individual citizens and enterprises.

6.3.2 Private law/execution

In the *phase of execution* the economic needs of the party against whom the execution is directed are normally taken into account to a certain extent. Property and income that are needed to secure at least a minimum of subsistence for the debtor are

---

[16] See for more detail e.g. Holzscheck - Hörmann - Daviter 1982 p. 282, 324 ff., Adler 1985 p. 16, 21, Trebilcock - Reiter - Laskin 1979 p. 28 ff., Holmila 1973 p. 17 and Holmila-McCafferty 1975 p. 27, 36.

excepted from distraint.[17]

In the discussion both of the possibilities of introducing general need-oriented protection for the debtor in private law and of the development of the principle of social force majeure, it has sometimes been asserted that these problems are such as should be solved in the phase of execution, not in the material assessment of the legal relationship. There has been a wish to *define out* the issue of the possibilities of considering the debtor's economic needs from the field of private law and make it into a pure question of execution with which private law does not need to occupy itself.

The most important counter-argument to such reasoning is the observation that the delay sanctions of private and procedural law may often themselves greatly aggravate the social problem that the payment difficulties represent. A debtor who gets into arrears incurs a number of supplementary costs: penal interest, legal expenses and so on or, if he attempts to avoid getting into arrears, costs for new and as a rule more expensive credits, new bills etc. These costs must often be met before a payment can be made on the main debt. The debtor may thus find himself placed in a position where his debt does not decrease; it may even increase despite continued payments. *Annette Kähler* describes the situation of those who get into this modern debt imprisonment as follows: "These debtors derive little enjoyment from life. It is not unusual for them to give up their job voluntarily because there is little incentive for them to earn when most of their wages are used to service debts they can never hope to repay. The next step in their downward spiral is for them to lose their house or flat. Finally,

---

[17] In Finland for example, the following are exempt from distraint: the debtor's and his family's necessary clothes, bedclothes, beds and indispensible furniture and household utensils, equipment necessary for work, and one month's provisions where this is deemed indispensible to the debtor. From the debtor's salary according to the main rule two-thirds shall be exempt from distraint, but always as much as he is considered to need for his own and his family's support. A greater part of the debtor's salary is exempt from distraint if his ability to pay is substantially reduced because of illness, unemployment or other special cause (*social force majeure*).

they have to be taken into care by the social welfare authorities".[18]

In view of this it is a matter of some urgency to introduce this problem into private law itself in order to protect the debtor already in an earlier phase, that is, before he has reached a state of economic breakdown. In the welfare state it would be more consistent to go in and provide substantive law with the social lubrication which is often no longer of any use in the execution phase.[19]

This is not of course to say that the execution phase would lack interest in respect of the development of debtor protection. On the contrary, the rules on this are very important: the development of consumer bankruptcy legislation in countries where such legislation does not exist would certainly mean a significant improvement in the situation of overindebted consumers. This theme falls outside the scope of the present work, however.

6.3.3 Legal consequences

The legal consequences that can be connected with the debtor's economic and other needs may be of many different kinds. This is shown, too, in the example material in Chapter V. In certain cases in the relevant statutes the legal consequence is clearly stated (reduction of compensation or penal interest, limitation of the effects of an agreed sanction, etc.). In other cases, such as application of the general adjustment rule in sec. 36 of the Contract Act, the concrete legal consequences may vary depending on the situation in the individual case (reduction of the sum of the performance due, the right to cancel contracts, other ways of dissolving the contractual obligation, etc.).

Because of the necessary connection of need-oriented debtor protection to *in casu* considerations, it is not possible to list

---

[18] Kähler 1984 p. 490. Reifner 1980 p. 355 refers to the same problem when he notes that one can use private law to create a social welfare case. See also Trebilcock - Reiter - Laskin 1979 p. 74.

[19] Reifner 1980 p. 387.

systematically the possible legal consequences of a need-oriented assessment. Suffice it to note here that the relationship between the debtor's needs and the burdensome character of the obligation on the one hand and the legal consequence on the other may be shaped legally in two different ways:

(i) The more radical possibility is to mitigate precisely the obligation that appears over-burdensome with regard to the debtor's needs. If, for example, an obligation to repay unjust enrichment appears excessively severe, the obligation may be reduced or removed. The debtor may also be given the right to terminate a contract that has become excessively burdensome, and it may also be declared that a contract term that binds him to an unfair extent shall carry no force. The legal consequence of the need-oriented assessment in this case is *mitigation of a burdensome obligation*.

A need-oriented assessment of this nature would appear very radical to the extent that, on the basis of such considerations, one could reduce the central element of the contract, the agreed payment (*the price*).[20] Need-orientation in the law of contract has indeed developed far if it appears legally possible to adjust, in relation to individual economically vulnerable customers, a price which in relation to customers in general can be considered fair and reasonable. Even if it would for this reason seem hard to defend such a general principle, one could nevertheless maintain that need-oriented reasoning should be granted particular weight at least when the issue is one of obtaining a socially important utility. In view of the special interest devoted to the problems of housing when discussing need-orientation, one could thus when adjusting e.g. rent, or price in cases of purchase of dwellings, require more consideration - alongside other circumstances - for the debtor's economic needs. Regarding performances within the framework of a social community, it is of course also very near at hand to

[20] That adjustment of unfair prices is in fact possible in Finnish law is clear from sec. 36 of the Contract Act. From this, however, it does not yet follow that account could be taken of the debtor's economic standing in the assessment of fairness.

observe both the creditor's and the debtor's economic and other needs. Here, need-oriented reasoning can more easily be rendered more primary.[21]

A less radical mitigation of a burdensome obligation enters the picture where a contracting party is granted the right to withdraw from a contractual relation on need-oriented grounds. The Finnish concrete legal material contains examples of granting or wishing to grant a party this right e.g. in cases of social force majeure (see V.8.2.iv and V.7.2.5). However, there is scant reason to limit the possibilities of a need-oriented dissolution of contractual obligation to cases covered by the doctrine of social force majeure. It can be imagined that *in casu* - on the basis of an overall assessment in which other circumstances are also considered - a party may be granted a right to withdraw from a contractual obligation on the basis of needs that were already present when the contract was concluded, or with reference to economic difficulties that have arisen later but which cannot be ascribed to the special events premised by the doctrine of social force majeure.

A party in an individual case could for example be given the right to cancel a contract entered into by him but not yet completed if his economic position or his situation in other respects is such that it cannot be considered fair to demand that he performs in accordance with the contract. In this case one could speak of a kind of *social right of cancellation*. In addition, a party to a long-term contract could be given a need-oriented possibility of withdrawing from such a contract with future effect. One could here speak of a *social right of termination*, which would imply that, on the basis of a party's economic and other needs, one gives him the right to terminate a current contractual relationship. This could, for example, take place formally through adjustment of contract terms concerning the duration of the contract[22] or through supplementing a contract with rules on the right to terminate.

---

[21] See as an example HD 1986 II 144 above V.8.2.i.

[22] Thus for example the case reported in V.8.2.ii.

Particularly in cases where the counter-party suffers no significant damage through the dissolution of the contractual relationship or where his damage is compensated to a reasonable extent, it appears hard to reject a social right of cancellation and of termination.

(ii) In other cases, however, one does not intervene against the obligation whose fulfillment has been made difficult by the debtor's poor standing, one only mitigates the consequences affecting the debtor by reason of the failure to perform. A debtor who has run into difficulties and cannot pay his debt cannot in this case demand reduction of the debt, only mitigation of the consequences that may affect him because of the breach of contract. The debt as such remains intact.

Such *mitigation of sanctions* is provided for in Finnish law, as the examples show, primarily in the rules on what is termed social force majeure. This does not prevent one from prescribing mitigation of consequences, which is after all a milder legal consequence than mitigating the actual burdensome obligation, in other need-oriented decisions as well.

The consequences of social force majeure will be discussed in more detail in the next chapter.

CHAPTER VII

SOCIAL FORCE MAJEURE

1. INTRODUCTION

Structuring the general principles of a branch of law anew may be expected to have a greater effect the more concisely the new principles can be formulated. The more clearly the new norms can be presented in the form of ordinary "rules" in the meaning *Alexy* and *Dworkin* give this term (see above II.1) the easier it is for the legal decision-maker to use the new instruments. In this chapter it will be shown how such a new, relatively precise legal principle can be created on the basis of a fragmented concrete legal material.

As will be shown below, an individual monetary debtor's payment difficulties are most often due to changes in his financial situation that are more or less independent of himself. The difficulties are a consequence of the debtor's unemployment, illness, divorce or other corresponding problems. In developing need-oriented debtor protection, therefore, the possibility of considering such *subsequent needs* as arise through events of this kind represents a central, practical problem area. As noted earlier, it is precisely in the regulation of subsequent needs that the possibility exists of carving out the need-oriented principles in more concrete form. One can discuss whether there is justification for recognizing a special principle of social force majeure and, if so, what it should contain. These problems are the subject of this chapter.

In the ideology of the welfare state, one of the chief goals given for social development is the attempt to increase citizens' security by creating safeguards against the consequences of illness, unemployment and old age. A principle of social force majeure appears to be a means, albeit relatively unimportant, of furthering this goal. The discussion of the principle thus also implies specification of the extent to which this element of welfare-state ideology should be allowed to influence the law of contract.

In view of the fact that a central general principle of traditional private law has been the maxim that "each and every person is responsible for his ability to pay", or "you've got to have money" (see above V.7.1), a general principle of social force majeure stands in clear opposition to the established system. In other words, development of such a principle offers a good example of a partial "switching of principles" of the type in which alternative dogmatics is interested.

The principle is here put into concrete form largely from a Nordic perspective.[1] At the level of the concrete norms, the arguments for a switching of principles must obviously be grounded in a national legal order. As will emerge below, however, corresponding lines of thought are also current in other countries.

2. THE CAUSES OF PAYMENT DELAY

A common misapprehension is that payment delays often depend on the debtor's unwillingness to pay. Empirical studies from a number of countries regarding the reasons why private persons have not fulfilled their debtor's obligations show, on the contrary, that delays are normally connected with the difficult economic circumstances the person has happened to fall into. In addition, the studies show that this economically vulnerable posi-

---

[1] As stated earlier, the concrete legal material regarding social force majeure reported in Chapter V also has equivalents in the other Nordic countries (with some reservation for Denmark).

tion is not as a rule a consequence of the person's incorrect financial planning (voluntary overindebtedness) but of changes in his economic situation that are more or less independent of his own action. The difficulties in fulfilling the obligations are most often a consequence of the debtor being afflicted by

- *unemployment*,
- *illness*,
- other *reduction in income*,
- *divorce* and other marital problems and/or
- increased *living* or other *costs*.

Perhaps the best known, albeit somewhat old, study in the field is *David Caplovitz'* Consumers in Trouble. Here the author noted the following distribution of primary reasons (often, many reasons were given) for default among consumers in the USA:[2]

Loss of income	43 %
Voluntary overextension	13 %
Involuntary overextension	5 %
Marital instability	6 %
Debtor's third parties (unreliable friends and relatives etc.)	8 %
Debtor irresponsibility	4 %
Creditor may be implicated	22 %

In over half the cases where the first reason for default was loss of income, this was because of an adverse employment change, and in a third of the cases because of illness of the chief wage earner.[3]

In an English study carried out by the National Consumer Council in 1969, consumers who had had difficulty in debt payment stated the following causes of this:[4]

---

[2] Caplovitz 1974 p. 53.

[3] Caplovitz 1974 p. 58.

[4] Quoted in Cranston 1984 p. 205. A number of later investigations in Great Britain have also demonstrated a close connection between payment delay and unemployment, see Adler 1985 p. 16 and also Conaty 1985 p. 94.

Illness	20 %
Unemployment	15 %
Over-commitment on credit buying	6 %
Marital difficulties	5 %
Defective goods and subsequent dispute with vendor	5 %
Industrial labour disputes	4 %
National financial situation	3 %
Miscellaneous causes	3 %
Unforeseen debts arising	1 %
Reasons unknown or not remembered	37 %

Lastly may be mentioned a fairly recent West German study which attempted to investigate, among other things, the origin of conflicts leading to summary proceedings (Mahnverfahren) for recovery of consumer credit.[5] As many as 83 % of the recipients of default summonses reported an income drop or extraordinary financial burdens during the period of the credit. The distribution of reasons given was:

Unemployment[6]	58 %
Accident	9 %
Short-time work	3 %
Wife stopped work because of child	8 %
Debtor stopped work because of child	4 %
Illness	27 %
Strike	1 %
Loss of overtime hours	12 %
Dependents' illness, incurring costs	6 %
Unanticipated costs of child's education	2 %
Substantial rise in living costs	28 %
Costs ensuing from divorce	18 %
Supplementary taxes	9 %
Expiry of surety	3 %

---

[5] Holzcheck - Hörmann - Daviter 1982 p. 339.

[6] In a study of cases where credit institutes had withdrawn a credit prematurely because of payment delay, the debtor's unemployment was found to a corresponding extent to be the most important cause of the delay. Among the cases where the social causes of the delay were known to the lender, there was unemployment in 56 % of the cases, see Holzscheck - Hörmann - Daviter 1982 p. 284.

Other family reasons (children, death, etc.)	7 %
Other private reasons (removal, loss of liberty)	7 %
Other job-related reasons (employer's bankruptcy, incapacity for work, change of workplace)	11 %
Other reasons (price rises, other debt)	4 %

The high percentages are explained by the fact that several events of the types mentioned often contributed to the household's economic collapse.[7]

While these observations cannot be transferred directly to present Nordic reality, there are good reasons for assuming that the situation does not differ significantly from that in other countries. The credit card explosion can, however, in the Nordic countries as elsewhere, be imagined to entail an increase in the proportion of cases where payment difficulties have arisen as a consequence of "voluntary" overindebtedness.

3. SOLUTIONS AND PROPOSALS OUTSIDE THE NORDIC COUNTRIES

3.1 Introduction

The problems treated in the present section are, as noted, international. On the one hand, the principle of each person being responsible for his ability to pay is a traditional basis of many systems of private law. On the other hand, studies carried out in many developed market economies indicate what is untenable in such a basis by showing how deficient ability to pay follows in the majority of cases from events over which the debtor has little control. In other words, the same conflict - a need of debtor protection against social force majeure, which cannot be met within the framework of traditional views on the debtor's obligations - is found in many legal systems. It is therefore of interest to see whether there has been an attempt in other (non-Nordic) legal systems to develop debtor protection in contract law for the case

[7] Hörmann - Holzcheck 1983 p. 465.

in question, and what methods have been chosen for this. The material lends itself, from a Nordic point of view, to use in two lines of reasoning, connected with the following questions:

(i) Has it been considered, and on what grounds, *legally possible* to develop *de lege lata* principles of the type dealt with here in legal systems that resemble the Nordic one? The question is of interest mainly in view of the possibilities of transferring the relevant reasoning to a Nordic legal environment.

(ii) Have there been *legislative* attempts to solve the problem in other countries? The material is intended chiefly to illustrate to what extent such a regulation is *socially possible*.

3.2 Re-interpretation of traditional principles

In *West Germany Udo Reifner* has attempted to re-interpret - using what he terms *social interpretation* - the formal regulations of the Bürgerliches Gesetzbuch in such a way that they can be used to generate a general principle for mitigation of sanctions regarding delayed payment of a consumer credit.

Reifner maintains that in the pertinent cases, where the social conditions of the debtor's obligation to perform become relevant, failure to pay, which is a necessary consequence of the debtor's embarrassment, does not express any special attitude on his part. According to the social interpretation advocated, the failure consists simply of the fact that no income over which the debtor has control has been received to cover his payment obligation. If the debtor fails to pay in time because of a subsequent need caused by unemployment, short-time work, illness, strike or further drains on his means available for consumption, he should thus not be considered to have rendered himself liable to *culpa* in the sense intended in sec. 276 of the BGB. This implies that the debtor in such a situation *is not in arrears* according to sec. 285 of the BGB and consequently cannot be charged with delay sanctions.

From the rules of the BGB also follow some delimitations

of the principle just mentioned:[8]

- If the relevant cause of the payment difficulties is brought about by the debtor, deliberately or through culpa, he should be liable.

- If the event was foreseeable when the contract was entered into, the debtor should be liable similarly.

- The debtor should do what he can to avert the damage, e.g. by offering part performance, and should in such a way that may be required of him use for payment other property at his disposal.

In certain cases it would also be possible according to Reifner to apply the provisions on impossibility (sec. 323-325 of the BGB). This would be possible either where the debtor has suffered lasting incapacity for work or when the whole contract period - at least, however, a time corresponding to two part performances by the debtor[9] - has elapsed. If the impossibility cannot be ascribed to the debtor as deliberate action or culpa he is only obliged to make over to the counter-party the unjust enrichment he has gained through being liberated from his obligation, i.e. as a rule to return the consumer goods purchased.[10]

According to Reifner these principles find expression in the actual consumer credit *contract*: when one applies for credit the lender requires particulars of the applicant's employer and salary on the one hand and of his household and expenses on the other. An *interpretation* of the contract based on an understanding of social context leads to a determination of the debtor's repayment obligation, according to which payment must be made from the income *available to the debtor* over and above his "fixed" expenditure.[11]

In the last analysis it is a matter of breaking through the

---

[8] Reifner 1979 p. 321.

[9] This condition is taken from hire-purchase law.

[10] See Reifner 1979 p. 321 ff.

[11] Reifner 1980 p. 377 ff.

"monetary veil" between consumption and work. From the consumer's point of view the prevailing principle "you've got to have money" is the same as "you've got to have a salary". This shows that the prevailing legal view, which does not recognize the existence of any right to work, is attempting wrongly to use on consumer credits a standard of measurement loaned from the sphere of capital.[12]

Reifner's proposal for re-interpretation has not been accorded an overwhelmingly positive reception in West German legal writing. Some authors ignore it while others reject it as foreign to the system of the BGB.[13] Yet there are also more positive voices. Thus, in the alternative commentary to the BGB, *Roland Dubischar*, for example, states in a reference to Reifner that there is reason, at least regarding consumer credits, to think over the premise "you've got to have money".[14] *Günter Hörmann*, who points out that Reifner's empirical assumptions have proved correct, also supports the latter's notions while expressing uncertainty concerning the possibilities of realizing them *de lege lata*.[15]

As a more moderate solution, *Dieter Medicus* has later proposed the use of the doctrine of the 'basis of the transaction' (Geschäftsgrundlage) to adapt the contract to some changes in the situation of the debtor. Expectations regarding the debtor's future income could be viewed as a basis of the transaction, which would make it possible to take into account such changes in his income situation that would entail its being 'too much to ask'[16] of the

---

[12] Reifner 1980 p. 375.

[13] See for more detail Hörmann 1987 p. 84.

[14] BGB-Kommentar p. 295, see also Brüggemeier in BGB-Kommentar p. 102.

[15] Hörmann 1987 p. 87, 456. As a further legal argument he adduces a decision of the Bundesgerichtshof, where the court referred to "the legal figure 'jeopardization of economic existence'" (p. 87).

[16] The terms *Geschäftsgrundlage* and *unzumutbar* are translated here in the same ways as in Zweigert - Kötz 1987 p. 213 f.

debtor to bind him to the contract in unmodified form. The doctrine implies that the content of a contract can be adapted to the changed circumstances.[17]

The West German discussion has been presented here at some length since it is here that the debate on the effect of changes in the debtor's economic and social situation on his obligation to perform has been most elaborated. Yet concrete examples from other countries could certainly be given too, where various general principles are used for ascribing legal relevance to such changes.[18]

3.3 Statutes and draft bills

In his analysis of the problems of consumer credit law, *Udo Reifner* has not been content to propose a re-interpretation of the BGB: his work also contains a detailed proposal for a statute including a provision on social force majeure.[19] However, no such legal rule has come into *West German* law, even though there has been some discussion on the need of a rule of this kind.

Particular mention may be made here of the discussion at the 53rd German Jurists' Day. A proposal had been laid before this forum to recommend the introduction of a rule into sec. 609a of the BGB to the effect that a debtor raising credit for personal use should not be liable for his incapacity to repay the debt in time if he has lost the part of his income available for him entirely or

---

[17] Medicus 1988 p. 503 ff.

[18] As just one example might be mentioned an *English* case where a woman who had concluded a contract to sell her house had subsequently suffered compound social force majeure: her leg had been amputated as a result of an accident, she had become pregnant and her husband went bankrupt and ended up in prison. The question was whether the purchaser of the house could obtain a decision on specific performance for the handing over of what had been sold. Even though specific performance for the sale of land is normally granted, the court refused to do so in this case since the consequence would be unjust against the vendor. The case, Patel v. Ali [1984] 1 All E.R. 978, is mentioned in Collins 1986 p. 198.

[19] Reifner 1979 p. 432.

partly because of circumstances such as unemployment, short-time work, illness, accident or industrial conflict.[20] The proposal was rejected after a vote at the Jurists' Day.[21]

French law on the other hand contains an express statutory rule connected with social force majeure. Article 1244 of the Code Civil has long afforded the possibility in certain cases of requiring from a court a maximum of one year's deferment of payment (*délai de grâce*). The new Consumer Credit Act refers to this rule and specifies that such deferment may be considered specially where the debtor has been dismissed from his employment.[22] When deferment is granted, the court can order that no interest shall accrue on the loan during the period of grace. The maximum period of grace is, after a new amendment,[23] two years.

The rules on *délai de grâce* are assumed to have little practical significance, which may be a result of the procedural threshold entailed by the link with a court hearing.[24]

The *British* Consumer Credit Act also gives the judge wide powers to modify an agreed repayment schedule.[25]

[20] The text of the proposal is given in ZERP Mat 3 p. 57. The proposal is motivated, with reference *inter alia* to Reifner, by Reiner Huhs in Verhandlungen des 53. Deutschen Juristentages p. K 211 ff.

[21] See Verhandlungen des 53. Deutschen Juristentages p. K 247, K 251.

[22] Loi no. 78-22 du 10 Janvier 1978, sec. 8.

[23] Loi no. 85-1097 du 11 Octobre 1985. See here e.g. European Consumer Law Journal 1986 p. 58 f.

[24] Hörmann 1987 p. 457.

[25] The Consumer Credit Act, 1974, sec. 129(2)a.

4. A GENERAL PRINCIPLE OF SOCIAL FORCE MAJEURE

4.1 Arguments for a "switching of principles"

The development of a principle by which the debtor's liability should be reduced if he for reasons of unemployment, illness or other corresponding circumstance is incapable of performing, has been inhibited by the principle that each person is responsible for his ability to pay. The circumstance that the debtor has got into payment difficulties through no fault of his own has, in the light of this principle, not traditionally been seen as a ground for exemption.

This tradition has also meant that it has been possible in the doctrine to stamp the new special rules on social force majeure that have entered concrete legislation as exceptional ones without broader scope.[26] Yet it has been impossible to preserve entirely the notion that events connected with the debtor's person should be irrelevant in the general principles concerning the consequences of changed circumstances.[27]

Any elevation of the doctrine of social force majeure to a general principle would thus appear clearly as a "switching of

---

[26] Thus in Finnish law e.g. Aurejärvi 1988 p. 71, where sec. 11 of the Act on Interest is stated to be a limited exceptional provision, and Taxell 1972 p. 227, who points out that sec. 2 of the Act on Hire-Purchase, as an exception from accepted rules of avoidance, cannot be applied analogously.

[27] When treating the question of impossibility as a precondition for exemption from liability, the "grand old man" of Finnish contract law, Lars Erik Taxell, 1972 p. 320, states for example that "Impossibility may depend on circumstances relating to the person of the debtor, e.g. *illness and accident*. If the contract requires a personal contribution from the debtor, it would not be correct towards him in such situations to insist upon full compensation liability. *To a certain extent*, but not generally, *this can also apply in some cases where the contract does not necessarily have to be fulfilled by the debtor in person*. The situations envisaged here usually concern a culpa liability on the part of the debtor... - illness and accident mean absence of culpa and thus give exemption from compensation liability" (translated here; present author's italics).

principles", in Nordic law, too. As shown already in Chapter VI several good reasons may be adduced for such a "switching of principles" in a more need-oriented direction. It has been noted in several contexts that such a development has specially favourable prospects in matters of regulation of subsequent needs. It emerges from the symptomatic criticism in Chapter V that contract legislation has been, and is being, successively extended with rules that admit mitigation of sanctions in such cases. The points of departure that have been confirmed in this legislation have also been observed to some extent in the practice relating to the general clauses of consumer law. As the regulations and the practice mentioned exhibit considerable *internal consistency*, it is easy to maintain that they are expressions of a new, growing *general principle*, which can also be cited outside the scope of the special rules just mentioned. In addition, one may refer to the fact that these rules, as already stated, are consistent with the general welfare-state ideology that characterizes our society.

4.2 Terminology

We have already used in several contexts the expression *social force majeure* as a collective term for the special rules on mitigation of sanctions in the case of subsequent needs.[28]

This term, which in Chapter V was used in the description of the concrete legal material, may be criticized as misleading. By force majeure is traditionally meant "a far-reaching and infrequent occurrence, coming from outside and entailing an insuperable obstacle to the debtor's performance",[29] "an overwhelming occur-

---

[28] See e.g. the Swedish report on reform of the rules on interest, SOU 1985:11, which explicitly states that a proposed Swedish rule on adjustment of interest - now enacted - and also sec. 11 of the Finnish Act on Interest apply to "what is normally termed social force majeure" (p. 119, see also p. 181). The term has earlier been used e.g. in Wilhelmsson 1984 p. 81 f. In addition, as mentioned earlier, it has also come into use in the application of the general clauses of consumer law (see above 8.2.iv).

[29] Rodhe 1956 p. 355.

rence, an infrequent event of an exceptional nature coming from outside".[30] Neither unemployment nor illness are "infrequent" or "of exceptional nature". Nor can illness always be described as "coming from outside". For this reason, the original of the present work uses the term "socialt prestationshinder" ("social obstacle to performance"). This term has now become accepted in Nordic discourse also.[31]

The change of term was not, however, intended to have any necessary consequences as to content that might, for example, prevent those developing the new doctrine from using, where possible, analogies from the general doctrine of force majeure. For this reason, and since "social obstacle to performance" is linguistically inconvenient, the term "social force majeure" has been retained in this English version even though it is misleading in the way noted above.

4.3 The scope of the doctrine

We have seen that the special provisions on mitigation of sanctions which in Nordic law could form a main basis of the principle of social force majeure have in many respects a limited scope. A development of a *general* principle of social force majeure involves being able to accord relevance to the debtor's subsequent needs even outside the direct scope of these provisions. A general principle could be applied not merely to such claims as are covered by the relevant sections of the legislation but also to other contract-law claims, and perhaps even to claims based on other parts of the law of obligations, too.

However, this does not preclude giving the principle certain limitations that relate to the scope of the special provisions on mitigation of sanctions. Hence the scope of application of the principle can be discussed in the following respects, among others:

---

[30] Taxell 1972 p. 120.

[31] See in particular the new investigation of social obstacles to performance, by Bärlund 1990.

(i) *The parties*. Some of the special rules on mitigation of sanctions affect only consumer relationships, and the cases where the concept of social force majeure has been used in the application of general clauses have also been consumer-law cases. Obviously, the *core area* for the principle of social force majeure must be within consumer law. However, this does not prevent one from attempting, in accordance with what has been said earlier, to seek to plead the principle outside this area, too.

The events one has wished to consider in various contexts as social obstacles to performance - unemployment, illness, etc. - are such as can affect individuals. When the principle of social force majeure is generalized outside the framework of consumer law the question becomes primarily one of an extension to other situations where individual persons are adversely affected by payment difficulties. It is precisely regarding such persons that the principle "you've got to have money" assumes the form "you've got to have a salary"[32] - a principle which, given today's social reality, is hard to maintain.

In accordance with the statements in Chapter VI above it is, moreover, obvious that a general principle of social force majeure must be grounded mainly in the notion that enterprises and other institutions should bear a social responsibility. In individual cases, claims that one should take social force majeure into account can certainly be based also on ideas of owners' social responsibility, on solidarity when accidents occur or on responsibility in a social community. In the working out of a more detailed principle of social force majeure there is nevertheless good reason to place the central relation in the foreground.

This implies that, from now on, the presentation will concern chiefly *private persons* as debtors *in relation to enterprises*, organizations and public bodies. However, this does not prevent one from advocating *in casu*, where necessary, the application of corresponding principles to relationships between private persons or, conceivably, from seeking support from analogies

---

[32] Reifner 1980 p. 375.

taken from the doctrine described here when developing protection of small enterprises. In the latter case, however, the relevant events must obviously differ from those where the debtor is a private person.

(ii) *Monetary obligations and obligations in natura*. Both the special legal provisions considered in Chapter V and the fairness decisions that have been mentioned concern cases where the debtor owes money. In relations between private persons and enterprises, the individual's obligation is in the majority of cases a monetary one. The centre of gravity of the principle of social force majeure must therefore, both in practice and in theory, lie upon monetary obligations.

Nevertheless, this should not exclude attempts to apply the principle to obligations *in natura*, too. Traditionally, rules concerning the debtor's liability have been more severe against monetary debtors than against other debtors. To the extent one accepts social force majeure as - in a wide sense - a ground for exemption in connection with monetary obligations, it is obvious that one must also, to at least the same extent, do the same in connection with obligations in natura. Another thing is that the relevance and consequences of social force majeure are not necessarily always the same for the different forms of obligation. Hence in the case of monetary obligations social force majeure often appears as an exception to a more or less strict liability, while for obligations in natura it may be conceivable to understand social force majeure as a sign of the absence of culpa.

4.4 Mandatory law?

The concrete substantive principles in the contract law of the Western legal systems are in the majority of cases non-mandatory in character, even though mandatory (peremptory) principles exist also. Somebody might therefore argue that, even if one would have to accept a principle of social force majeure, it would, in theory at least, be non-mandatory (dispositive) and hence could be excluded by agreement.

Yet on such a basis alone, it is impossible to resolve the question of the relationship between the terms of a contract and the principle of social force majeure. For one thing the extension of the possibilities of fairness assessments in contract law has to some extent erased the clear borderline between mandatory and non-mandatory law: particularly in cases where the dispositive rules may be said to contain a legal-political value judgment, which is definitely true of the principle of social force majeure, they have been viewed in modern Nordic legal writing as "semi-peremptory"[33] rules which greatly influence the interpretation as well as the adjustment of contracts. Secondly, the significance of the principle treated here depends greatly on *what type* of contract term is required for the principle to be disregarded. Is a specific term required for excluding application of the principle, or does it also give way to general terms on the period of duration of the contract, its binding nature, etc.? It is obvious that the question of the relationship between the principle of social force majeure and the content of the contract must be treated with more sophistication. Different kinds of contract terms may have different significance.

(i) *General terms on the obligation to perform, the duration of the contract, etc.* In the principles concerning standard form contracts, the assumption in the Nordic countries has been that departures from non-mandatory law to the disadvantage of the counter-party should be clearly stated in the standardized terms. This principle is considered to apply in attenuated form to all contracts: in the interpretation of contracts in general a result should be sought that corresponds as well as possible to what follows from dispositive law.[34] The more the non-mandatory rules express legal-political evaluations considered to be acceptable in the legal order, the greater weight they should be accorded.

Such considerations can be used to reinforce the normative

---

[33] See e.g. Ramberg 1986 p. 37.

[34] See for further details the large work on the interpretation of contracts by Huser 1983 p. 539 ff.

significance of the principle of social force majeure. If for example the debtor has undertaken merely to perform at a certain point in time, it should not yet follow from this contract - even if the principle of social force majeure would be considered dispositive - that the time for performance could not be postponed on the ground of social force majeure. And further: if the debtor has in a long-term contract agreed on a certain period of duration, this should not prevent him - when conditions for this obtain - from terminating the contract prematurely with reference to social force majeure. In such cases one could well maintain that the question of the effect of social force majeure had been left open in the contract. The contract could therefore be *supplemented* with this principle.[35]

(ii) *Specific clauses on social force majeure*. The "switching of principles" goes a step further if one were to assume that not even specific clauses on the effect of social force majeure take precedence over the general principle expounded here. Even if one would not like to go as far as to declare openly that the principle of social force majeure is mandatory, the same result can, however, always be achieved by adjusting the contract with the support of the contract-law general clause in sec. 36 of the Contract Act, or of some other corresponding general clause. The dispositive ("semi-peremptory") principle can here be adduced as a basis for the assessment of fairness.

In practice the question is of scant significance: such clauses are certainly, today at least, extremely rare in contract practice.

---

[35] The borderline between interpretation and supplementation is well known to be diffuse, see e.g. Huser 1983 p. 127.

5. THE PREREQUISITES OF SOCIAL FORCE MAJEURE

5.1 Introduction

A more accurate hammering out of the new need-oriented ideas to form a special principle presupposes the specification of the prerequisites for the application of this principle and an analysis of its legal consequences.

In the light of the concrete legal material presented above in Chapter V, and of the general principles on the effects of force majeure etc., it is possible to develop fairly precisely for Finnish law the necessary conditions that should be met for a debtor to be permitted to plead social force majeure.

Four prerequisites can be distinguished. A relevant social obstacle to performance obtains, if (i) the debtor has been hit by a particular *occurrence*, which occurrence (ii) has in a certain way *caused* his delay in payment and this course of events (iii) *could not be foreseen* by the debtor and (iv) it occurred through *no fault* of the debtor.

As will emerge from, *inter alia*, the references to *Udo Reifner*'s analysis in what follows, these conditions, even if found through analysis based on national symptomatic criticism, are hardly typically Nordic; they reflect questions one is forced to decide about wherever one wishes to enter a debate on the regulation of social force majeure.

5.2 Relevant occurrences

The occurrences considered as relevant in the concrete legal material on mitigation of sanctions were listed above in Chapter V, section 7.3.ii. The legislation notes particularly the debtor's illness and unemployment. In those of the Consumer Ombudsman's decisions that refer to social force majeure, the Ombudsman has also stressed precisely these circumstances. In addition to them, however, he mentions other special circumstances which, arising through no fault of the debtor's, negatively affect his payment ability. This formulation appears to strike home at what is important in the description of the occurrences that ought to be able to constitute social force majeure. In other words, there should have been a *particular occurrence* that has led to the debtor's difficulties: if for example the difficulties have arisen because the debtor has overestimated his financial strength and become overindebted for this reason, social force majeure should not obtain.[36] In addition, this particular occurrence should clearly be of such a nature that it can *affect the debtor's payment ability* negatively, as a rule either because his income sinks or because his expenditure rises.

There is little to be gained at this stage by listing further criteria for the occurrences that may be relevant. In the same way that "one cannot clearly separate the events that constitute force majeure"[37], one should not seek any firm demarcation of the occurrences relevant to social force majeure. Detailed exemplification is enough for the needs of legal practice, without risking the rigidity an "exhaustive" definition could entail.

Udo Reifner also leaves his delimitation of relevant occurrences open. Alongside certain occurrences listed he also mentions that *new charges upon the debtor's funds for consumption* may be relevant. Their relevance must, however, be assessed *in casu*, with consideration of how clear the social nature and statistical necessity of the actual occurrences appear in reality and can for this reason be ascribed to the creditor's sphere of liability.[38]

Using the concrete legal material, the examples of relevant occurrences can be grouped as follows:

(i) *Changes in the debtor's state of health*. The debtor's illness and other physical injury affecting him afford perhaps the most typical example of an occurrence that can be relevant here.

---

[36] See also on the interpretation of the concrete legal material Wilhelmsson - Sevón 1983 p. 146 and OLJ 16/1985 p. 212.

[37] Taxell 1972 p. 125.

[38] Reifner 1979 p. 327.

Both physical and mental illness should naturally be adducible.

(ii) *Changes in the debtor's work situation.* The other type example of a relevant occurrence mentioned in the legislation is the debtor's unemployment. It is self-evident that other comparable circumstances in the field of working life, such as short-time and reduced wages and the disappearance of customary possibilities of overtime work, should be recognized as relevant to the extent that the other conditions for social force majeure are met. A reduction in income resulting from a lockout should also meet the requirements for an occurrence to be relevant. The same is true of a strike.[39] The situation is, however, complicated here by the fact that such a reduction of income always depends to some extent upon the employee's own action; this aspect is treated in more detail below.

If the debtor in question is a private trader, it is possible that a relevant reduction in income may be caused by other factors such as his bankruptcy,[40] a significant reduction in new orders, or other similar circumstances that affect his work situation in a negative manner.

(iii) *Changes in the debtor's housing situation.* The particular interest in a party's housing situation that appears in connection with many need-oriented regulations in the law of obligations may also be ascribed weight in social-force-majeure reasoning. A debtor whose tenancy has been terminated or who for some other reason has lost his dwelling can for this reason incur such new financial burdens - e.g. through being forced to rent new, more expensive housing or even to buy an apartment or a house while meeting the costs of a temporary residence and of moving - that the changes in his housing situation could very well be considered as an acceptable ground for pleading social force

---

[39] See also Reifner 1979 p. 326 f.

[40] OLJ 16/1985 p. 212 f.

majeure.[41]

(iv) *Changes in the debtor's family circumstances.* Different kinds of change in the debtor's family circumstances and in relation to persons close to him in general can lead both to increases in his outgoings and reductions in his "income" in the sense of available means. As an occurrence which is relevant with respect to the principle of social force majeure, mention has therefore been made of the debtor's divorce, for example, and the death of a family member with whom the debtor has had a shared economy.[42] If a family member or other person close to the debtor suffers illness or accident, this could also be brought in as an occurrence that can constitute social force majeure, to the extent the occurrence leads to a reduction in the household income or an increase in its expenses.[43]

If the illness and death of a member of the debtor's household can represent a relevant occurrence it is, further, hard to see that the unemployment or unanticipated reduction in income of such a person could not be adduced in the debtor's favour.

Lastly, reference may be made to the criterion for poor economic strength noted in connection with adjustment of damages: the debtor's maintenance burden. The advent of a new maintenance obligation could well be conceived to represent an occurrence of the type that can be relevant in the present connection.

(v) *Changes in the debtor's property circumstances.* As mentioned in the Introduction, the relevant occurrence should be such that it can entail a reduction in the debtor's income or an increase in his expenses. As we have seen above, the concrete

---

[41] See also corresponding statements regarding hire-purchase in Hakulinen - Raninen 1968 p. 80 and regarding insurance in ÖLJ 16/1985 p. 212.

[42] Thus the Swedish report SOU 1985:11 p. 182.

[43] See as regards hire-purchase Eklund - Nordström 1957 p. 111 and also Hakulinen - Raninen 1968 p. 80, who, among the relevant outgoings, also mention the help one feels obliged to give a close relative or friend who has suffered an accident.

examples of social force majeure that can be noted on the basis of the concrete legal material in Chapter V are also of this type. There is no example to show that reduction in the debtor's property would have been accorded relevance in the present connection.[44] It is for this reason harder to maintain, on the basis of the symptomatic criticism, that an event that merely leads to a reduction in the value of the debtor's property and the income associated with this should as such be able to constitute social force majeure. The empirical and theoretical reasons - the untenable nature of the phrase "you've got to have a salary" - that support the principle of social force majeure hardly justify such an extension of its scope, either.

One could nevertheless imagine *individual cases* where it would appear very natural to grant the debtor the right to plead social force majeure in the case of a change in his property circumstances. If for example a person without other source of income than a small pension arranges a consumer credit and plans to repay this by realizing his small property, and he then loses this e.g. through some unfortunate occurrence or through the company in which he had invested his savings going bankrupt, then one would be tempted to give him the right to plead this as social force majeure.

5.3 *The requirement on causal connection*

The circumstance that a general force-majeure event occurs does not necessarily lead to one being able to plead the legal consequences of force majeure. It is required that the event has been the cause of the inability to perform.[45]

A corresponding requirement that there should be a causal connection would also appear natural in a principle of social force

---

[44] Divorce and homelessness, and so on, can indeed lead to or be connected with changes in a party's property circumstances; as has emerged, however, it is, rather, the increased outgoings caused by these occurrences that have been the focus of attention.

[45] See e.g. Taxell 1972 p. 120.

majeure. An occurrence of the kind mentioned earlier could not be pleaded as social force majeure if the occurrence had not *caused* the debtor's performance difficulties.

In the concrete legal material this requirement as to causal connection has been formulated in different ways in different statutes. In some, one operates with a three-link chain of causality: particular event --> payment difficulties --> delay,[46] while in others the chain is shorter: particular event --> delay.[47] In the majority of cases these formulations lead to the same result. The most important difference is obviously where an occurrence of the character mentioned has not created payment difficulties in an economic sense but only entailed a *physical obstacle* to payment. One example is the case where the debtor is confined to bed by sudden illness so that he is prevented from making the payment in time. The shorter of the two causal chains obviously includes such a situation while the longer, with payment difficulties as a middle link, appears to leave out these cases.[48] The material used as the basis for creating the principle of social force majeure has concentrated chiefly on the question of the effect of economic obstacles to performance.[49] The core of the principle of social force majeure obviously ought to cover situations where a relevant occurrence has led to such worsening in the debtor's *economic situation* that his possibilities of performing have thereby been limited. Yet this does not prevent the principle here described from being applied *mutatis mutandis* to some extent even in cases where a relevant occurrence physically prevents the debtor from performing.

When judging whether a sufficient causal connection of the

---

[46] Thus e.g. sec. 2 and 11 of the Act on Hire-Purchase, and sec. 11 of the Act on Interest.

[47] Thus e.g. Ch. 7, sec. 16 of the Consumer Protection Act.

[48] Cf., however, the report OLJ 16/1985 p. 211 f., where such a formulation is *interpreted* to cover physical obstacles, too.

[49] See also the definition of relevant occurrence above, where the focus is upon the possibilities of the event to affect the debtor's ability to pay.

kind described above should be considered to exist, the most important question becomes the degree of financial embarrassment the occurrence must cause the debtor for him to be considered to have an acceptable reason for his non-performance. In the *travaux préparatoires* to the relevant special provisions, there are passages which show that the economic difficulties need not be so great that the debtor can be described as unable to pay. According to the *travaux préparatoires* to the Act on Interest, there may be adjustment, as already mentioned, "as soon as the debtor has been unable to pay the debt punctually without jeopardizing his reasonable housing and other living conditions".[50] Using an analogous term from the Nordic general principles on relative obstacles to performance, one could perhaps speak of a "personal limit to sacrifice",[51] below which the debtor is not obliged to lower his living standard for the purpose of making the performance possible.[52]

Accepting this implies that the effect of a social-force-majeure occurrence depends greatly on the debtor's economic standing in other respects. If a debtor afflicted by illness or unemployment has property that can be used for completing his performance without this jeopardizing his reasonable housing and other living conditions, he cannot plead social force majeure. In this respect the principle is a clearly need-oriented one in the sense used in the present work. The principle protects only the *debtor with limited means*.

---

[50] Reg.prop. 109/1981 p. 23.

[51] The Nordic principles on relative obstacles to performance cover situations where a party could in theory fulfill a contract but this would involve "disproportionately large efforts or expenses". It is asserted that a party is not obliged to meet obligations however burdensome, but that a "limit to sacrifice" can be drawn somewhere, see e.g. Taxell 1972 p. 126.

[52] The same purpose underlies Reifner's (1980 p. 378) interpretation of the debtor's payment obligation, according to which it should cover only the income *available*.

5.4 *The requirement on unforeseeability*

The legal effect of ordinary force majeure is normally not considered to come into play if a party anticipated or could anticipate the event in question when the contract was entered into.[53] A corresponding limitation would obviously be natural in the principle of social force majeure also.[54]

It should be noted here that heavy emphasis on the unforeseeability criterion can easily weaken the significance of a principle of social force majeure. This is especially true if one posits already more abstract foreseeability as an obstacle to adducing the principle. For example, an employee in an economic sector in crisis could never obtain support from this social instrument. One should not normally, therefore, if wishing to give the principle of social force majeure some practical significance, require that the debtor *ought* to be able to foresee events into which he has no insight. As a rule one should consider only factual knowledge;[55] the debtor should not be obliged to consider the risk that, e.g., international economic developments may render him unemployed in the future.

5.5 *The requirement on absence of fault*

In the special provisions on mitigation of sanctions in the concrete legal material it is required that the debtor has got into payment difficulties chiefly through no fault of his own. This requirement can more or less self-evidently be generalized to apply

---

[53] Taxell 1972 p. 120 f.

[54] Reifner 1979 p. 321, as mentioned earlier, in his model also starts from the notion that the debtor should bear responsibility if the unfortunate occurrence was foreseeable at the time when the contract was concluded.

[55] In this connection, the *travaux préparatoires* to Ch. 7, sec. 16 of the Consumer Protection Act also, quite correctly, speak about the debtor having been "aware" that an obstacle will arise. See Reg.prop. 88/1985 p. 32.

to the principle of social force majeure in general. If the payment difficulties are caused mainly by the fault of the debtor - he has for example resigned from his job without cause and thereby become unemployed - he would not be able to plead social force majeure.[56]

This apparently clear rule would not, however, if taken over-literally, lead to acceptable results in all situations. A good example here is divorce, which was mentioned as one alternative when relevant occurrences were described. It is obvious that one ought to be able to refer also to a divorce that has come about with the debtor's consent, even though strictly speaking one can in this case say that his payment difficulties caused by the divorce are self-inflicted. After all, the underlying cause of the divorce need not be ascribable to the debtor. And even were this the case it is hardly suitable to make the issue of who is responsible for a divorce a relevant question of dispute in contract-law proceedings between one of the spouses and an outsider, the creditor.

Another similar example is the debtor's participation in a strike. Here, too, the payment difficulties result from a measure that the debtor undertakes voluntarily. However, at least in cases where the strike has been called by an organization to which the debtor belongs and whose decisions he cannot influence, the voluntary character is in practice more theoretical than actual. In other cases also, the situation is often that the employee's solidarity with workmates morally obliges him to take part in the strike. For these reasons, the requirement that the payment difficulties should have arisen mainly through no fault of the debtor's ought not to prevent the debtor from pleading a strike as social force majeure.[57]

Lastly, there is reason to maintain that the requirement on absence of fault does not necessarily refer merely to the question of how the payment difficulties have arisen. The debtor can naturally also be imagined to have a general obligation to attempt to

[56] In the same vein for West German law Reifner 1979 p. 321.

[57] See also Reifner 1979 p. 326 f.

overcome these difficulties. If, for example, after becoming unemployed, he refuses for no good reason to accept new employment,[58] this could lead to the loss of his right to plead social force majeure in respect of the time after which the new employment would have led to improvement in his ability to pay.

6. LEGAL CONSEQUENCES OF SOCIAL FORCE MAJEURE

6.1 General

6.1.1 Possible legal consequences

The general concept of force majeure has as a rule been used in connection with certain particular consequences of breach of contract. It is used primarily in relation to the regulation of a party's liability in damages: force majeure limits a possibly strict liability. In addition, the principle has been adduced e.g. to prolong the time of performance or to limit the obligation to pay penal interest. In contract practice, it naturally happens that other legal consequences are also linked with force majeure.

The legal consequences of social force majeure that emerge from the special provisions on mitigation of sanctions in the concrete legal material are partially of a different kind. Here, too, reduction of penal interest and damages is possible; in addition to this, social force majeure can lead to a limitation of the possibilities of claiming any special sanction for delayed payment agreed upon by the parties. What is common to both these provisions and the general principles of force majeure is that the occurrence in question leads to a mitigation of the sanctions connected with the debtor's delay. The selection of the consequences particularly noted in the concrete legal material appears, however, not to have been made on any uniform and rational principle. It therefore seems reasonable, as a kind of *starting hypothesis*, to generalize:

---

[58] Reifner 1979 p. 328 mentions culpable neglect to resume work.

social force majeure may be conceived of as leading to mitigation of *all* the sanctions that may be aimed against the debtor because of delay. In relation to each type of sanction one can then discuss in more detail how far one should modify this starting point and/or introduce special conditions for pleading social force majeure.

The analysis of the effect of social force majeure should not, however, be limited to cases where the debtor claims *mitigation of sanctions*. As we saw earlier, there also occur in the law of obligations need-oriented regulations and cases in which consideration of the debtor's needs has permitted justification of a *mitigation* of the *burdensome obligation* itself. Hence one may ask how far social force majeure could be imagined to have an effect in mitigating performance also. It emerges from the Consumer Ombudsman's decisions reported in the concrete legal material that one can in a natural manner link at least certain legal consequences with such effects to social force majeure. The debtor could under certain conditions be given the right to withdraw from the contractual relationship. This section concludes with a more detailed discussion of the conditions under which such a solution can appear to be suitable.

6.1.2 Consideration for the counter-party

When assessing the legal consequences of social force majeure, one cannot overlook the interests of the party against whom the principle is pleaded. In the actual provisions underlying the principle, the advantage of this party have been regularly noted to some extent. This becomes evident in different ways in the different provisions.[59]

---

[59] In sec. 11 of the Act on Interest the counter-party is not explicitly mentioned. However, since this provision does not *oblige* the court to undertake adjustment when the requirements in it are fulfilled, but only states that adjustment "*can*" take place, it is obvious that the assessment can also allow some consideration of the fairness of the decision in relation to the counter-party. Under sec. 11 of the Act on Hire-Purchase the bailiff may grant a stay of execution for reasons of social force majeure "insofar as the seller's right to the goods is not jeopardized or

When private debtors plead social force majeure against enterprises or similar organizations or bodies, it is often hardly consonant with a need-oriented attitude to give significant consideration to the advantage of the enterprise since, as we have seen, the enterprise is in most cases able to fragment the social risk. Obviously, the formulation "clearly unreasonable" in Ch. 7, sec. 16 of the Finnish Consumer Protection Act is based on such a line of thought. One should, then, in the cases mentioned here, assume that the question of the effect of social force majeure is to be decided primarily on the basis of the interest of the *debtor* afflicted by the occurrence. Only in *exceptional cases* should consideration of the interests of the enterprise lead to modification of the legal consequences of social force majeure in some respect.

6.2 Mitigation of sanctions

In theory the problem of a debtor's possibility of avoiding sanctions in cases of social force majeure may be solved in two different ways. On the one hand, the question may be regarded as one of the due date of performance: one may imagine that the presence of social force majeure should lead to *postponement of the date of performance*, which in turn would automatically lead to a similar postponement of the creditor's possibilities of claiming sanctions. If the debtor is prevented by social force majeure from performing, he would not fall into arrears at all.[60] On the other hand, one may assume that the debtor who has not been able to perform punctually because of social force majeure is still

---

his right in other respects unreasonably set aside". Lastly, Ch. 7, sec. 16 of the Consumer Protection Act contains a rule that more resembles a general clause: the debtor may plead social force majeure "unless, with consideration to the length of the delay and the other circumstances, this would clearly be unreasonable for the creditor". This rule, too, appears as a limited exception from the main rule stated in the section. That it may be brought in only in special cases is clear from the use here of the exceptional formulation "*clearly* unreasonable".

[60] Thus - on account of sec. 285 of the BGB - Reifner 1979 p. 319 ff.

regarded to be in delay. One then considers only the consequences of the delay: what consequence(s) can be mitigated because of the obstacle in the case?

Even though in contract practice regarding ordinary force majeure one may find clauses according to which force majeure shall lead to postponement of the due date,[61] the effects of force majeure have in Nordic law usually been assessed from the latter of the two angles just mentioned. The special provisions in the concrete legal material on mitigation of sanctions in cases of social force majeure are designed in this way, too: the application of the provisions leads to mitigation of certain sanctions without this affecting determination of the due date itself. In the cases regulated by statute, social force majeure does not lead to postponement of the obligation to perform, merely to mitigation of the sanctions mentioned in the acts.

If one chooses such a differentiated angle of attack, which is one that accords with the analytical view of the legal relationships of private law prevailing in the Nordic countries, one must in the development of the general principle of social force majeure analyse the effect of such an obstacle to performance individually for each delay sanction. This analysis is also required by the fact that the *general* conditions for the different sanctions vary.[62]

What has been said is illustrated here with the help of some considerations regarding the two most important sanctions on breach of contract: damages and avoidance. It should not, however, be understood from this that the principle of social force majeure could not be used in the assessment of the prerequisites for other sanctions.

As stated earlier, ordinary force majeure has been understood primarily as a ground for liberating the debtor from *liability*

---

[61] See e.g. Hellner 1984 p. 246.

[62] The right to claim penal interest, and the right to claim other sanctions, arise, for example, in many cases at different times in Finnish law; see Wilhelmsson - Sevón 1983 p. 97 f.

in damages.[63] Considering the rationale of the special provisions on mitigation of sanctions - to protect the debtor against supplementary burdens in cases of certain unfortunate occurrences - it should be easy to justify social force majeure, too, having this legal consequence.

Nationally, the concrete legal material affords a good point of departure for reasoning in this manner. One can refer in particular to sec. 11 of the Act on Interest, which admits adjustment of penal interest in cases of social force majeure. It can be maintained that it is unacceptable, if one is to have some consistency in the system of contract law, for the monetary debtor in a contractual relationship to be relieved of the obligation to pay penal interest on the plea of social force majeure simply to be met with a claim for compensation which perhaps, at least partly, covers the damage that the penal interest would otherwise have covered. And moreover, if one concedes, on the grounds just given, a right for the monetary debtor to plead social force majeure, it is hard to see that one should not concede such a right to a debtor *in natura* as well: as a rule the liability of monetary debtors is judged more strictly than that of debtors in natura, not the other way round.

For the most basic type of contract, sale of goods, which in Finland as in Norway and Sweden is expressly regulated in detail in a new modern statute, the Sale of Goods Act, special problems arise, however. This is because the prerequisites for the buyer's and the seller's liability to pay damages have been specially regulated without social force majeure being mentioned. These problems are not insurmountable, but since their practical significance will decline sharply in the near future, at least as far as Finnish law is concerned, following the intended introduction into the rules on consumer sales in the Consumer Protection Act of an express rule to the effect that social force majeure limits the consumer's liability to pay damages (see above V.7.2.5), the

---

[63] See e.g. Taxell 1972 p. 320 ff.

possible solution models will not be described in detail here.[64]

In the Nordic countries as in many other countries - as also reflected in e.g. the United Nations Convention on Contracts for the International Sale of Goods - the general precondition for *avoidance* of a contract is fundamental breach of contract. If this precondition is fulfilled, avoidance may be resorted to in theory regardless of the cause of the particular breach of contract.

This point of departure - the irrelevance of the cause of the breach - has not been completely adhered to in modern Nordic doctrine, however.[65]

Where the debtor is afflicted by social force majeure, situations can easily arise where a limitation of the right to avoidance would appear justified from a social point of view. Argument in favour of such a limitation could be supported partly by anal-

---

[64] Three strategies for overcoming the apparent conflict between the Sale of Goods Act and the principle of social force majeure, in the latter's favour, are conceivable:

(i) One can maintain that the Act is *not* intended to be exhaustive and hence that the doctrine of social force majeure can be applied as a *supplement* to the Act.

(ii) One could *interpret* the liability rule of the Act which, modelled on the United Nations Convention on Contracts for the International Sale of Goods, rules out liability for impediments beyond the control of the party, which he could not reasonably be expected to have taken into account or to have avoided or overcome, so that social force majeure is perceived as a relevant impediment; thus Bärlund 1990.

(iii) One could employ the general clause of the Sale of Goods Act on adjustment of unreasonable damages as *gateways* for the principle of social force majeure into the rules on damages in the law of sale of goods.

[65] Taxell 1972 p. 226 writes: "In special situations there is reason to consider whether the right to avoidance should be set aside on the ground that the debtor has not negligently caused the breach of contract. Among other things, one can refer to a case where, although the breach is fundamental, avoidance would mean a disproportionately great financial loss for the debtor. As one should in such situations weigh the parties' interests against each other, it may be correct to refuse the creditor the right to avoidance *with reference partly to the financial effects avoidance would have for the debtor* (present author's italics), and partly to the absence of negligence on his part. Here one must also observe whether the creditor's interest can be sufficiently met in other ways than through avoidance." (translated here).

ogies from certain hire-purchase provisions that have as their main purpose to prevent the seller from being able to repossess the goods from the buyer - an effect of avoidance - in a case of social force majeure and thus from inflicting on the buyer the economic loss repossession normally involves.[66]

It should thus be possible to limit the right of avoidance at least in certain cases where it would obviously entail financial loss for the debtor. Some concrete examples may illustrate how this principle could be applied.

A decisive step in the process leading to economic collapse of a debtor afflicted by social force majeure is taken when his creditors begin to *call in* his *debts prematurely*. Where possible, the principle of social force majeure ought to be adducible as protection against such claims.

Once again, such an attempt could in Nordic law be grounded in parallels to the concrete legal material. One can find here, as we have seen, provisions on social force majeure that explicitly strike at contract clauses, according to which future installments become payable immediately upon delay of payment of any installment. Avoidance without support of any specific contract clause can have the same effect as a clause of the kind just mentioned. In such a case, the philosophy underlying the said provisions could be referred to as an argument for limiting the right to avoidance. If in the case of a bank loan (which is not covered by the specific provisions referred to) a debtor gets into arrears regarding a repayment, the circumstance that the delay is due to social force majeure ought to limit the bank's right to avoidance or termination because of the delay.

It is not merely the continuation of credit agreements that is important in a personal economic crisis. Private persons are

---

[66] As another concrete example, reference can be made to a case from the Swedish Market Court, (S)MD 1979:3, where the Court decided upon the fairness of a contract term of a purchase of real estate according to which the seller should have immediate right of avoidance if there was delay in payment of the price. The Court found the term unfair because, among other things, the buyer should as acceptable excuse for the delay be able to plead illness or comparable circumstance.

parties to many other more or less permanent contracts which are of essential significance in their lives in general. Such contractual relationships should be maintained as far as ever possible if one wishes to prevent the effect of creating social drop-outs to which financial problems can often lead. This effect in persons suffering from unemployment, illness and so on comes to light in very painful ways if, for example, electricity, heating and telephone connections are cut off. In contractual relationships regarding such "*necessary*" utilities, a social application of the law would presuppose at least a temporary limitation of the right to avoidance where the debtor can plead social force majeure. A principle of this kind must naturally include a corresponding limitation of the supplier's right to withhold his performance.[67]

6.3 Dissolution of the contractual relationship by the debtor

As mentioned earlier, the possibilities of pleading social force majeure should not be limited to situations where the debtor is claiming mitigation of the sanctions for delay. At least in some cases, one could imagine granting him the right to withdraw entirely from the contract on a plea of social force majeure. As this legal consequence is more radical than mitigation of sanctions, however, it is presumably necessary, in consideration of the counter-party's interests, to accept more often that the desired legal consequence does not follow.

What follows outlines some possibilities of developing the principle of social force majeure in the direction indicated here. Because the concrete legal material where the dissolution of contractual obligations has been associated with social force majeure

[67] In a British report from 1983 the National Consumer Council/Welsh Consumer Council stresses: "We reaffirm our view...that the fuel industries should collect their debts through the courts, like other creditors. Disconnection should be used only as a last resort, on the express authority of the courts, following the debtor's failure to keep to the repayment arrangements imposed upon him by the court" (quoted in ZERP Mat 3 p. 89).

is limited in extent,[68] the presentation will not go much further in concrete terms than the description of the general social right of cancellation and of termination (see above VI.6.3.3).

Contract practice contains general force-majeure clauses that lay down that the contract may be cancelled when an event referred to in the clause has occurred. The question of how far *cancellation of contract* should be considered possible where there are no clauses of this kind has been much discussed in Nordic law,[69] but no completely clear rules have been developed.[70]

One could well maintain that social force majeure ought to constitute a special circumstance of such a kind as should give the person afflicted by the occurrence the right to cancel his contract. At least in cases where the counter-party suffers no appreciable damage from the cancellation, it is hard to see why such a right could not be accepted. Also in cases where the counter-party does suffer damage but can take account of the "risk of cancellations" in his costing, a right of cancellation would scarcely seem objectionable. In certain cases an acceptable compromise can be a requirement that, as a condition for cancellation, the customer should pay the counter-party a certain (limited) compensation.[71]

---

[68] Note, however, that many cases from the other Nordic countries can be mentioned where the Consumer Ombudsman has succeeded in pushing through changes in general conditions of contract to entitle the consumer to terminate the contract in cases of social force majeure. The cases are reported together in Bärlund 1990 p. 44 ff.

[69] See e.g. Lyngsø 1971.

[70] Taxell 1972 p. 165 draws up the following general guideline for the assessment: "A party should be granted the right to annul a contract when he has an actual need of legal protection which may be suitably met by dissolving the contractual relationship. Such a need may normally be said to presuppose *special circumstances* (present author's italics). The right to annulment must not be completely arbitrary. One condition for annulment is that the contractual obligation can be eliminated in such a way that the counter-party's interest in it is sufficiently well catered for." (translated here).

[71] This has been the course adopted in the draft bills on consumer sales and purchase of dwellings recently put forward in Finland, see above V.7.2.5.

Cancellation can take place before the parties have performed. In contracts where the parties are to perform at different points in time, as in credit sales, a party who has already received a performance but whose own performance is still outstanding may possibly find himself in a situation where he wishes to plead social force majeure and return the performance received.[72] Consideration of the counter-party's interests obviously implies, however, that it must be more difficult to gain acceptance of such a *right of return* than for a right of cancellation of the character described above. In cases where, for example, goods sold can be returned to the seller essentially unchanged and undiminished,[73] a right of return associated with social force majeure might be considered.

In long-term contracts, a *right of termination* can make urgent measures of reorganization possible for a debtor afflicted by a crisis. The threshold for such a social right of termination can obviously be set lower than for a social right of cancellation. The cases reported in the concrete legal material that concern the effect of social force majeure on contractual obligation recognize precisely such a right of termination.[74] In line with the above, a right of termination in cases of social force majeure would be particularly easy to justify in cases where no appreciable damage to the counter-party arises because of the termination and in cases where the latter would have been able to cost the "risk of terminations". In other cases it is perhaps necessary to accept the compromise of a limited termination fee.

Even though the concrete legal material on dissolution of contractual obligation for reasons of social force majeure is

---

[72] As was seen earlier, Reifner 1979 p. 321 ff. is prepared to allow a consumer such a right of return.

[73] This expression is used in the regulation of the right of return in home and mail order sales in Ch. 6, sec. 4 of the Consumer Protection Act.

[74] In one such decision reported above (V.8.2.iv) the Consumer Ombudsman maintained that in consumer sales there is a move towards accepting that social force majeure, especially in long-term contracts, entitles the consumer to terminate the contract on payment of reasonable compensation.

limited, the foregoing brief considerations show clearly that the new principle has here a potential for significant new applications. This concluding section demonstrates very concretely the way alternative dogmatics has its effects: from disparate provisions on mitigation of sanctions, a principle can be built up that *makes it legitimate* also to discuss, within legal dogmatics, the debtor's right to withdrawal from a contractual relationship when certain relevant events occur.

CHAPTER VIII

EFFECTS OF AN ALTERNATIVE DOCTRINE

1. INTRODUCTION

1.1 The Problem

On the definition adopted in the introduction to this work, alternative dogmatics is characterized among other things by the belief that through legal-dogmatic activity one can bring about changes in society. An alternative dogmatics is intended to be employed in some sense in legal practice: a purely academic discourse on new principles of law cannot satisfy the proponent of alternative legal dogmatics.

This is not of course to say that the decisive test of the value of a new alternative collection of principles should be the rapidity with which it becomes generally accepted in court practice. The new doctrine may very well have significant practical effects even though this test gives no appreciable result. Assessment of the relation of the new alternative principles to legal practice presupposes a broader perspective.

First, one should be aware that a reorganization of principles in legal dogmatics need not necessarily be employed directly in legal practice. The chain of effect of such new principles is often *indirect*. The new proposals for systematization perhaps first stimulate only academic discussion, which may leave traces in textbooks and teaching, whence the ideas finally flow out into practice. Sometimes the new ideas may be used first in the drafting of statutes: a progressive legislator may gain from the doctrine both inspiration and support for his new way of thinking. Alternative dogmatics may make it possible for the legislator partly to clothe reorganizations in the more acceptable raiment of codification.

Hence, the practical significance of a new set of principles should not be measured over too short a time span. It may not gain a more radical practical importance until decades after it was first formulated.[1] The legal ideology, on the level of which systematic alternative dogmatics works, often changes but slowly.

In addition - and this is yet more important - there is reason to bear in mind that such a more radical impact does not necessarily in practice represent a goal of alternative legal dogmatics. Expectations regarding such effects are hard to reconcile with the view of the law that underlies alternative dogmatics. The new principles are, as propounded earlier, merely a proposal made at the moment for systematizing the contradictory legal material. They cannot claim to create the impossible in the form of a new harmony which would definitively bridge the internal contradictions of the law. Hence alternative dogmatics fulfils the practical function sought for it as soon as it is able to offer tools for exploiting these contradictions for emancipatory ends in the hands of a judge or other legal decision-maker willing to use such tools.

The introductory chapter contained a description of how the discussion of alternative dogmatics flourished in the Nordic countries during the 1970s and the 1980s. The phenomenon has a clear connection with hopes that a legal dogmatics of this kind will have practical effects in the ways described above. This chapter will briefly analyze what developmental traits in modern society and the law may justify such a hope. The analysis is carried out against the background of observations concerning the corpus of

---

[1] As a comparison it can be noted that Zitting's (1951) analytical criticism of the conceptual-juridical concept of ownership, a pioneering work in Finland, is not considered to have become accepted in the reasoning practice of the Supreme Court until the 1970s.

theory outlined in the present work. The purpose is to describe, in the context of this work, certain preconditions for the practice of a social private law.

1.2 An example: the case of social force majeure

Among the changes of systematization outlined above in this work, the principle of social force majeure is the one that has received most concretion. A brief survey of the growth of the concrete legal material on which the alternative principle is grounded, and of the expansion of the material after the principle had been presented, indicates some circumstances of importance for the question of how an alternative dogmatics can have effects.

The first expression of the notion that what is termed social force majeure, i.e. unemployment, illness and similar negative, unforeseen occurrences afflicting a debtor, ought to lead to certain mitigations of the obligations upon such a debtor, or limitations in the sanctions of breach of contract that may be directed against him, is found in certain individual provisions on consumer credit and penal interest (see V.7.2.). Supplementing these, some cases have been noted in the concrete legal material where the consumer authorities, supported by general clauses of consumer law, have granted relevance to social force majeure (V.8.2.iv). This concrete legal material, where noted at all in legal writing, has been described as limited exceptions from the principle that each person is responsible for his ability to pay.

By formulating the doctrine of social force majeure as a general principle,[2] it has been possible to support the development of such notions at the legislative level as well as in practice. The resystematization has succeeded in bringing about both direct and indirect effects of the types mentioned in the introduction to this chapter.

In legislative work, the explicit doctrine of social force majeure has found expression, among other ways, in certain

[2] Wilhelmsson 1987, Chapter 5.

provisions of the new proposals on consumer sales and purchase of dwellings (see in more detail V.7.2.5.). In the commentaries to these it has been possible to make express reference to "social obstacles to performance",[3] that is to the terminology used in the formulation of this doctrine (see above VII.4.2.). It has been possible to link the proposals to legal doctrine.

In legal practice the formulated principle of social force majeure has been employed chiefly by the consumer authorities. At a Nordic level, the interest of these authorities is demonstrated by the fact that the Nordic Consumer Ombudsmen have initiated a joint Nordic research project on "social obstacles to performance" financed by the Nordic Council of Ministers. The consumer authorities have expected this project to provide them with stronger arguments in their negotiations concerning contract terms, again based on the general clauses of the consumer legislation. The aim of the project was not, however, to function only as a gatherer of arguments for the Consumer Ombudsmen. Some officials have also expressed the hope that the project would to some extent persuade general legal opinion to become more sympathetic towards the principle of social force majeure. The project has resulted in a report which, among other things, recommends that the Consumer Ombudsmen should seek to achieve a general contractual granting of certain rights of cancellation or termination to consumers in the event of social force majeure, and that contracts for the supply of electricity, heating, water and telephone should forbid the supplier to make use of disconnection if the consumer is afflicted by social force majeure.[4]

All these new elements in legislation and practice naturally increase the weight of the general principle of social force majeure, which in turn makes it easier to have it accepted in practice, and so on. Alternative theory and critical practice support each other. This makes possible a continual advancing of the positions of the new principle.

---

[3] OLJ 9/1988 p. 28, KM 1989:47 p. 107.

[4] Bärlund 1990 p. 82.

The pattern of development can be illustrated with the figure below:

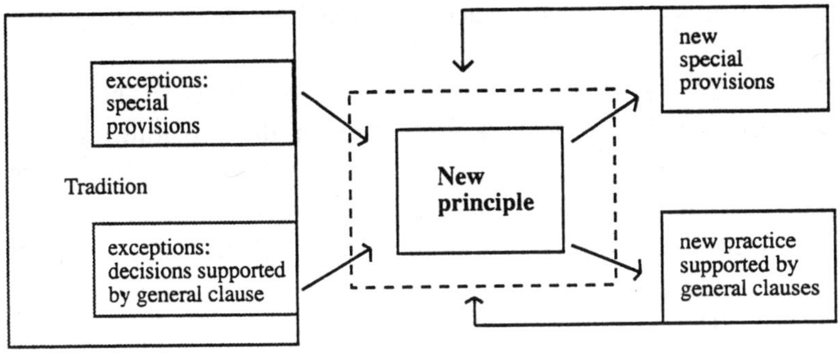

This brief and simplified case study indicates at least two special circumstances that appear important with regard to the effects of an alternative dogmatics. First, the role, noted earlier, of the general clauses as gateways for a new way of thinking emerges clearly here, and secondly the significance of special authorities such as the consumer authorities as motors of a development of the law is illustrated.[5] These circumstances are touched upon more closely in the next section.

2. PREREQUISITES OF AN ALTERNATIVE PRACTICE

2.1 Introduction

An alternative dogmatics must naturally have soil in which to grow in the social conditions of the society in which it is intended to operate. Without some form of social base or "social demand" the new dogmatics is of hardly any significance.

---

[5] Reception of the new principle has, in fact, been by no means unanimously positive, see for example the reserved reaction in Taxell 1988.

This necessary link with social development will not be analysed here. Instead, attention is directed to certain features associated with the legal apparatus itself (in a broad sense) which can be presumed to influence the effects of an alternative legal dogmatics.

In the light of the experience reported earlier in this chapter and of the general discussion of the possibilities of an alternative legal dogmatics, one can distinguish at least three different kinds of circumstance that can promote the effectiveness of a legal dogmatics of this kind. These prerequisites of a critical practice are here termed

(i) personal,
(ii) institutional and
(iii) legal-technical.

2.2 *Personal prerequisites*

In Italian discussion, it has been claimed that *the proletarianization of the judicature and the bureaucrats* offers a basis for an alternative view of the law.[6]

In the Nordic countries, too, one could imagine that the fact that those trained to be lawyers are recruited from all social levels, albeit with considerable over-representation of the upper levels,[7] in combination with the sinking salary level and social status of judges and bureaucrats, could create the soil for a new social awareness to develop, at least within sections of this group. Yet there is nothing automatic about this: another possible reaction to the development is a growing petit-bourgeois conservatism among those affected.

In any event it is obvious that the judicature in the Nordic countries has become increasingly heterogeneous as to background

---

[6] See e.g. Eriksson 1977 p. 40.

[7] Particularly in the highest instances there are still relatively few judges from the lower social levels, see e.g. for the Norwegian Supreme Court Østlid 1988 p. 136.

and values, and that this is reflected in the legal decision-making of the lawyers.[8] This growing heterogeneity of values among lawyers and judges is probably connected not only with the broadened access to legal education for less privileged classes but also with the supposed general decline of common values in modern societies.

This disintegration of personal legal values is obviously one of the most important reasons why alternative dogmatics is today really considered to have certain practical breakthrough possibilities. It can, without aspiring to hegemony, represent a tool in the hands of those judges and bureaucrats whose value systems it suits.

Here there may also be reason to note the strong levelling out of the sexes taking place in, for example, the Finnish courts. This can advance the effectiveness of an alternative women's-law dogmatics.

Considering the more *indirect* effects of the formulation of an alternative corpus of principles, the composition of the community of legal scholars is also of significance. Here, too, the changes of the last decades in several Nordic countries have been great. The preconditions exist for an alternative-dogmatic discourse in legal research,[9] which in the longer term may strengthen the legitimation of alternative dogmatics.

---

[8] In an analysis of the voting behaviour of Norwegian Supreme Court judges in certain cases with dissenting opinions, Østlid 1988 p. 138 notes, e.g., that judges with conservative preferences are more inclined to vote for more stringent sanctions than judges in the radical grouping. - Even in a, party-politically, relatively homogeneous circle such as the Finnish Supreme Court - with only a few leftist members - systematic variations occur in voting behaviour. This emerges e.g. from Bruun 1986, who has analysed the various judges' voting behaviour in labour law cases.

[9] A good expression of this is the recent Nordic collected volume on the alternatives of legal dogmatics, Tuori (ed.) 1988.

2.3 *Institutional prerequisites*

The modern state has since its inception been perceived as a monolithic whole with *one* collection of goals for its activity and *one* collection of values upon which the activity is based. This view, which presumably from the beginning exhibited traces of fiction, was understandable as long as the state was primarily assumed to act as a liberal night-watchman state. The fiction becomes the more difficult to maintain when one is describing the modern state, which performs greatly varying tasks in all areas of social life. Different public departments and other institutions work increasingly towards their own goals, self-assumed or given from outside, and safeguard their own interests; to put it briefly, exercise their *own* power which is not necessarily linked closely or coordinated with that of other organs of state.[10] One can speak of *the disintegration of the state* into several more or less well-knit centres of power: "Society consists of a constellation of governments rather than an association of individuals held together by a single government."[11]

This disintegration is institutional in character and hence does not have as a necessary precondition the disintegration of the common personal value base among judges and bureaucrats spoken of above. Naturally, however, growing heterogeneity of values can support this institutional disintegration.

The disintegration of the state is not merely internal, but also implies that the borderline between state and society becomes less and less clear. Corporativistic solutions, where representatives of different interests (organizations) are drawn directly into state decision-making - such models are known to be common in e.g. Nordic labour and consumer law - are blurring the borderline between the state interest and the private. Even if, for example, a merchants' or a consumers' representative in the Market Court is acting formally under judicial responsibility and as such should

---

[10] See also e.g. Graver 1989 p. 57 ff.

[11] Unger 1976 p. 193.

avoid partisan positions, his task is nevertheless at the same time to channel into the decision-making the view of the correct order of things that prevails in his background environment.

The unity of the law is connected with the monolithic character of the state. The disintegration of the state must, to some degree, also imply a disintegration of the law.[12] In postmodern conceptions of law *legal pluralism* becomes a key concept: "We live in a time of porous legality or of legal porosity, of multiple networks of legal orders forcing us to constant transitions and trespassings."[13]

The growing legal pluralism connected with the disintegration of the state might be recorded in the form of an increasing replacement of traditional state law by other small group normative orders in the minds of ordinary people. At least in some fields of law the alienation of many groups in society from state law is obvious (though other fields, like consumer law, point in another direction). Within the domain of state law the disintegration thesis again is connected with insights concerning, among other things, the dissolution of the mythical unitary "legislator" into several public, semi-public or private national and international bodies issuing legal or law-like norms.

The legal pluralism is, however, obviously not restricted only to the sphere of creation of new norms. Another aspect of it, which is of special interest in this context, is an assumed *disintegration of the application of the law.* Different authorities and courts, which are linked to different power centres, do not necessarily apply the law in the same way.[14] The concrete contents of the law become more and more related to each authority. What is

---

[12] In the words of Joerges 1989 p. 634: "Under the new conditions of the 'society of organizations', law can no longer represent a coherent social order".

[13] Santos 1987 p. 298.

[14] See also Teubner 1989 p. 414 ff. on the separation of legal fields, each field being "administered by specialized legal experts, who identify with the corresponding social spheres at least as strongly as with the law", above Chapter II, footnote 30.

understood as an acceptable argument in the Market Court perhaps awakes no response in the Supreme Court, and the practice of the Consumer Complaints Board may very well even systematically differ from the assessments made in the general courts.[15]

A reference to the concept of "polycentrism in the doctrine of legal sources", launched by *Henrik Zahle*,[16] is pertinent in this connection. With this concept the author has expressly attempted to bring out the tendencies towards a more authority-specific doctrine of the sources of law that is becoming visible in modern society. When the different sources of law have different significance for different authorities - the administration, for example, sees itself as to some extent bound by administrative practice while the courts do not - the unified concept "law in force" disintegrates into a spectrum of "laws in force" supported by different authorities with varying roles in the application of the law.[17]

To the extent such a disintegration of the state and the law takes place, it does of course extend the possible effectiveness of the alternative dogmatics. The new tools this dogmatics offers can, even when rejected by the majority of the legal audience, be received within those niches of administration and justice whose goals and interests they may further. Thus for example, as noted earlier, the principle of social force majeure has been well received by the consumer authorities despite more reserved reactions from other quarters.

2.4 *Legal-technical prerequisites*

As mentioned in the introductory chapter to this book, one of the common features of different forms of alternative dogmatics is the emphasis on the judge's wide discretion when applying the law. This realization is a necessary prerequisite for speaking of an alternative legal dogmatics.

---

[15] Certain examples of this are given in Wilhelmsson 1989 p. 202.

[16] Zahle 1986.

[17] Graver 1989 p. 60.

The assertion that the law is indeterminate need not of course be understood to mean that the discretion of the judge is unlimited. The very concept of *legal* decision-making contains by definition some demarcation of the alternatives available to the decision-maker. If every logically conceivable decision alternative in all situations were also acceptable as a legal decision, the specification "legal" would be meaningless. There are bounds to what can be considered a legal decision.[18]

The existence of such limits has earlier been indicated with the term "legally possible". For alternative dogmatics, the realization that a broad spectrum of solutions to a problem can be classified as "legally possible" is sufficient.

If one starts in the way indicated with the idea that there *are* limits, albeit very unclear, to the legal decision-maker's discretion, one may also presume that the scope of this discretion is not necessarily constant at different times and in different places.[19]

---

[18] I do not necessarily wish to play here upon the traditional distinction between "hard cases", where the judge has wide discretionary powers and "easy cases" in which only one solution is considered legally possible, as the "easy cases" also, when analysed more closely and using an alternative reasoning, can often be made "hard". Rather, the "legally impossible" alternatives never arise as cases or in connection with cases since it is obvious to all members of the legal culture in question, regardless of value background, that these alternatives lie outside the sphere of the legally possible. Anyone would consider it patently non-legal if a Finnish court today should sentence a person to death since this sanction is forbidden by law; but a court is never called upon to consider this alternative since no prosecutor or plaintiff would conceive of making such a demand. Even though the death-penalty alternative is a factual possibility, it is excluded as a legal alternative. The freedom of action of the courts is further limited not merely concerning the possible final results of proceedings. Important here is the circumstance that the way of justifying a legal decision is also hedged about with certain limits. A hard private-law case may be decided with reference to, e.g., guilt, risk reasoning, principles of protection or other similar arguments. On the other hand the same decision would be considered legally inacceptable if the argument ran "The case should be decided in A's favour because B smells".

[19] See e.g. Atiyah - Summers 1987 p. 75 ff., who attempt to show that the flexibility of rules is much greater in American law than in English.

Different circumstances can influence this discretion. In a strongly legalistic legal culture like the Finnish, the design of the legislation is of substantial importance for how even critical lawyers understand the freedom of action.

In view of this it seems evident that the changes in modern legislation and legal thinking described in Chapter III, which have been labelled e.g. shifts from a formal to a substantive rationality or from a "law of legal security" to a "law of control", are of considerable relevance when the possibilities for an alternative doctrine are being discussed. The obvious changes in legislative technique, which involve the regulation of at least private law being realized to an increasing degree through flexible provisions (general clauses) in which courts and other law-applying authorities are explicitly granted broad discretionary powers,[20] are making it easier to give alternative legal ideas that grounding in legislation which is an essential value in a legalistic legal culture. The general clauses can be presumed to function as entrance gateways for such new general principles as alternative legal thinking is seeking.

The concrete legal material referred to in this book shows clearly the importance of the changes in legal technique that have taken place in modern Nordic society. The general clauses of both tort law and contract and consumer law have proved to be usable tools for slipping the new values into private law.

3. CONCLUDING REMARK

The three circumstances mentioned above, namely the changes in the social composition of the judicature, the institutional disintegration of the state and the law and the flexibilization of legal technique, afford opportunities for the realization of an emancipatory dogmatics of the sort sketched here. However, they afford opportunities for many other things, too. The heterogeneity

---

[20] Teubner 1989 p. 410 speaks of "a new and disturbing quality of indeterminacy in law".

of the judicature may permit the generation of authoritarian currents, parts of the state machinery may represent strongly conservative values and the general clauses may also be used for purposes of suppression.[21]

There is therefore reason to repeat here by way of conclusion what was maintained earlier (section II.5): perhaps the most central question when discussing possibilities of working out and implementing alternatives to traditional legal dogmatics concerns determination of the *values* upon which the work is based. The worth of an alternative dogmatics should be assessed primarily on the basis of an evaluation of the politico-moral choices underlying the new principles. The goodness of the alternative systematization lies in the goodness of its values.

* * *

This book is written before the massive changes in the countries of Central and Eastern Europe. The effects of the changes on the Western societies is still to be seen. The strong revival of old-fashioned market-liberalism in those countries may strenghen similar tendencies in our part of the world. The "alternative" values of the near future may turn out to be rather anti-welfarist. On the other hand the death of "real socialism" may in the long run enlarge the opportunities for promoting new emancipatory ideals as well. There is still room for a critical private law as part of such an emancipatory enterprise.

---

[21] An extreme example of this is given by the illustrative analysis of the role of the general clauses in the application of the law in the Third Reich, in Rüthers 1968 p. 210 ff.

BIBLIOGRAPHY

Aarnio, Aulis,

Mitä lainoppi on? (What is legal dogmatics?). Helsinki 1978.

- " - *Denkweisen der Rechtswissenschaft*. Wien 1979.

- " - *Oikeussäännösten tulkinnasta* (On the Interpretation of Legal Rules). Helsinki 1982.

- " - *The Rational as Reasonable*. A Treatise on Legal Justification. Dordrecht 1987.

Adler, Michael,

The Economic and Social Situation of Consumer Debtors in Great Britain. *Zentrum für Europäische Rechtspolitik* (Bremen) *Mat 6* (1985) p. 12-24.

Alexy, Robert,

Rechtsregeln und Rechtsprinzipien. *Archiv für Rechts- und Sozialphilosophie* Beiheft nr. 25 (1985) p. 13-29.

Aro, Pirkko-Liisa,

Om tillämpning av SBL § 8 (A Case on Adjustment of an Unfair Contract. The Finnish Promissory Notes Act sec. 8). *Tidskrift, utgiven av Juridiska Föreningen i Finland* (Helsinki) 1974 p. 171-187.

Assmann, Heinz-Dieter - Brüggemeier, Gert - Hart, Dieter - Joerges, Christian,

Wirtschaftsrecht als Kritik des Privatrechts. Königstein/Ts. 1980.

Atiyah, P.S.,

The Rise and Fall of Freedom of Contract. Oxford 1979.

- " - *Freedom of Contract and the New Right*. Stockholm 1989.

Atiyah, P.S. - Summers, Robert S.,

Form and Substance in Anglo-American Law. Oxford 1987.

Aurejärvi, Erkki,
Oikeustointen kohtuullistamisen yleiset opit ja yrittäjien väliset sopimukset (The General Principles concerning Adjustment of Contracts and Contracts between Enterprises). *Lakimies* (Helsinki) 1979 p. 725-745.
- " - *Velvoiteoikeuden oppikirja* (Textbook on the Law of Obligations). Jyväskylä 1988.
Bayles, Michael D.,
Principles of Law. A Normative Analysis. Dordrecht 1987.
Bengtsson, Bertil,
Om jämkning av skadestånd (On Adjustment of Damages). Lund 1982.
BGB-Kommentar,
Kommentar zum Bürgerlichen Gesetzbuch. Band 2. Allgemeines Schuldrecht. Reihe Alternativkommentare. Darmstadt 1980.
Blegvad, Britt-Mari,
Nonet/Selznick og Teubner: Ret, og teori og empiri (Law, Theory and Empiric Knowledge). In: Asmund Born - Nils Bredsdorff - Leif Hansen - Finn Hansson, *Refleksiv ret*. København 1988 p. 151-172.
Broekman, Jan M.,
Legal Subjectivity as a Precondition for the Intertwinement of Law and the Welfare State. In: Gunther Teubner (ed.): *Dilemmas of Law in the Welfare State*. Berlin 1986 p. 76-108.
Bruun, Niklas,
Työoikeudellinen lainkäyttö ja tuomarin arvostukset (Practice in Labour Law and the Values of the Judge). *Työoikeudellisen Yhdistyksen vuosikirja* (Helsinki) 1986 p. 49-56.
Bruun, Niklas - Wilhelmsson, Thomas,
Rätten, moralen och det juridiska paradigmet (Law, Morals and the Juridical Paradigm). *Svensk Juristtidning* (Stockholm) 1983 p. 701-713.
Brüggemeier, Gert,
Probleme einer Theorie des Wirtschaftsrechts. In: Assmann - Brüggemeier - Hart - Joerges 1980 p. 9-81.

Brüggemeier, Gert,
"Wirtschaftsverfassung und Staatsverfassung" - Mischverfassung des demokratischen Interventionskapitalismus" - "Verfassungstheorie des Sozialstaates". Drei Modelle der Verflechtung von Staat und Wirtschaft? - Eine Problemskizze. In: *Rechtsformen der Verflechtung von Staat und Wirtschaft*, herausgegeben von Volkmar Gessner und Gerd Winter. Opladen 1982 p. 60-73.

- " - Überarbeitung des Schuldrechts - Herausforderung oder Überforderung des Gesetzgebers? *Kritische Justiz* 1983 p. 386-395.

Bärlund, Johan,
Sociala prestationshinder i konsumentavtal (Social Obstacles to Performance in Consumer Contracts). NÄK rapport 1990:6 (Nordic Council of Ministers). Köpenhamn 1990.

Caplovitz, David,
Consumers in Trouble. A study of Debtors in Default. New York 1974.

Collins, Hugh,
The Law of Contract. London 1986.

Conaty, Patrick,
The need for money advice centres. *Zentrum für Europäische Rechtspolitik. Mat 6* (1985) p. 91-103.

Cranston, Ross,
Consumers and the Law. Second ed. London 1984.

Dalberg-Larsen, Jørgen,
Retsdogmatik, legalstrategi og marxisme (Legal Dogmatics, Legal Strategy and Marxism). *Retfaerd* (Århus) 12 (1979) p. 80-92.

- " - På vej frem mod det gode samfund eller fuld fart tilbage? (On the Way towards the Good Society or Full Speed Backwards?). *Retfaerd* (København) 32 (1986) p. 6-22.

Dalton, Clare,
An Essay in the Deconstruction of Contract Doctrine. *The Yale Law Journal* 94 (1985) p. 997-1114.

Damm, Reinhard,
Verbraucherrechtliche Sondergesetzgebung und Privatrechtssystem. *Juristenzeitung* 1978 p. 173-180.

Dauner-Lieb, Barbara,
Verbraucherschutz durch Ausbildung eines Sonderprivatrechts für Verbraucher. Systemkonforme Weiterentwicklung oder Schrittmacher der Systemveränderung? Berlin (West) 1983.

Derleder, Peter,
Antizipatorische Elemente der Privatrechtsentwicklung? In: N. Paech - G. Stuby (Hg.): *Wider die "herrschende Meinung".* Beiträge für Wolfgang Abendroth. Frankfurt am Main 1982 p. 215-227.

Dworkin, Ronald,
Taking Rights Seriously. London 1981.

Dübeck, Inger,
Store selskaber og samfundet (Large Corporations and Society). Om samfundsansvarlighed i amerikansk selskabsret: en komparativ studie. *Tidsskrift for Rettsvitenskap* (Oslo) 1989 p. 305-332.

Eckhoff, Torstein,
Kan vi laere noe av kvinneretten? (Can We Learn Something from Women's Law?). *Retfaerd* (København) 31 (1985) p. 82-90.

Eckhoff, Torstein - Sundby, Nils Kristian,
Rettssystemer (Systems of Law). Oslo 1976.

Eidemüller, Horst,
Rights, Systems of Rights, and Unger's System of Rights. *HiMoN Discussion Papers* 137/89. Center for Studies on Changing Norms and Mobility. Siegen 1989.

Eklund, Rudolf - Nordström, Torkel,
Lagen om avbetalningsköp (The Act on Hire-Purchase). 2 uppl. Stockholm 1957.

Eriksson, Lars D.,
Magistratura democratica och den italienska juristoppositionen (Magistratura Democratica and the Italian Lawyer's Opposition). *Oikeus* (Helsinki) 1/1977 p. 37-43.

- " - Utkast till en marxistisk jurisprudens (Sketch on a Marxist Jurisprudence). *Retfaerd* (Århus) 11 (1979) p. 40-53.

- " - *Marxistisk teori och rättsvetenskap* (Marxist Theory and Legal Science). Helsinki 1980.

- " - Kvinnorätten i det rättsvetenskapliga projektet (Women's

Law in the Project of Legal Science). *Retfaerd* (København) 31 (1985) p. 91-98.

Eriksson, Lars D.,
Till teorin om den reflexiva rätten (On the Theory of Reflexive Law). In: *Samfunn Rett Rettferdighet. Festskrift til Torstein Eckhoffs 70-årsdag*. Otta 1986 p. 281-292.

Eräsaari, Risto,
Sosiaalivaltio ja sosiaalipolitiikan itseymmärrys (The Social State and the Self-understanding of Social Policy). Helsinki 1984.

Esser, Josef,
Grundsatz und Norm in der richterlichen Fortbildung des Privatrechts. 2. Auflage. Tübingen 1964.

Esser, Josef - Schmidt, Eike,
Schuldrecht. Band I. Allgemeiner Teil. 6 Aufl. Heidelberg 1984.

Ewald, Francois,
A Concept of Social Law. In: Gunther Teubner (ed.), *Dilemmas of Law in the Welfare State*. Berlin 1986 p. 40-75.

Friedman, Lawrence M.,
Legal Culture and the Welfare State. In: Gunther Teubner (ed.), *Dilemmas of Law in the Welfare State*. Berlin 1986 p. 13-27.

Gilles, Peter,
Zu neueren Verbraucherschutzgesetzgebung in ihrem Verhältnis zum klassischen Privatrecht. *Juristische Arbeitsblätter* 1980 p. 1-8.

Godenhielm, Berndt,
Om jämkning av skadestånd i inomkontraktuella förhållanden (On the Adjustment of Damages in Contractual Relations). *Tidskrift, utgiven av Juridiska Föreningen i Finland* (Helsinki) 1975 p. 400-414.

Goodrich, Peter,
Reading the Law. Oxford 1986.

Graver, Hans Petter,
Refleksiv rett og makt (Reflexiv law and Power). In: Asmund Born - Nils Bredsdorff - Leif Hansen - Finn Hansson (eds.), *Refleksiv ret*. København 1988 p. 83-110.

Graver, Hans Petter,
Normative systemer - skisse til en oppløsning av rettsbegrepet (Normative Systems - a Sketch on the Dissolution of the Concept of Law). In: Ellen Margrethe Basse (ed.), *Regulering og styring - en juridisk teori- og metodebog*. København 1989 p. 53-68.

Groth, Ulf,
Schuldnerberatung als Aufgabe der Sozialarbeit. In: Günter Hörmann (Hrsg.), *Verbraucherkredit und Verbraucherinsolvenz*. Bremen 1986 p. 368-380.

Habermas, Jürgen,
Erkenntnis und Interesse. Frankfurt am Main 1968.

- " - *Theorie des kommunikativen Handelns I-II*. Frankfurt am Main 1981.

- " - Law as Medium and Law as Institution. In: Gunther Teubner (ed.), *Dilemmas of Law in the Welfare State*. Berlin 1986 p. 203-220.

Hakulinen, Y.J.,
Obligationsrätt I. Allmänna läror (The Law of Obligations I. General Principles). Tammerfors 1962.

Hakulinen, Y.J. - Raninen, Huugo,
Osamaksukauppa (Hire-Purchase). Tampere 1968.

Hart, Dieter,
Zur konzeptionellen Entwicklung des Vertragsrechts. Die Aktiengesellschaft. *Zeitschrift für das gesamte Aktienwesen* 1984 p. 66-80.

Helin, Markku,
Käsitteistä päättelemisestä (On Drawing Conclusions from Concepts). In: *Juhlajulkaisu Simo Zitting 1915 - 14/2 - 1985*. Vammala 1985 p. 82-92.

- " - *Lainoppi ja metafysiikka* (Legal Dogmatics and Metaphysics). Vammala 1988.

Hellner, Jan,
Speciell avtalsrätt I. Köprätt (Special Contract Law I. Sale of Goods). Stockholm 1982.

- " - *Speciell avtalsrätt II*. Kontraktsrätt (Special Contract Law II. The Law of Contract). Stockholm 1984.

- " - *Skadeståndsrätt* (The Law of Torts). 4. uppl. Stockholm 1985.

Henf, Frieder,
Billigkeit und zivilrichterliche Argumentation. Diss. Kiel 1978.
von Hippel, Eike,
Der Schutz des Schwächeren. Tübingen 1982.
Holmila, Marja,
Selvityksiä ulosottotoiminnasta Helsingissä, Nurmijärvellä ja Kontiolahdella (A Study on Execution in Helsinki, Nurmijärvi and Kontiolahti). OLJ 16/1973.
Holmila-McCafferty, Marja,
Selvityksiä ulosottoperinnän kohdentumisesta (A Study on the Subjects of Execution). OLJ 7/1975.
Holzscheck, Knut - Hörmann, Günter - Daviter, Jürgen,
Praxis des Konsumentenkredits in der Bundesrepublik Deutschland. Köln 1982.
Hopt, Klaus,
Nichtvertragliche Haftung ausserhalb von Schadens- und Bereicherungsausgleich. Zur Theorie und Dogmatik des Berufsrechts und der Berufshaftung. *Archiv für die civilistische Praxis* 183 (1983) p. 608-720.
Huser, Kristian,
Avtaletolking (Interpretation of Contracts). Bergen 1983.
Hydén, Håkan,
Ram eller lag? Om ramlagstiftning och samhällsorganisation (Framework or Law? On Framework Legislation and the Organization of Society). Civildepartementet. DsC 1984: 12. Stockholm 1984.
Hönn, Günther,
Kompensation gestörter Vertragsparität. München 1982.
Hörmann, Günter,
Verbraucher und Schulden. Baden-Baden 1987.
Hörmann, Günter - Holzscheck, Knut,
Consumer Credit in the Federal Republic of Germany. *Journal of Consumer Policy* 1983 p. 457-468.
Joerges, Christian,
Politische Rechtstheorie and Critical Legal Studies: Points of Contact and Divergencies. In: Christian Joerges - David M. Trubek (eds.), *Critical Legal Thought: An American-German Debate*. Baden-Baden 1989 p. 597-643.

Kangas, Urpo,
Lesken oikeudellinen asema (Legal Status of Widowed Persons). Vammala 1982.
Karisto, Antti,
Elinolojen muutossuunnat Suomessa (The Trends in the Change of Living Conditions in Finland). Sosiaalihallituksen julkaisuja 3/1985. Helsinki 1985.
Karisto, Antti - Takala, Pentti - Haapola, Ilkka,
Elintaso, elämäntapa, sosiaalipolitiikka (Standard of Life, Way of Life, Social Politics). Juva 1984.
Kennedy, Duncan,
Form and Substance in Private Law Adjudication. 89 *Harward Law Review* 1976 p. 1685-1778.
- " - Distributive and Paternalist Motives in Contract and Tort Law, with Special Reference to Compulsory Terms and Unequal Bargaining Power. 41 *Maryland Law Review* 1982 p. 563-658.
Kilian, Wolfgang,
Kontrahierungszwang und Zivilrechtssystem. *Archiv für die civilistische Praxis* 180 (1980) p. 47-83.
Kindermann, Harald,
Die Antwort des Bürgerlichen Gesetzbuchs auf die soziale Frage. *Rechtstheorie* 12 (1981) p. 209-225.
Kivimäki, T.M. - Ylöstalo, Matti,
Suomen siviilioikeuden oppikirja. Yleinen osa (Textbook in Finnish Private Law. General Part). 4. painos. Juva 1981.
Kivivuori, Antti,
Suomen vahingonkorvauslainsäädännön kehitys I (The Development of Finnish Legislation on Tort Law I). Joensuu 1969.
- " - Yksityisoikeuden yleisten oppien kriisi? (Crisis of the General Principles of Private Law?) *Studia Juridica 1983.* Helsinki 1983 p. 53-60.
KM 1957:8,
Huoneenvuokralakikomitean mietintö (Report of the Rent Act Committee). Helsinki 1957.
KM 1977:30,
Kulutusluottotoimikunnan mietintö (Report of the Consumer Credit Committee). Helsinki 1977.

KM 1989:47,
Ehdotus asuntokauppalainsäädännöksi. Asuntokauppatoimikunnan mietintö (Proposal for Legislation on Purchase of Dwellings. Committee Report). Helsinki 1989.

Kom.bet. 1965: A4,
Skadeståndskommitténs betänkande (Report of the Tort Law Committee). Helsingfors 1965.

Kosonen, Pekka,
Hyvinvointivaltion haasteet ja pohjoismaiset mallit (The Challenges of the Welfare State and the Nordic Models). Tampere 1989.

Krämer, L.,
EEC Consumer Law. Bruxelles - Louvain-la-Neuve 1986.

Kähler, Annette,
Consumers and Debt in the Federal Republic of Germany. *Journal of Consumer Policy* 1984 p. 487-495.

Köndgen, Johannes,
Selbstbindung ohne Vertrag. Tübingen 1981.

Lieb, Manfred,
Grundfragen einer Schuldrechtsreform. *Archiv für die civilistische Praxis* 183 (1983) p. 327-366.

Lindell-Frantz, Eva - Roos, Carl Martin,
Generös avtalstillämpning (Generous Application of Contracts). Lund 1985.

Lyngsø, Preben,
Afbestillingsret (The Right of Cancellation). København 1971.

Mathiesen, Thomas,
En marxistisk jurisprudens? (A Marxist Jurisprudence?). *Retfaerd* (Århus) 15 (1980) p. 70-74.

- " - "Styringsjuss", "rettssikkerhetsjuss" - og det gode samfunn ("Law of Control", "Law of Legal Security" - and the Good Society). *Retfaerd* (København) 28 (1985) p. 12-25.

Medicus, Dieter,
"Geld muss man haben". Unvermögen und Schuldnerverzug bei Geldmangel. *Archiv für die civilistische Praxis* 188 (1988) p. 489-510.

Mollnau, Karl A.,
Empirische Sozialerkenntnis und Rechtswissenschaft.

Rechtstheorie Beiheft 9 (1986) p. 157-170.

Montgomery, Robert,
Handbok i Finlands allmänna privaträtt. Första delen. Inledande läror. I (Handbook in Finnish General Private Law. First Part. Introductory Principles. I). Helsingfors 1889.

Mäkipää, Eila,
Henkilövahinkojen korvauskäytäntöä (Practice in Compensating Personal Injuries). Oikeuspoliittisen tutkimuslaitoksen julkaisuja 69. Helsinki 1984.

Nilsson, Edvard - Strömbäck, Erland,
Konsumentförsäkringslagen (The Act on Consumer Insurance). Helsingborg 1984.

Nousiainen, Kevät,
Kvinnan och domstolsprocessen (Woman and the Court Procedure). *Retfaerd* (København) 31 (1985) p. 70-80.

NU 1984:5,
Nordiska köplagar. Förslag av den nordiska arbetsgruppen för köplagstiftning (Nordic Sale of Goods Acts. Proposal of a Nordic Working Group). Stockholm 1985.

OLJ 8/1982,
Thomas Wilhelmsson - Kirsti Rissanen - Rauno Vanhanen: *Kulutusluottotyöryhmän mietintö* (Report of the Working Group on Consumer Credit).

OLJ 16/1985,
Jussi Järventaus: *Ehdotus henkilövakuutuslaiksi* (Proposal on an Act on Insurance of Persons).

OLJ 18/1985,
Ilkka Cantell: *Lausunnot pohjoismaisen kauppalakityöryhmän ehdotuksesta*. Tiivistelmä (Opinions Delivered on the Proposal of the Nordic Working Group on a Sale of Goods Act).

OLJ 3/1988,
Ehdotus vahinkovakuutuslaiksi. Työryhmän mietintö (Proposal of a Working Group on an Act on Insurance of Property).

OLJ 9/1988,
Leif Sevón - Thomas Wilhelmsson - Pauliine Koskelo: *Ehdotus kuluttajansuojalain muuttamisesta* (Proposal on the

Amendment of the Consumer Protection Act).
Portin, Göran,
Om jämkning av oskäliga avtal (On Adjustment of Unfair Contracts). *Tidskrift, utgiven av Juridiska Föreningen i Finland* (Helsinki) 1974 p. 323-335.
Preuss, Ulrich K.,
The Concept of Rights and the Welfare State. In: Gunther Teubner (ed.), *Dilemmas of Law in the Welfare State*. Berlin 1986 p. 151-172.
Pöyhönen, Juha,
Om teoretiska förutsättningar för en marxistisk rättsdogmatik (On Theoretical Prerequisites for a Marxist Legal Dogmatics). *Retfaerd* (Århus) 15 (1980) p. 75-83.
- " - Refleksiivinen oikeus - vihreän liikkeen oikeusideologiaa? (Reflexive Law - the Legal Ideology of the Green Movement?). *Oikeus* (Helsinki) 1985 p. 127-138.
- " - *Sopimusoikeuden järjestelmä ja sopimusten sovittelu* (The System of Contract Law and the Adjustment of Contracts). Vammala 1988.
Ramberg, Jan,
Allmän avtalsrätt. Del I (General Contract Law. Part I). Stockholm 1986.
Rebe, Bernd,
Privatrecht und Wirtschaftsordnung. Bielefeld 1978.
Reg.prop. 187/1973,
Regeringens proposition till Riksdagen angående lagstiftning om skadestånd (Government Bill; Act on Torts).
Reg.prop. 90/1974,
Regeringens proposition till Riksdagen med förslag till revision av lagstiftningen om barns ställning (Government Bill; Legislation on the Position of Children).
Reg.prop. 8/1977,
Regeringens proposition till Riksdagen med förslag till konsumentskyddslagstiftning (Government Bill; Consumer Protection Legislation).
Reg.prop. 109/1981,
Regeringens proposition till Riksdagen med förslag till räntelagstiftning (Government Bill; Act on Interest).

Reg.prop. 247/1981,
Regeringens proposition till Riksdagen med förslag till lagstiftning om jämkning av rättshandlingar (Government Bill; Adjustment of Contracts).

Reg.prop. 205/1983,
Regeringens proposition till Riksdagen med förslag till lagstiftning rörande utvecklande av anställningstryggheten (Government Bill; Legislation Concerning Employment Security).

Reg.prop. 127/1984,
Regeringens proposition till Riksdagen med förslag till revidering av hyreslagstiftningen (Government Bill; Rent Act).

Reg.prop. 57/1985,
Regeringens proposition till Riksdagen med förslag till lagstiftning om jämställdhet mellan kvinnor och män (Government Bill; Act on Equality between Women and Men).

Reg.prop. 88/1985,
Regeringens proposition till Riksdagen med förslag till lagstiftning om konsumentkrediter (Government Bill; Legislation on Consumer Credit).

Reg.prop. 49/1986,
Regeringens proposition till Riksdagen med förslag till en personregisterlag och lagar som har samband med den (Government Bill; Registration of Persons Act).

Reg.prop. 93/1986,
Regeringens proposition till Riksdagen med förslag till köplag (Government Bill; Sale of Goods Act).

Rehbinder, Manfred,
Status - Kontrakt - Rolle. In: *Berliner Festschrift für Ernst E. Hirsch*. Berlin (West) 1968 p. 141-169.

Reich, Norbert,
Zivilrechtstheorie, Sozialwissenschaften und Verbraucherschutz. *Zeitschrift für Rechtspolitik* 1974 p. 187-194.

- " - *Markt und Recht*. Neuwied und Darmstadt 1977.

- " - Reflexives Recht? Anfragen an eine neue Theorie von Gunther Teubner. *Zentrum für Europäische Rechtspolitik* (Bremen) *Mat 4* (1984) p. 269-290.

Reich, Norbert,
Yhteiskuntatieteet ja lakien uudistaminen: kokemuksia sopimusoikeuden sääntelystä kuluttajan eduksi (Social Sciences and the Reform of Legislation: Experiences of Regulating Contract Law to the Advantage of the Consumer). *Lakimies* (Helsinki) 1985 p. 191-217.
Reifner, Udo,
Alternatives Wirtschaftsrecht am Beispiel der Verbraucherverschuldung. Darmstadt 1979.
- " - Verbraucherverschuldung und Arbeitslosigkeit - Soziale Problematik und zivilrechtliche Bewertung. In: *Arbeitslosigkeit als Problem der Rechts- und Sozialwissenschaften*. Baden-Baden 1980 p. 355-387.
Reuter, Dieter,
Die ethischen Grundlagen des Privatrechts - formale Freiheitsethik oder materiale Verantwortungsethik? *Archiv für die civilistische Praxis* 189 (1989) p. 199-222.
Reynolds, Francis,
The Applicability of General Rules of Private Law to Consumer Disputes. In: Steve Anderman (ed.), *Law and the Weaker Party*. Volume II. Abingdon 1982 p. 91-110.
Rodhe, Knut,
Obligationsrätt (The Law of Obligations). Lund 1956.
Rottleuthner, Hubert,
Richterliches Handeln. Zur Kritik der juristischen Dogmatik. Frankfurt am Main 1973.
- " - Theories of legal evolution: between empiricism and philosophy of history. *Rechtstheorie* Beiheft 9 (1986) p. 217-230.
Rüthers, Bernd,
Die unbegrenzte Auslegung. Zum Wandel der Privatrechtsordnung im Nationalsozialismus. Tübingen 1968.
Santos, Boaventura De Sousa,
Law: A Map of Misreading. Toward a Postmodern Conception of Law. *Journal of Law and Society* 1987 p. 279-302.
Saxén, Hans,
Skadeståndsrätt (The Law of Torts). Åbo 1975.
- " - *Tillägg till Skadeståndsrätt* (Supplement to The Law of

Torts). Åbo 1983.
Schmidt, Eike,
Von der Privat- zur Sozialautonomie. *Juristenzeitung* 1980 p. 153-161.
Schmidt, Jürgen,
Vertragsfreiheit und Schuldrechtsreform. Berlin 1985.
Schuhmacher, Wolfgang,
Review of Barbara Dauner-Lieb, Verbraucherschutz durch Ausbildung eines Sonderprivatrechts für Verbraucher. *Zeitschrift für das gesamte Handelsrecht und Wirtschaftsrecht* 1986 p. 284-289.
Simitis, Konstantin,
Verbraucherschutz. Schlagwort oder Rechtsprinzip? Baden-Baden 1976.
SOU 1985:11,
Ny räntelag. Betänkande av räntelagsutredningen (New Act on Interest. Report by a Swedish Committee). Stockholm 1985.
Stang Dahl, Tove,
Innledning til kvinneretten (Introduction to Women's Law). In: Stang Dahl (ed.): *Kvinnerett I*. Oslo 1985 p. 13-109.
Summers, Robert S.,
Two Types of Reasons of Substance in Common Law Cases. *Archiv für Rechts- und Sozialphilosophie* Beiheft 11 (1979) p. 217-229.
Sv. Prop. 1975:12,
Regeringens proposition med förslag till lag om ändring i skadeståndslagen (1972:207), m.m. (Swedish Government Bill; Amendment of the Act on Torts).
Taxell, Lars Erik,
Avtal och rättsskydd (Contract and Legal Protection). Åbo 1972.
- " - Sociala drag i avtalsrätten (Social Features in Contract Law). In: *Lov, Dom og Bok, Festskrift til Sjur Braekhus 19. juni 1988*. Otta 1988 p. 525-534.
Teubner, Gunther,
Substantive and Reflexive Elements in Modern Law. *Law & Society Review* Vol. 17 (1983) p. 239-285.

Teubner, Gunther,
Prozeduralisierung. *Zentrum für Europäische Rechtspolitik* (Bremen) *Mat 4* (1984) p. 91-92.
- " - After Legal Instrumentalism? Strategic Models of Post-Regulatory Law. In: Gunther Teubner (ed.), *Dilemmas of Law in the Welfare State*. Berlin 1986 p. 299-325.
- " - Introduction to Autopoietic Law. In: Teubner (ed.), *Autopoietic Law: A New Approach to Law and Society*. Berlin 1988 p. 1-11.
- " - "And God Laughed..." Indeterminacy, Self-reference and Paradox in Law. In: Christian Joerges - David M. Trubek (eds.), *Critical Legal Thought: An American-German Debate*. Baden-Baden 1989 p. 399-434.

Tolonen, Juha,
Siviilioikeuden yleisten oppien kriisi (The Crisis of the General Principles of Private Law). *Oikeus* (Helsinki) 1/1973 p. 11-19.

Tonner, Klaus,
Verbraucherrecht und Selbstregulierungskonzepte. *Kritische Justiz* 1985 p. 107-125.

Trebilcock, M.J. - Reiter, B.J. - Laskin, J.B.,
Debtor and Creditor. Cases, Notes, and Materials. Toronto 1979.

Tuori, Kaarlo,
Alternativ eller kritik, snäv eller utvidgad doktrin? (Alternative or Critique, Narrow or Extended Doctrine?). In: *Rättsdogmatikens alternativ* (Tammerfors 1988) p. 181-210.
- " - (ed.), *Rättsdogmatikens alternativ* (The Alternatives of Legal Dogmatics). Tammerfors 1988.

Unger, Roberto Mangabeira,
Law in Modern Society. New York 1976.
- " - The Critical Legal Studies Movement. *Harvard Law Review* 1983 p. 563-675.

Vallauri, Luigi Lombardi,
Difficulties and Possibilities of a Non-Reductive Conception of Welfare. *Archiv für Rechts- und Sozialphilosophie* Beiheft 24 (1985) p. 190-196.

Verhandlungen des 53. Deutschen Juristentages. Berlin 1980.

Band II. München 1980.
Westerlind, Peter - Beck-Friis, Jörgen - Sköllerholm, Ove, *Kommentar till konsumentkreditlagen* (Commentary to the Consumer Credit Act). Lund 1980.
Westermann, Harm Peter,
Sonderprivatrechtliche Sozialmodelle und das allgemeine Privatrecht. *Archiv für die civilistische Praxis* 1978 p. 150-195.
- " - Verbraucherschutz. *Gutachten und Vorschläge zur Überarbeitung des Schuldrechts herausgegeben vom Bundesminister der Justiz.* Band III. Köln 1983 p. 1-122.
Wieacker, Franz,
Industriegesellschaft und Privatrechtsordnung. Frankfurt am Main 1974.
Wiethölter, Rudolf,
Entwicklung des Rechtsbegriffs. In: *Rechtsformen der Verflechtung von Staat und Wirtschaft*, herausgegeben von Volkmar Gessner und Gerd Winter. Opladen 1982 p. 38-59.
- " - Materialisierungen und Prozeduralisierungen von Recht. *Zentrum für Europäische Rechtspolitik* (Bremen) *Mat 4* (1984) p. 25-64.
- " - Materialization and Proceduralization in Modern Law. In: Gunther Teubner (ed.): *Dilemmas of Law in the Welfare State.* Berlin 1986 p. 221-249.
- " - Proceduralization of the Category of Law. In: Christian Joerges - David M. Trubek (eds.): *Critical Legal Thought: An American-German Debate.* Baden-Baden 1989 p. 501-510
Wilhelmsson, Thomas,
Mietteitä amerikkalaisesta realismista (Thoughts on American Realism), *Oikeus* (Helsinki) 2/1976 p. 51-57.
- " - Om tro och heder i finsk avtalsrätt (On Faith and Honour in Finnish Contract Law). *Oikeustiede-Jurisprudentia* (Helsinki) XI (1978) p. 35-88.
- " - Siviilioikeuden yleisten oppien kriisistä (On the Crisis of the General Principles of Private Law). *Studia juridica 1983.* Helsinki 1983 p. 37-49.

Wilhelmsson, Thomas,
Standardavtal (Standard Form Contracts). Vammala 1984.
- " - Den nordiska rättsgemenskapen och rättskälleläran (The Nordic Legal Community and the Doctrine of the Sources of Law). *Tidsskrift for Rettsvitenskap* (Oslo) 1985 p. 181-197.
- " - Legal Analysis and the Relative Autonomy of the Law. *Rechtstheorie* Beiheft 9 (1986) p. 119-126.
- " - *Social civilrätt* (Social Private Law). Vammala 1987.
- " - Bedürfnisorientierung im Schuldrecht. *Demokratie und Recht* 1987 p. 175-186 (1987b).
- " - Alternative Use of the Law - a Different Model of Legal Dogmatics? In: *Reason in Law*. Proceedings of the Conference Held in Bologna, 12-15 December 1984. Volume Two. Milano 1988 p. 257-266.
- " - *Konsumentskyddet i Finland* (Consumer Protection in Finland). Helsinki 1989.
- " - Social Force Majeure - a New Concept in Nordic Consumer Law. *Journal of Consumer Policy* 1990 p. 1-14.

Wilhelmsson, Thomas - Sevón, Leif,
Räntelag och dröjsmålsränta (The Act on Interest and Interest on Delayed Payments). Vammala 1983.

Wüstmann, Ephard,
Rolle und Rollenkonflikt im Recht. Berlin (West) 1972.

Vähätalo, Kari,
Pitkäaikaistyöttömät (Long-Term Unemployed). Työvoimaministeriö. Työvoimapoliittisia tutkimuksia nro 30. Helsinki 1982.

Yablon, Charles M.,
The Indeterminacy of the Law: Critical Legal Studies and the Problem of Legal Explanation. *Cardozo Law Review*, vol. 6, 1985 p. 917-945.

Zahle, Henrik,
Polycentri i retskildelaeren (Polycentrism in the Doctrine of Legal Sources). In: *Samfunn Rett Rettferdighet. Festskrift til Torstein Eckhoffs 70-årsdag*. Otta 1986 p. 752-756.

ZERP Mat 3,
Günter Hörmann (Hrsg.): *Konsumentenkredit und Schuld-*

betreibung. Materialien zu einer Tagung. Bremen 1984.
ZERP Mat 4,
Gert Brüggemeier - Christian Joerges (Hrsg.): *Workshop zu Konzepten des Postinterventionistischen Rechts*. Bremen 1984.
Zinke, Horst,
Der Erkenntniswert politischer Argumente in der Anwendung und wissenschaftlichen Darstellung des Zivilrechts. Berlin (West) 1982.
Zitting, Simo,
Omistajanvaihdoksesta (On the Change of Owner). Vammala 1951.
Zweigert, Konrad - Kötz, Hein,
Introduction to Comparative Law. Volume II. Second Revised Edition. Oxford 1987.
Østlid, Henry,
Dommeratferd i dissenssaker (Judge Behaviour in Cases with Dissenting Opinions). Oslo 1988.

FINNISH STATUTES

Act on Equality between Women and Men	Laki naisten ja miesten välisestä tasa-arvosta / Lag om jämställdhet mellan kvinnor och män 8.8.1986/609
Act on Hire-Purchase	Laki osamaksukaupasta / Lag om avbetalningsköp 18.2. 1966/91
Act on Interest	Korkolaki / Räntelag 20.8. 1982/633
Act on Procedure for Termination of Contracts of Employment	Laki työsopimuksen irtisanomismenettelystä / Lag om förfarandet vid uppsägning av arbetsavtal 3.2.1984/124
Act on Torts	Vahingonkorvauslaki / Skadeståndslag 31.5.1974/412
Child Maintenance Act	Laki lapsen elatuksesta / Lag om underhåll för barn 5.9. 1975/704
Code of Inheritance	Perintökaari / Ärvdabalk 5.2. 1965/40
Consumer Protection Act	Kuluttajansuojalaki / Konsumentskyddslag 20.1.1978/38

Contract Act	Laki varallisuusoikeudellisista oikeustoimista / Lag om rättshandlingar på förmögenhetsrättens område 13.6. 1929/228
Criminal Code	Rikoslaki / Strafflag 19.12. 1889/39
Insurance Contracts Act	Vakuutussopimuslaki / Lag om försäkringsavtal 12.5. 1933/132
Labour Contracts Act	Työsopimuslaki / Lag om arbetsavtal 30.4.1970/320
Marriage Act	Avioliittolaki / Äktenskapslag 13.6.1929/234
Promissory Notes Act	Velkakirjalaki / Lag om skuldebrev 31.7.1947/622
Registration of Persons Decree	Henkilörekisteriasetus / Personregisterförordning 30.4. 1987/476
Rent Act	Huoneenvuokralaki / Hyreslag 10.7.1987/653
Sale of Goods Act	Kauppalaki / Köplag 27.3. 1987/355

ABBREVIATIONS

HD	Högsta domstolen / Supreme Court (Finland)
Kom.bet.	Kommittébetänkande / Proposal of State Committee (Finland)
KM	Komiteanmietintö / Proposal of State Committee (Finland)
MD	Marknadsdomstolen / Market Court
NU	Nordisk Utredningsserie / Nordic Series of Reports, Nordic Council
OLJ	Oikeusministeriön lainvalmisteluosaston julkaisu / Publication of the Law Drafting Department of the Finnish Ministry of Justice
Reg.prop.	Regeringens proposition / Government Bill (Finland)
SOU	Statens Offentliga Utredningar / Proposal of State Committee (Sweden)
Sv.Prop.	Government Bill (Sweden)

INDEX

Law and Philosophy Library

Managing Editors:
Alan Mabe, *Florida State University, Tallahassee, Florida*
Aulis Aarnio, *University of Helsinki, Finland*
Conrad D. Johnson, *University of Maryland, Maryland*

Publications:

1. E. Bulygin, J.-L. Gardies and I. Niiniluoto (eds.): *Man, Law and Modern Forms of Life.* With an Introduction by M. D. Bayles. 1985 ISBN 90-277-1869-5
2. W. Sadurski: *Giving Desert Its Due.* Social Justice and Legal Theory. 1985 ISBN 90-277-1941-1
3. N. MacCormick and O. Weinberger: *An Institutional Theory of Law.* New Approaches to Legal Positivism. 1986 ISBN 90-277-2079-7
4. A. Aarnio: *The Rational as Reasonable.* A Treatise on Legal Justification. 1987 ISBN 90-277-2276-5
5. M. D. Bayles: *Principles of Law.* A Normative Analysis. 1987 ISBN Hb: 90-277-2412-1; Pb: 90-277-2413-X
6. A. Soeteman: *Logic in Law.* Remarks on Logic and Rationality in Normative Reasoning, Especially in Law. 1989 ISBN 0-7923-0042-4
7. C. T. Sistare: *Responsibility and Criminal Liability.* 1989 ISBN 0-7923-0396-2
8. A. Peczenik: *On Law and Reason.* 1989 ISBN 0-7923-0444-6
9. W. Sadurski: *Moral Pluralism and Legal Neutrality.* 1990 ISBN 0-7923-0565-5
10. M. D. Bayles: *Procedural Justice.* Allocating to Individuals. 1990 ISBN 0-7923-0567-1
11. P. Nerhot (ed.): *Law, Interpretation and Reality.* Essays in Epistemology, Hermeneutics and Jurisprudence. 1990 ISBN 0-7923-0593-0
12. A.W. Norrie: *Law, Ideology and Punishment.* Retrieval and Critique of the Liberal Ideal of Criminal Justice. 1991 ISBN 0-7923-1013-6
13. P. Nerhot (ed.): *Legal Knowledge and Analogy.* Fragments of Legal Epistemology, Hermeneutics and Linguistics. 1991 ISBN 0-7923-1065-9
14. O. Weinberger: *Law, Institution and Legal Politics.* Fundamental Problems of Legal Theory and Social Philosophy. 1991 ISBN 0-7923-1143-4
15. J. Wróblewski: *The Judical Application of Law.* (*In preparation*)
16. T. Wilhelmsson: *Critical Studies in Private Law.* A Treatise on Need-Rational Principles in Modern Law. 1992 ISBN 0-7923-1659-2

KLUWER ACADEMIC PUBLISHERS – DORDRECHT / BOSTON / LONDON